FOREWORD

ABOUT FIFTEEN YEARS AGO I agreed to have some of my spoken messages put into print in the form of a book *Come! Live! Die!*, now entitled *Hunger for Reality*. To my amazement, since then I have received over 14,000 personal letters, most of which I have tried to answer. That book has now been translated into over twenty languages, so these letters have come from all over the world. It is especially with these people in mind that I have gone ahead with this new book.

As I reread, added to, and subtracted from the material Tony Collins took and compiled from my message tapes, I almost decided to cancel the project. To my mind, there are already so many better books than this one. Being able to mention some of them in this book has helped me to press on with it. Mainly, however, it has been the perseverance and hard work of Tony that has made this book a reality.

I am constantly challenged by the way I see God use the printed page. Even in the past weeks I have found myself making a deeper commitment to the distribution of Christian literature. This firstly means prayer for people to develop a greater spiritual appetite. When this happens, people may even take down from their shelves great books that have been sitting there for years and begin to read them.

It is my prayer that people will not just read books, especially this one, but that they will learn to be a blessing to others by distributing books. Remember there are tens of millions who have never read a single Christian book, or even a portion of Scripture, for that matter. We can, and must, do something about this.

This book is basically for people who already know Christ as their Lord and Savior. Unless you have at least begun in your Christian life through true faith in Christ, you may find it a little difficult to understand. On the other hand, I thought this was also true of my last book, and, to my amazement, a good number have come to know Christ through reading that. . . . So where you go from here is really up to you. And remember, what you do with the message of these pages will determine whether many other people will ever hear the message of Christ at all. God wants to use weak ordinary people to do great things for him. God wants to use you!

George Verwer

the **REVOLUTION** *of* **LOVE**

*Molding our lives
to mirror God*

CONTENTS

ACKNOWLEDGMENTS

The message of this book would not have been possible without the dedication of my dear wife, Drena, who has stood with me now in the battle for twenty-nine years.

My thanks also go to my editor, Dr. Ruth March, for her tireless efforts to transform my spoken messages into print.

INTRODUCTION

THIS BOOK IS A COLLECTION of messages that were first given in spoken form. Two are being republished, and the rest have never been published before. *Revolution of Love* was originally part of the "orientation material" that was given to young people joining Operation Mobilization for one-month summer campaigns in Europe in the early 1960s and reflects many of the early emphases of OM. The emphasis on "Spiritual Balance" came later on in the ministry of OM, and these messages were then published together in book form in 1977 under the title *Revolution of Love and Balance*.

The name "Operation Mobilization" came from the vision that God gave a small group of students from Europe and America back in the late 1950s. We felt that if Christianity was a spiritual revolution, a "revolution of love," then the important thing was to obey what the Lord Jesus had told us to do in living for him and going and teaching people in all nations of the world to be his disciples. We felt that many of the young people, who in those days were sitting in the large churches of the USA, Britain, and Europe, could be mobilized to tell those who did not know about the good news of Jesus Christ and the need for repentance and a personal faith.

I felt strongly about the need for prayer and evangelism because, without the faithfulness of one elderly woman in the States, I would never have known about the joy of knowing God in a personal way. I was brought up in a home where such things were not talked about. Then, one day, I received a Gospel of John through the post. This Christian lady had seen me going to my high school and had already started to pray that I should become a Christian.

She had to pray for several years before anything happened at all. Then, in March 1955, the evangelist Billy Graham came to Madison Square Gardens. For the first time I heard and responded to a clear message on the salvation that God has made available to us through Jesus Christ, and I surrendered my life to him.

Some people ask if that sort of decision of total commitment can really last. I would like to tell you that what happened to me that night so many years ago has been a reality in my heart and life for every single day since. I can assure you that it is not some late adolescent escape from guilt, but it is a true, living, and real experience with God himself made possible through what Jesus Christ has done on the Cross.

When we presented the challenge of those who had never heard to the young Christians of the western world in the 1960s, they responded in the hundreds. Today, many thousands of young people have spent time with OM, as it is usually known, in one of the short-term or longer-term options, and "OM graduates" are found in almost every Bible college or missionary society in the world.

The message contained in "A Wide-Open Heart" was first given to a group of OMers and other Christian workers in Peshawar, Pakistan, early in 1988. The refugee crisis in Pakistan means that Christians from many different backgrounds and organizations are working together in service and evangelism, so that a broad-minded attitude is particularly important. We in OM have always taken a strong stand against extremism, and this plea to be open-hearted in the work of God reflects that view.

"Real People, Real Power" and "New Generation—Unfinished Task" were messages from OM's leadership training conference at Birmingham in March 1988. This conference is not primarily for OM leaders but for young people in positions of responsibility in churches, Christian unions, and Christian organizations. I feel that these two powerful messages on discipleship and power in the Christian life and on the challenge of mission in the world today, are relevant not only to these young people but to many in the church today.

Finally, "Accepting Yourself and Others" is taken from a seminar given to our local OM teams here in Bromley, in the spring of 1988. This seminar helped to answer the need of many people to learn to accept their own personalities as God accepts them, and therefore to learn to accept other people in the same way.

I share these messages with you with the hope that, as you study them, they will help you to be a true spiritual revolutionary for Jesus Christ.

George Verwer
Bromley, Kent
January 1989

1

the REVOLUTION of LOVE

JESUS CHRIST WAS A REVOLUTIONARY—the greatest and most complete revolutionary this world has ever known. Not a political revolutionary, but a spiritual revolutionary.

And I believe that Christianity is a "revolution of love," a revolution that the Holy Spirit wants to bring about in our hearts and lives as he radically changes the way that we think and act. I am convinced that there is nothing more important in all the world than this.

As we see the state of the church worldwide and the state of many believers today, it is easy to become discouraged. We look for discipleship; we look for those who are working together in unity, in prayer, in power and we see quarrels and divisions, complacency and mediocrity.

Many people are asking, "Why is the church in such a state? Why is Christianity today making so little impact?"

Some people think that somehow we have missed some essential teaching or experience, and if we can only rediscover this secret through new meetings and books, deliverance and restoration will once again be brought to the church.

Now it seems to me that it would not be very fair of God to keep secret the most basic ingredient of Christian effectiveness. And, in fact, I do not believe this ingredient is a secret at all.

Let us look at Galatians 5:22–26:

> But the fruit of the Spirit is love, joy, peace, patience, kindness, goodness, faithfulness, gentleness and self-control. Against such things there is no law. Those who belong to Christ Jesus have crucified the sinful nature with its passions and desires. Since we live

by the Spirit, let us keep in step with the Spirit. Let us not become conceited, provoking and envying each other.

The fruit of the Holy Spirit is love. But what does the Bible mean here by love? In 1 John we find a clear and simply-stated definition: God is love.

In other words, true love is from God; it does not exist apart from him. We know that God is One. Therefore, we cannot think of God the Father without thinking of love; we cannot think of the Lord Jesus Christ without thinking of love; we cannot think of the Holy Spirit without thinking of love. There is no separation. God does not send love. He does not manufacture it. God *is* love.

Now that appears to be a very simple statement, but I am convinced that only an extremely small percentage of believers have really come to grips with this truth.

The Basic Message

This is, I believe, the basic ingredient that is largely lacking in Christianity today, and the lack of it is the source of most of our problems. It is the cancer that is eating away at the church, but it is no secret. In fact, it is so non-secretive that it is written on almost every page of the New Testament. And yet, because our hearts are so hard and cold, and because we are so self-centered, we do not see (or we do not really believe) that the basic message of the New Testament is *love!*

I am absolutely convinced that most of us miss this most obvious and often-repeated message, even while we are laying great emphasis on what is an "orthodox" interpretation of the Bible, what is "biblical teaching."

Well, I would like to ask, "What *is* biblical teaching?" We have long discussions on the Second Coming, on the meaning of the crucifixion, on the Church, the Holy Spirit, and so on. But what about love and humility and brokenness? These usually go into a separate category, but I want to tell you that if your teaching does not include love and humility and brokenness, then your teaching is not biblical.

There are thousands, even millions, of people who claim to be "orthodox Christians" because they cling to a certain set of beliefs in accordance with the Bible. They are aware that they do not practice much humility, but they do not think that makes them any less orthodox. They are aware that they do not really love other Christians (especially those who are different from them), but that does not cause them to think their teaching is not biblical.

They may admit that they know nothing of serving others and considering others better than themselves, yet they consider themselves Bible-believing, orthodox Christians.

They could not be more wrong! This is not Christianity but a travesty of Christianity—thinking we can be orthodox without having humility, thinking we can call ourselves as Bible-believing Christians though our lives do not show love or the other fruit of the Spirit. In fact, I believe that this is the greatest error that has ever hit the church of Jesus Christ!

Teaching cannot be separated from practical living. I cannot see Jesus Christ as some sort of split personality, partly doctrinal and partly moral, trying to bring two separate realms of truth into our minds. He is not on one occasion satisfying our intellectual curiosity by teaching us things *about* God, and in a separate exercise meeting our moral need by trying to make us more like the character of God. You cannot have a correct understanding about God without wanting to live in a way that pleases God.

"Oh," someone says, "there is a good, evangelical Christian who has a very good understanding of the Bible. He doesn't have much love for others and he's not very humble, but he certainly understands the Bible." I tell you, he does *not* understand the Bible if he does not love other Christians. What do we read in 1 John 4:8? "Whoever does not love does not know God."

There is no more biblical teaching than love, and, apart from love, there is no biblical teaching. Love is the foundation of all other biblical teaching, and you cannot build the building of biblical truth without that foundation.

The Wise Man

Let's turn to some verses that teach us a lot about this revolution of love and how it works out in everyday life. James chapter 3, beginning at verse 13: "Who is wise and understanding among you?"

Well, who *is* wise and understanding among you? Is it the person who knows all the answers? Is it the person who has the solution to every problem, the one who always knows which way to go, how to tell people about Christ, how to hand out literature? Is this the person who has true wisdom? Possibly. But not necessarily.

The passage goes on, "Let him show it by his good life, by deeds done in the humility that comes from wisdom." In other words, God says to the man who has the correct theory and who knows what the Bible teaches, "All right, let's see it in your life. First, above everything else, let's see it lived out. If a man is truly wise, then he is truly humble."

Reading on in James, we find that certain things mean that a person cannot have true wisdom; just "spiritual cleverness." "But if you harbor bitter envy and selfish ambition in your hearts, do not boast about it or deny the truth." If we show off our great knowledge and understanding of the Bible, and yet our lives are not filled with humility and love, but with bitterness and pride, we are actually lying against the truth with our lives. And how do you think non-believers feel when they see Christians saying one thing and living another?

James goes on to explain bluntly where this false "wisdom" comes from. "Such 'wisdom' does not come down from heaven but is earthly, unspiritual, of the devil." It must indeed please the devil with the damage it can cause.

An Illustration

Let me illustrate this kind of "spiritual cleverness" with an incident that occurred in our work some time ago. A team member made a mistake when doing something practical. Naturally, one of his colleagues was keen to put him right.

Very quickly he said, "This is wrong. You should not have done it that way." The first team member said defensively, "Well, I was told to do it that way." The second, even more heatedly, said, "Well, I know it is not right. This is what you should have done." And soon they had a full-scale argument.

Later on, I was able to have a talk with the one who claimed to be right. I said to him, "Do you still feel you were right in that situation?"

"Absolutely," he said. "I was right and everybody else knows I was right!" And, indeed, he had managed to convince everyone else that he was right—not only on the practical point but in the way he had acted.

Then I said, "Tell me, when you spoke to him, were you controlled by the Holy Spirit or by your emotions?"

He stopped at that and thought for a minute. "Well, I don't suppose that I was really what you would call controlled by the Holy Spirit."

I said, "Well, then, you were controlled by your emotions." He was a bit hesitant but said, "All right, I admit that I was controlled by my emotions and not by the Holy Spirit, but I was still right."

So I said, "But surely the word of God says that those who are controlled by their sinful nature cannot please God!" (Romans 8:8)

He wasn't right! The way I think, the way I believe Christ thought, the way I believe the New Testament teaches, he was absolutely wrong in the way he had acted, because even though he was telling what he believed to be the truth, he was saying it without love, and the Bible teaches that you cannot tell the truth without love and still please God.

We ask, "Is it true? Is it theologically accurate? Is it orthodox?" And all the time God is looking at the state of our hearts and our lack of love for our brothers and sisters. I believe that the curse of today is orthodoxy without love, orthodoxy without power, orthodoxy without the life of our Lord Jesus Christ!

When we as Christians try to communicate in areas that have been traditionally Roman Catholic or Muslim or Communist, we must always remember that no matter how right we are about an issue, the minute we act without love, we are being controlled by our own nature and not living in Christ, and that is sin. No matter how much "truth" comes from our mouths about the need for repentance and faith in Christ, and about the inability of any other religion or philosophy to bring people to God, if it is spoken without love it will not please God.

That is what the Bible is saying in these verses. This "wisdom" that does not come with kindness and gentleness and love is not wisdom. It is unspiritual, devilish. Some of the most horrible and unbelievable situations can arise in the church amongst those who have "lip truth" but do not live the truth.

The next verse says, "For where you have envy and selfish ambition, there you find disorder and every evil practice." Where there is no true love, where there is no true wisdom, you cannot hope to have Christians working together in an orderly way. In the work of Operation Mobilization, we have seen again and again that no matter how much people know about the Bible, if they are not living it out in their lives, there will soon be disorder, confusion and pain.

Pure and Peace-Loving

True wisdom, on the other hand, will never bring confusion: "But the wisdom that comes from heaven is first of all pure" (verse 17). God's wisdom is primarily not orthodox, but pure. And whenever what we say and do, is not pure, then it is not from heaven, but is mere earthly "spiritual cleverness."

God's wisdom is also peace-loving (verse 17). Alan Redpath says that when you know you are not controlled by the Spirit, when you know you are a little upset, then just do not open your mouth! I like the way he puts it: "At that moment, literally force yourself back into the will of God." Force yourself back into the will of God, and then speak. But never open your mouth when you are not controlled by the Spirit, for, no matter how hard you try, you will never speak with true wisdom.

How many times have you hurt someone because you spoke too soon? Husbands and wives, how many times have you hurt your partner because you did not keep quiet a few minutes longer, until you were in control of your tongue? I have lost count of the number of times I could have kicked myself just because I did not wait a little longer before I spoke.

James reminds us, "The wisdom that comes from heaven is first of all pure; then peace-loving, [then] considerate." Considerate wisdom—gentle, the King James version says. I wish many young people would study this verse. It is easy to be a "keen Christian" when you are young—and we are grateful for that. When you are young and energetic, it seems that the world is just waiting to be conquered in the name of Jesus Christ. You cannot imagine why it has taken so long.

But when we reach the age of thirty or thirty-five, or after the first child has arrived, suddenly it becomes a bit harder to raise the enthusiasm for yet another outreach or yet another meeting. Suddenly we are a bit more understanding of others and a bit slower to condemn them for their apathy. Finally, we have to admit that so often we have been working in the energy of our own nature. Youthful energy! Youthful enthusiasm! But where was the gentleness that should have gone with the energy? Remember, the wisdom that comes from heaven is always considerate of others.

How Do You Respond?

God's wisdom is also "submissive." Now this is an emotive word. Does the Bible mean we should be some kind of doormat for others to step on? Certainly not. In fact, when you look a little more deeply into the meaning of this word, you find that it could have been translated "easily persuaded." So "submissive" in this context means that we should not be stubborn when we are wrong; we should be easily taught and corrected.

How do you respond when, for instance, you are helping to make tea after a church meeting and someone says, "Oh, you shouldn't have used that water—it wasn't really boiling. Pour it all out and start again. And why have you used these teaspoons? We always use the ones in this box . . ." Are you willing to be corrected?

Or what if you have been playing the guitar for your music group in the morning service and someone comes up to you and says, "That chorus you were playing at the beginning was much too slow . . . and I don't like the one we finished with, it's too noisy for the older people. And the way you were standing was all wrong; we couldn't see your face at the back . . ." What would you say? You need to be close to the Lord to accept criticism, however well meaning it may be.

I believe that one of the greatest tests in the Christian life comes when we are confronted with correction and criticism. When we are criticized, rightly or wrongly, then we must learn to lean not on other people's opinion of our work, but only on Jesus. Possibly that is why God sometimes allows the props to be knocked from under us and puts us under fire in the form of criticism. We need to learn to work only for his "Well done, good and faithful servant."

This passage gives us some other ways to test true wisdom. Next, James says, "the wisdom that comes from heaven is . . . full of mercy and good fruit, impartial and sincere." Full of mercy— towards those who are weak, those who are insecure, those who have done wrong; full of mercy and full of the fruit of the Spirit. It is impartial and sincere, without hypocrisy.

This is true biblical teaching—truly orthodox belief. And I pray that if anyone can show me that this is wrong thinking or that I am misinterpreting the New Testament, and that it is possible for me to understand the Bible without peace, purity, gentleness, and so on, that they will show me. But please do not try to tell me that some Christian you know has a good understanding of the Bible but a miserable, loveless life, because I will just not believe you. Biblical teaching and true, God-given wisdom always comes with a Bible-linked life. And all true Christian work will reflect this partnership of biblical teaching and biblical living.

Explosive Message

Perhaps the clearest explanation of what is meant by the "revolution of love" is found in 1 John 3. This letter is so loaded with revolution and dynamite that, if taken seriously, it makes the writings of Karl Marx look like a damp squib.

I will never forget a young, red-hot Communist who came into our Operation Mobilization office in the North of England many years ago. We read this letter with him and showed him the teachings of Jesus, and two weeks later he got down on his knees in the kitchen and gave his life to Christ. I tell you, the message of 1 John could have been written yesterday, so relevant is it to today's generation!

Now let's see what God says to us through 1 John 3:11: "This is the message you heard from the beginning: We should love one another."

What are we as Christians trying to get over to people? Sometimes it seems that our first message is "believe." Believe in the Lord Jesus and you will be saved. Believe in the Lord Jesus and afterwards everything will be fine. But when I read the word "believe" in the New Testament, I find something that is like an atomic bomb. When a man really believes in Jesus Christ, it is revolution becoming operative, a revolution of love. You cannot separate the one from the other.

We know that true belief must include repentance. But what does "repent and believe" really mean? Does salvation come when we first believe, or only when we have shown God the evidence of our changed lives? The Bible teaches clearly that salvation comes through faith alone. But real belief brings revolution. It results in a changed life. There is no such thing as real belief which does not change the believer. "Believe on the Lord Jesus and you will be saved." Doing good will never save you, no matter how hard (or long) you work, or how much you achieve. But when you have believed, you are going to do good as a result, because the Holy Spirit, who lives in you as a Christian, wants to do good through you.

The Holy Spirit

Many years ago, when the gifts of the Holy Spirit were not talked about in most churches as freely as they are now, a friend came to me with stories of wonderful experiences some people had had in the Holy Spirit. I have to admit that I was a bit skeptical. I asked her, "When the Holy Spirit works in such a mighty way, shouldn't the people who have had such experiences afterwards be filled with love and joy and peace? Shouldn't they leave everything they have for Christ's sake, as we are told the early Christians did in the book of Acts? Shouldn't they even be willing to lay down their lives for others?"

Now I think my friend knew perfectly well that not all the people who had had these experiences "in the Spirit" showed the evidence of a "revolution of love" in their lives, and that some Christians who did show this evidence had never had this sort of experience. So she said to me, "Sometimes the Holy Spirit comes just to give us joy and a wonderful experience of blessing." I said to her, "You mean that sometimes the Holy Spirit comes apart from his holiness?" And she had no answer to that.

I strongly believe that all Christians should seek to be filled with the Holy Spirit. But I tell you, the Holy Spirit does not come apart from his holiness. The emphasis is not on "Spirit" but on "Holy," and he cannot divide up his gifts and his character. Therefore, it is possible to measure people's true depth of experience with the Spirit (although it would be more correct to say the Spirit's experience with people) by the way that they live day by day.

You cannot separate the word "believe" in its biblical context from the word love. Don't try! How many men are there in our churches, leaders some of them, who speak to a congregation from the word of God, but in their homes know nothing more about loving their wives than the man in the next house who cannot stand his! And they go on and on, continuing to think they are spiritual men with just a besetting sin of not being able to really love their wives. I find this absolutely heart-breaking! To me it is completely incompatible to say that you are a spiritual person and then not be able to get on with your family or even your neighbor!

If your "besetting sin" is that you cannot love people, you are in serious trouble. I do not mean to say that it will always be easy to love people, or that you will not have battles about it. In fact, you will find that the devil will fight you tooth and nail in this area, often twenty-four hours a day. But this should not discourage you, for the word of God clearly teaches that we are to love one another.

We cannot have fellowship with God without having fellowship with our brothers and sisters in Christ. We cannot love God without first loving our fellow-Christians.

Look at 1 John 4:20:

> If anyone says, "I love God," yet hates his brother, he is a liar. For anyone who does not love his brother, whom he has seen, cannot love God, whom he has not seen.

The popular idea today seems to be that if we love God enough, we will eventually love our brothers and sisters in Christ. But this is not what the verse says. It states clearly that if there is any brother or any sister who we do not love, actively, operationally, then our relationship with God is seriously wrong.

I am convinced that many of our prayers do not get any higher than the ceiling because of our lack of love and hardness of heart. If some of the prayers we hear in prayer meetings today were being answered, the world would have been evangelized long ago. Fantastic things are asked of God. "Lord, we claim this country for you." "We believe, Father, that you will open a way into China." "Lord, we trust you to bring a hundred new people to the meeting tonight." And on and on we go, and yet all the time there are other Christians in the same prayer meeting whom we cannot stand. Oh, not that we don't love them . . . we would just rather not sit next to them. Of course we don't hate them—it is just that our personalities conflict!

Love Your Enemies

There are dozens of watered-down phrases for not loving other people. "Oh, I love him in the Lord, but I don't like his mannerisms. . . . Susie is all right, but she is so hard to get to know. . . . So-and-so has emotional problems, and such-and-such comes from such a *difficult* background . . ."

In the sight of God it is all hypocrisy. God never said in the Bible, "Love your brother if he is a keen Christian, well-dressed, a good evangelist . . . and if he gets on with you." No! In fact, Christ told us in the Sermon on the Mount that real love does not begin until we love our enemies!

This whole concept of loving our enemies is, for the average person of today, nothing but an out-dated theological phrase, so impossible for human nature to attain that it is often not taken seriously even among Christians.

We know so little of it, so little of really loving people who cannot tolerate us, who speak evil of us, spite us, do not like us, or the way we operate.

Christians who live in cultures that are opposed to all Christian work and often all foreigners must learn the hard way what loving their enemies really means, if they are to go on loving even those who persecute them for Christ's sake. Meanwhile, we in the West often cannot love even the people around us, who do us no harm at all!

Some time ago, someone told me flatly that he loved everybody. I said to him, "I find that hard to believe." But he was insistent that he loved everybody. Now I happened to know of at least one person to whom he didn't bother to say "hello" in the morning. He could pass this person several times a day, never showing kindness—not a smile. So I mentioned this person's name and asked, "Do you really love him?" He said, "Of course I do. Well, I mean, I love all the believers."

It was all in the head! There is no love without action. Potentially that Christian may have loved everybody. Theoretically he may have loved everybody. But it was not a reality.

God's Work

Who is it that brings about this revolution of love? When you became a Christian, the Holy Spirit of God came to live within you, with all his potential for this tremendous life of love. The Holy Spirit is there, just waiting to take possession of you and make you more loving. He is just waiting to move you to volunteer to do some shopping for the older people in your church, or to help clean out the gutters. But what happens? Our pride, stubbornness, and self-centeredness soon get in the way and stop the action of the Holy Spirit in our lives.

Jesus Christ said, "Love your neighbor as yourself." Now, it's very nice that we Christians have been given the truth. But what has been the result in the practical realm? What has it been in India, for instance? Certain missionaries went with their heads in the clouds, taught, "Love your neighbor as yourself," but then shut themselves away from the people in their missionary compounds, and put locks on all the doors. And in Africa, what have been the results? Well, in many places, the missionaries have said, "We love our neighbors as ourselves. But, well, the colored people had better use the back doors, and clean the houses, and be the nannies for the little white children."

What, then, does all this talk about love really mean? "Love your neighbor as yourself." Well, how do you love yourself? How did you love yourself this morning? You got out of bed groggily, wiped all the sleep out of your eyes, went to the mirror and said, "Oh, how I love you! You are so wonderful; I love you, I love you, I love you so much!" Did you? Well, if you do that too many mornings someone might call in a psychiatrist for you. That is not the way we love ourselves! That is the way we love our neighbors. "The Lord bless you, dear brother. Yes, yes, the Lord bless you. The Lord do wonderful things for you!"

We sign our letters "love in Christ" and think, "Well, that's another one out of the way." But that is not the way we love ourselves. Perhaps we can understand love better if we use the word "care." You have been caring for yourself all day long, ever since this morning when you woke up and your self-love automatically went into action. You had a wash, maybe used a few creams and lotions, and put on the proper amount of clothes to keep your body warm. Shortly after getting out of bed, you had a little pain in your stomach—very slight, but enough to get you into action. Immediately you started toward the kettle and the cereals and bread and jam.

If you are really honest, you will probably have to say that as you came to the table you were not wondering if you could make some coffee or tea for anyone else, or if you could make a start on the washing-up. No. You sat down, and, noticing that there was no margarine on the table, you began to look for some in the fridge. You were taking care of yourself automatically.

I am not saying that this is wrong. Neither does Jesus. It is wonderful that Jesus knows all about us, all about the human mind. If we could only grasp this truth, we could burn most of the psychiatry books in a big rubbish bin.

God doesn't say that you should not love yourself. But he does say that you should love your neighbor in the same way as you love yourself. He does not say that you should not have breakfast, but he does say you should be concerned about your neighbor's breakfast as well.

I pray that the Spirit of God will show you what this revolution of love really is—what it means to obey the command of Jesus Christ to love your neighbor from the time you get up in the morning until you go to bed at night. Only this will make an impact on such a materialistic age as this one! Our books and leaflets will not do it. Our Bibles will not do it. Jesus said, "All men will know that you are my disciples if you love one another." Not if you know all about the Bible and are fired with great enthusiasm. No! They will know it if you love one another. This is the greatest challenge in the word of God—to love people as Christ loved them, to love them as we love ourselves, to care for people as we care for ourselves.

Surrendering Everything

The only logical outcome of such love is to surrender everything to God, I believe that when someone falls in love with Jesus, it can be compared in some ways to a young man falling in love with a girl he has dreamed about all his life. The day they are married, he transfers his bank account and puts it in her name, and he takes out an insurance policy in her name. In other words, because he loves her, he gives her all he has.

A lot of Christians have trouble with this sort of teaching. Anything that involves money or possessions is very sensitive, and I do not want to judge or condemn anybody. Christians have very different ideas about what is meant by "stewardship" of money and possessions and what is meant by "giving up everything." One Christian will sell his home and give the money to missions or to the poor. Another will keep a beautiful home and use it to show others the gift of hospitality.

I am not saying that God cannot use your possessions for his work and for his glory, once they have been surrendered to him. But I am saying that we must first give all control of our possessions and our money to God. I know that it is difficult. Often we hold back because we have not yet learnt to trust God with our whole lives. It is easy to sing "Jesus, I love you" and hard to hand over a bank account. I believe that often those who hold back have not yet fallen in love with Jesus Christ. Once our relationship with him is right, we are no longer afraid of his control. Then we can lay everything at his feet.

The man who does not know the joy of giving has not yet begun to live, for it is, just as the Bible says, more blessed to give than to receive. It is a revolutionary principle of life that our greatest joys come from giving. It is completely contrary to our human nature. By nature we grasp everything to ourselves and we become the center. But when we become Christ-centered, it is just like a centrifugal force, like a whirlwind throwing everything outward and leaving Christ alone, our one supreme love.

"Love your neighbor as yourself," said Jesus. And on another occasion he illustrated in the parable of the Good Samaritan who he meant by our neighbor and what he meant by love. Care for your neighbor as you care for yourself. That is why I find it hard to eat breakfast without praying for India, why I find it hard to take a piece of bread and a sip of tea without a pain in my heart for those who have no food.

We who claim to have the truth, we evangelicals, we Bible-believers, have become hardened to the need of mankind. In recent years movements like "Live Aid" and "The Race Against Time," which are not even specifically Christian, have overtaken many

Christian groups in mobilizing aid for the starving in Africa and
Asia. Sometimes I feel ashamed of the complacency of Christians,
while these young people are making such efforts. If I asked you
to distribute leaflets and promised to give you five pence a leaflet,
how many leaflets would you give out? If I said I would give you
£50 cash for every person you bring to Jesus Christ, maybe you
would be motivated to go out and tell others about the gospel a
little more! Is this really the way we should react? We all know it
is not. No one can put a value on a soul. We need to see where we
are before God. Look at 1 John 3:14;

> We know that we have passed from death to life, because we love
> our brothers. Anyone who does not love remains in death.

That is quite blunt, isn't it? You say, "Oh, but I have been born
again." But how were you born again? Putting your hand up in
a gospel meeting did not make you born again. Saying "Jesus,
I believe in you" did not make you born again. You were only
born again and freed from spiritual death when you repented of
your former lack of love and trusted in Jesus to give you his Holy
Spirit, to produce his fruit of love in your heart for your brothers
and sisters.

There are many people in our churches today who have made
so-called decisions at some time in their lives, who have claimed
to be Christians for many years and yet have never show any
evidence of repentance, and whose lives are filled with a bitterness and a lack of love towards other Christians. This is a delu-
sion—the largest, most detestable sugar-coated pill the devil ever
gave out! There is no conversion without revolution. There is no
conversion that does not produce the seed of a loving life, tiny
though it be in the beginning.

Look at verse 16:

> This is how we know what love is: Jesus Christ laid down his life
> for us. And we ought to lay down our lives for our brothers.

This is how we know God loves us. This is how we know the
love of God; the way we perceive it; the way we understand it. He

laid down his life for us. He died for us; he did something. He did not sit up in glory and sing, "My earthlings, I love you, I know you are mine." He did not do that. That is what we do. We sit in our meetings and sing, "My Jesus, I love you," yet often we are not on speaking terms with the man in the seat beside us. Anyone who can sing that without going out from that meeting to show love in his life has passed through a religious pantomime that is an insult to Almighty God. And I am convinced that the world will never be evangelized unless we experience the love of God in our hearts towards others!

Now, I am not going to give you some sort of list of steps to take so that you can experience the love of God. There are no short cuts in the Christian life. I am not going to tell you about some new gift or prayer style or experience that will lead you closer to God. These things have their place. But the first step to being filled with God's love is to want it! Want to be like Jesus! Want to know this life-changing love! Want him with a spiritual hunger that will get you so absolutely starved for God that eventually through knowing him, his love will be poured out into your life!

> Blessed are those who hunger and thirst for righteousness,
> for they will be filled. (Matthew 5:6)

It is a universal law that when you want something badly, whether it is good or bad, if you continue to crave that thing, desire for it will take hold of your subconscious mind and eventually you will be motivated to get it. How many times has it happened that someone has asked you the name of a person and you have said, "I have his name right on the tip of my tongue . . . now what is it?" You were motivated to want to know that name. You tried again, "What is that person's name?" And again, "Now what is his name?" And then you forgot about it for a while. You thought you had forgotten about it. But you had fed a wish into your inner being, into your subconscious mind, and the wheels started going. Ten minutes later, completely without conscious effort, what came into your mind? The person's name!

This hunger, this deep craving, can be used for evil as well as for good. Many years ago a young university student in Texas called Charles Whitman went up into a tower on the university campus one day and began to shoot people at random. This thought had come into his mind many times before. He had even mentioned it to his psychiatrist. But I am sure that the first time it occurred to him he was shocked and thought, "I could never do anything like that." Nevertheless, the thought continued to come to him more and more frequently. He suppressed it and suppressed it until finally it took possession of him totally, and he was powerless against his craving.

This is what happens when you crave something. Every time you want something that is not of God, you sow a thought. Maybe you have a desire you wouldn't admit to your best friend or your husband or wife. Maybe it is new clothes, maybe it is marriage, maybe it is recognition. Perhaps it is even something legitimate, if God were to give it to you. But the craving is so strong in you that you begin to think, "Other people have it," and the seed of envy is sown in your heart. And then you think, "Why can't I have it?" and the seed of bitterness is sown.

Probably all of us have had thoughts like that at one time or another. But remember that if you go on allowing these thoughts to have possession of your heart and mind, they will take control of you. Soon the things of God will start to mean less and less to you, and in the end God may let you have your desire. But at what price?

Brokenness

In the same way I am convinced that if you want a life of love, if you want to be conformed to the image of Jesus Christ, if you want to join that remnant of people who are fed up with words, hymns, and hypocrisy, if you want reality and revolution in your life, then you will get it. If you are starved for such a life, then you will get it. "Blessed are those who hunger and thirst for righteousness, for they will be filled."

It will take time. Perhaps you have heard this before and you say, "Last year I heard a message like this and I prayed and wept and rededicated myself before God. I said, 'Lord, I want to be loving, I want to be humble, I want to be gentle, I want to be a servant.'" And now you look back at the past year, and it is not very impressive. Do not be discouraged. What God wants of us is *brokenness*. He wants us to realize that in our own nature we cannot please him, that we cannot love our brothers and sisters, that from the time we get up in the morning until we go to bed at night we live a life of utter selfishness, except when God interrupts us. Do you want this? Do you want to know something of loving your enemies? Do you want to know something of being a servant, something of being easily taught and corrected, of weeping for people who are without food and without Christ?

I will never forget a one-day campaign we had in Bombay, when we were challenged to distribute half a million Christian leaflets in one day. After we had distributed some four hundred thousand leaflets throughout the day, we then had a meeting in the evening. And as we closed that meeting we said that if anyone was motivated to go back into the streets with leaflets, we still had a few left—about a hundred thousand! There were several volunteers. I had absolutely no desire to go out that night with more leaflets. It was 11 p.m., we had started the day at 5 a.m., and I had worked through the night before on the maps of the city. I was tired. I did not feel any love tingling through me. And as I started out, I just had to stop where I was and turn my eyes towards Jesus. I saw him walking an extra mile for me—I saw him going up Calvary's hill to the cross for me. That was love! It was not cheap sentiment. It was not a letter signed, "I love you." It was action. And I said to myself that if Jesus could go the extra mile for me, then surely he would help me go the extra mile for those others whom he loved. Love is action! "If you love me, keep my commandments."

We went out into the streets of Bombay again, and around midnight I could see for about a quarter of a mile in front of us thousands of men and women sleeping on the pavement. I've never before seen such a sight in my life. I had two big bags filled with leaflets, and for the first time in my life, I went from bed to bed, giving out leaflets!

This world in which we live is a sick world. It is a world of misery and tragedy such as most of us cannot begin to imagine. Millions are sleeping on pavements, starving to death, knowing nothing of the love of God for them. The church sings, "My Jesus, I love you." And at the same time a couple of thousand people a day slip away into eternity. And we say that we love them. I say we don't. If we loved them with Christ's love, we wouldn't stop until we had sold a million books and distributed a hundred million leaflets and laid down our lives in every kind of service and action to help them. And as we did it, our tears would bathe these lost souls. I know too little about it. I have wept little over souls and much over my unloving heart. But I can say right now before God, "I *want it!* You can take all that I have! You can take my family (and I do not say this lightly), *but I want a life of love! I want God!"*

If you can say this with me, I believe that God will answer you! But if what you want is not God but Christian service, Christian activity, or Christian fellowship, no matter how good those things may be, then I do not believe you will ever be truly satisfied.

> *Lord, we cry to you to teach us to love, to break us of self, pride, stubbornness, that the love of Christ, poured out into our hearts through the Holy Spirit, might be operative daily, hourly, moment by moment.*
>
> *We cry to you to teach us to love our enemies, to love our critics, not in word, but in deed also. We cry to you that we want this life of love, and we want you, for you are love! Amen.*

2

Spiritual **BALANCE**

LEARNING ABOUT THE REVOLUTION of love is something that is essential for all Christians, whether they have been following the Lord for five days or fifty years. Learning about the principles of spiritual balance is part of growing up as a Christian— moving towards spiritual maturity. In spiritual balance, biblical passages that give different aspects of the truth are kept together; not being watered down, but seen in context and in the perspective of God's whole revelation.

Spiritual balance, like spiritual revolution, is something that must be real for each one of us. If we only understand the principles of it in our heads, then our discipleship will not withstand the test of time and suffering. I am completely convinced that discipleship is not just for "full-time" Christian workers. Discipleship is for every believer. Discipleship is not just for people who are living in a Christian community or a Bible college. It is for believers everywhere. Discipleship is not a set of rigid rules. The principles of discipleship are more flexible and adaptable than many of us would dare to admit.

The unreal expectations of a few Bible verses taken out of context can lead people into spiritual frustration. Only by balancing one strong biblical truth with another will we come to spiritual reality.

Flexibility

The first area of conflict which often arises with keen, young Christians is that of flexibility: how much to try to convince others of the great teaching they may have received or the great experiences they have had, and how much simply to accept all Christians as they are. This is a conflict that may appear when young Christians have been for their first period of training with Operation Mobilization or their first term with a college Christian union or their first Bible conference. Naturally, they may come back brimming with ideas to their home churches and begin to tell much older Christians just where they have been going wrong and how they should change. And, just as naturally, the older Christians may react with some resentment.

This is a situation in which the need for balance is obvious. It is good for young Christians to have strong beliefs and to be constantly learning and sharing what they have learnt. But what happens when others are not so keen to listen?

As disciples of Christ, our chief rule must always be love, and love brings with it sensitivity to the needs of others. When we are in a church meeting or a committee, and we find ourselves disagreeing violently about some matter of priorities or finance or church politics, and we feel the anger welling up within us, love restrains us. Love causes us to think before we speak. Most of us realize our tongues run faster than our brains, and that this can get us into trouble. True disciples are adaptable and flexible, although they do not compromise their beliefs.

If you spend time working with any Christian group you may find that you build up strong convictions on minor issues, just because that is the way that group does things. But if you then go on to join another group or return to work in your local church, you may find they have different convictions on these points, or that they do not consider these things important. This can become very frustrating and may place a barrier between you and your new area of work and Christian service, unless your attitude is one of spiritual balance. Unless you are flexible, adaptable, and loving, you will not be able to fit into another fellowship easily.

There is nothing wrong with having strong convictions, so long as we remember that we are still learners. A humble attitude will stop us thinking that we have the answers to every situation and make us flexible to the convictions of others.

God uses men of completely opposite convictions. There is one man of God who visited us on the M.V. *Logos* once to do some preaching, and during his sermon smoked a pipe all the time. Now this is something that most of us involved in OM would find completely unacceptable. Yet, although he believes and acts differently to us, he is a man who is being wonderfully used of God.

God is so great and so mighty that he will always carry on the work of his kingdom, and he will use people despite their mistakes, weaknesses, and even wrong ideas and minor beliefs. Sometimes we will have to say, "Others may, I will not." This is very different than saying, "I will not, so no one else will either!" which is using our own weaknesses to judge and condemn others.

Work and Rest

Another area in which Christians often have great difficulty is the need to strike a balance between working as hard as possible, yet leaving time to be relaxed and rested. The importance of relaxation is becoming more recognized today. There have been too many Christians, especially leaders, whose ministry or families have collapsed under the strain, simply because they never learned to relax.

Some Christians think that there is too much to do to relax; that if they are truly disciplined, they should be able to work all the time. But this is not the way God has made us. A time of relaxation helps us to build up our physical, emotional, and spiritual strength and power so that we can then go on to accomplish more in a week than we would otherwise have done in a month.

Different people relax in different ways. Some people need complete separation from work to relax. Some need a week's holiday every so often, others can just take off a few hours, while others can just change from one sort of work to another. Some people's attitude to work is much more relaxed from the start, and they never become so uptight as some others. We need to realize that it is God who is in charge, and that we are not indispensable.

When we can trust God enough to relax, we will become more, not less, disciplined. It is easy to produce a false discipline, working ceaselessly, and being present at every meeting just to impress others. This sort of attitude should never be encouraged. God, who looks at the heart, knows whether our work is first of all for him or for other people.

It is self-discipline that will last, not some discipline that is imposed by others. Of course there are times when we need to accept the discipline of the church or community. This is only part of our own self-discipline. And of course there will be times when we fail and fall short of our own standards. But I know of no better way of learning than through failure.

Concern and Inner Peace

To be able to learn through failure takes another area of balance: the ability to balance concern and inner peace. It is good to be concerned that things are done in the right way and that people are living in the right way, but it is not good to have unhealthy anxieties. If we know that we are working with God and that he is in control, it is possible to have peace within ourselves when other things are going wrong.

Without an inner compulsion to get things done in the best possible way, many Christian leaders would not achieve what they do for God.

But that compulsion must not become an obsession; it must be kept under God's control.

If we do not learn to have inner peace when things go wrong, we will become impatient with those around us. Look instead at how the Lord Jesus dealt with his stumbling, fumbling disciples. They said and did many stupid things, but he did not become impatient with them but forgave them everything.

Perfection Through Failure

When we learn to have inner peace because we know we are complete in God's own Son, we will be able to obtain a balance between aiming at perfection and coping with failure. To be perfect should be the aim of every true Christian: to live a life in the

Spirit, not to offend anyone, to love everyone as Christ loves us, to do all things in the right way, and to glorify God in our every action.

But each of us must also learn to accept failure, especially our own failures, mistakes, and shortcomings. We must know what to do when we fail. Wallowing in "repentance" that is mostly made up of self-pity is not the answer, for it merely paralyzes our effectiveness. We refuse to get on with the work of God, imprisoning ourselves in a self-imposed purgatory, while the devil chuckles with delight.

Avoiding failure is not the answer either. Many Christians are so afraid of failure that they simply lower their aims. "We won't have a prayer meeting in case nobody comes." "We handed out leaflets last year and someone laughed at us, so we won't do it again."

To be afraid of failure in this way is to dishonor God. Fred Jarvis has said, "The greatest sin of Christians is not failure, but aiming too low." We must not try to diminish God by our own lack of faith. We must have high aims but be able to accept our own failure.

Some Christians tend towards a perfectionist attitude and may have impossibly high aims for themselves while worrying over every slip and fall. Others will simply avoid failure by compromising and lowering their aims so that they achieve nothing at all for God. The difference is often not one of spirituality but of temperament. The only answer is to have spiritual balance.

Sometimes Christians live a whole day in frustration because they were unable to get their "quiet time" first thing in the morning. They really believe that the devil is going to pounce on them extra hard. Actually the Bible does not even mention having a "quiet time." The devil is going to attack us anyway whether we miss our "quiet time" or not. Let us aim for perfection but not become obsessive over it.

We must learn to handle our mistakes. Sometimes our expectations are unreal. With young people who have not had much experience of Christian work but who have read inspiring Christian

books and been to impressive Bible conferences, there are bound
to be disappointments and frustrations. These things are a normal
part of the Christian life, particularly in a group situation.

We should learn to take Christian biographies with a pinch of
salt. They are often so concerned to tell us all about this great man
or woman of God that they select only the good points, leaving
out the difficulties and weak points. This is particularly true of
books written some years ago. The impression given is of a life
free from any mistakes and failure, and this can be very discour-
aging to young people who then find that the Christian life is not
quite like that.

The inner history of many missions and societies is not always
pleasant and inspiring. Some of the greatest men and women of
God had amazing inconsistencies and weaknesses. But God used
them despite their mistakes, for in Christ he made them perfect. In
1 Corinthians we read about the most unspiritual Christians in the
New Testament. Yet Paul opens his letter by saying he is writing
to those who are sanctified. It is clear from the letter that some of
these people were living in sexual sin and doing all kinds of things
against God, but the apostle Paul knew how to handle people's
failures. He encouraged them to keep aiming for perfection, but
he also showed them how to pick themselves up and keep going
when they failed. This balance is the only way to achieve spiritual
maturity.

Spiritual Maturity

There is a lot of spiritual immaturity in the Christian world,
particularly in the realm of material possessions. It is amazing
how easily we get the "I want" bug, just because we see that someone else has something and not because we need it. Generally, if
we really need something God will give it to us. But often it is
only when we see somebody else with something that we suddenly realize we want it as well. We may start to envy someone
else's food or clothes or music system. This is not genuine need;
it is simply jealousy.

God's way is much more revolutionary than the materialistic

way of life we are used to. The apostle Paul lived this out; he chose to go without some things that other Christians thought were essential. Don't base your spiritual life on even the most dedicated Christian you know. Base it instead on the word of God and what the Lord Jesus reveals to you. Perhaps the Lord has shown you things you should not do, such as drink alcohol or spend money on luxury items. Then you meet some apparently mature Christians who are doing these things. This can be most upsetting, and you may begin to wonder if you were right to obey God.

Firstly, remember that these Christians may not be as spiritually mature as they appear. Often people with strong, outgoing personalities gain reputations as keen Christians, when in reality they are depending on natural ability rather than a close knowledge of God. Secondly, remember that we all have strengths and weaknesses in different areas. Just because these Christians have a weakness in this particular area does not mean that they are not strong in other areas. In fact, some Christians are able to stay close to God while doing some things that for most of us would cause problems. We must not judge others but must obey what God shows us about the way to run our own lives.

Let us beware of getting worked up by the way people spend money. This is always a sensitive area. There are some people who will spend more money in one week for a hotel room and food than some of us would spend in a month. Yet God is using them. How can this happen? It can happen because God is sovereign, God is great, God is a God of love, God is a God of mercy, and he looks upon our hearts. Let us look to God and live our lives the way he shows us, being able to say, "Others may, but I cannot." This is the sign of true spiritual maturity.

Spiritual Balance

Learning about spiritual balance enables us to learn to distinguish the difference between what is biblical principle and what is personal conviction. It is possible to find a Bible verse to support almost anything, but only if you are willing to take isolated Bible verses out of context.

Certain things we do in life do not come directly from biblical principles. The larger principle of love guides us to do things in the most convenient and practical way. If we are spiritually mature, we can accept this, even if it means things are not always done in the way that we would prefer.

Having a balanced attitude to important biblical principles leads us from spiritual immaturity to maturity; from frustration to fulfillment. Only when we learn to be adaptable yet strong in our beliefs, to work hard yet to relax in God, and to aim at perfection through failure will we become effective and used by God.

> *Lord, teach us about spiritual balance. Let us not look to others for our example, but to you alone; learning to follow your word, not just the passages that we have selected to suit our own abilities or temperament, but in its glorious and complete whole.*

> *Amen.*

3

a **WIDE-OPEN** *heart*

"*ALL MEN WILL KNOW* that you are my disciples, if you love one another" said Jesus (John 13:35). Is this the way the rest of the world looks at the Christian church? Or do they merely see divisions and intolerance, criticism and narrow-mindedness?

The narrow-mindedness of Christians is not a new problem:

> "Teacher," said John, "we saw a man driving out demons in your name and we told him to stop, because he was not one of us." "Do not stop him," Jesus said, "No one who does a miracle in my name can in the next moment say anything bad about me, for whoever is not against us is for us. I tell you the truth, anyone who gives you a cup of water in my name because you belong to Christ will certainly not lose his reward." (Mark 9:38–41)

Now the Bible teaches us that the way to God is a narrow road. And yet we do not have the right to try to make it narrower than it really is by excluding everybody who does not think and believe exactly as we do. Sometimes we are so narrow-minded and so rigid that our hearts are not wide open to what God is doing. Our hearts are closed, as Paul wrote to the Christians at Corinth:

> It is not we who have closed our hearts to you; it is you who have closed your hearts to us. I speak now as though you were my children: show us the same feelings that we have for you. Open your hearts wide! (2 Corinthians 6:12–13, GNB)

Narrow-mindedness is the opposite of an open heart, the opposite of Christian love. God's love, by contrast, always believes the best of others:

> Love is patient, love is kind. It does not envy, it does not boast, it is not proud. It is not rude, it is not self-seeking, it is not easily angered, it keeps no record of wrongs. Love does not delight in evil but rejoices with the truth. It always protects, always trusts, always hopes, always perseveres. Love never fails. (1 Corinthians 13:4–8)

If we really believed these verses, it would be a joy to work together with Christians from other denominations and different backgrounds; to learn from individuals and groups who may have different emphases and experiences of the Holy Spirit, of sanctification, of mission and evangelism. Instead, we bicker and fight over these and every conceivable minor issue. I believe strongly that a lack of understanding is a basic cause of this narrow-mindedness, and that it is essential for us to look at these issues that divide Christians with honesty and with love. This is the only way in which we will learn to have a wide-open heart.

Labels

Our fondness for putting labels on people, for assuming that people will live up (or down) to our stereotyped image of their spiritual background or denomination, has probably caused more damage than any other issue in the church. For a start, it is harder to generalize now than at any other time in history. There are evangelical people and Bible-believing people and charismatic people in almost every denomination you can find.

Often we criticize; but in fact we are very ignorant of what other people believe. For instance, I know a lot of people who are very negative about the charismatic movement but, in fact, are very ignorant of what that movement actually means and what it includes.

And what happens to the people who are criticized in a situation like this? Often they in turn become more narrow-minded. Especially if they feel they're under attack, especially if they feel threatened. They react defensively, either by the spoken or written word, in a way that may not help the situation. This is the way divisions and prejudices start. I've made some mistakes in this area myself. I've said some things about people and groups that were perhaps less than best, and sometimes those things have been remembered ever since.

The word of God teaches that love covers over all wrongs. I strongly recommend that you read *Love Covers* by Billheimer.[1] The word of God also teaches that different Christians can and should have fellowship together. This means that we should know how to compassionately disagree.

Someone asked me recently, "How exactly do you compassionately disagree?" Let me give you an example. Maybe I have a strong conviction that I should wear red socks. Then one day a Christian friend comes to me and says, "Brother, I don't believe you should be wearing those red socks. I believe you should be wearing yellow socks." What do you think I should do in that situation? Do I immediately say, "Yes, my friend, you are right. I see it all now. All these years I have been disobeying God by wearing red socks." Not at all! There is no reason why I should not follow my own convictions in relatively minor matters. Or do I say to my friend, "If that is the way you feel, we can no longer have fellowship together. Until you repent of your yellow socks, I will not work with you." No! He also has the right to his own opinion. Neither do we spend weeks and months ignoring the needs for evangelism, service, and prayer while we argue out this matter of socks. No, we agree to disagree. I still love my friend, I still fellowship with him, and I still work with him, however much we compassionately disagree.

Now I know that this is a very trivial illustration. But I believe that the same principle can apply to many other things that Christians may feel are much more important, although not as important as the basic doctrines such as the divinity of Christ, the inspiration of the Scriptures, and the need for all people to repent and believe. These things, the things that you will find in the doctrinal statement of most evangelical churches or organizations, are basic. But there are many other things that are not basic. And if you are to have anything to do with Operation Mobilization or any other Christian organization, sooner or later you will see things that you don't like. Don't let that hinder you! I see a lot of things in OM that I don't like, and I'm still working with them. My wife sees a lot of things in me that she doesn't like, but she hasn't abandoned me!

Doctrine

Now, says someone, it is all very well learning to compassionately disagree over socks, hymn books, or orders of service. But what about much more important matters? What about people who deny the lordship of Christ, the full inspiration of the whole Bible, or the need for mission and evangelism. Surely our attitude to them must be one of absolute rejection!

We are on a narrow road as Bible-believing Christians when it comes to these basic beliefs. And it is right that we should have clear in our minds what is a minor, negotiable matter and what is beyond negotiation and debate—the basic beliefs of our faith. It is normal to have struggles with people over these basic teachings; the church in New Testament times was constantly struggling in this area. In some cases, we may have to separate from someone in terms of working together. I'm not saying that we can always work with everyone. We need to have our principles. We need to have our standards. But when we decide that we can't work with a particular Christian, it doesn't mean that we get arrogant with him; that we become unloving. It means that we compassionately disagree.

We had a big meeting once with a particular group, and we had to make the decision that we would not work together unless they changed their position on a number of areas. The biggest one was that at that time they taught that to be a disciple you had to leave secular work. Nobody was a true disciple unless they left secular work. Now although that is not as fundamental as the divinity of Christ, it was still a basic divergence, because one of the strongest messages in OM is that you can be a disciple back in your home town, working in an office, a factory, or a school, wherever God puts you.

But we came out of that very difficult meeting with love for one another. And in fact I have continued my friendship with the leader of that group, and we've corresponded ever since. Sometimes we need to just let these things go and be past history. Not to hold anything against anybody, just continue to pray and press on with the work.

Most evangelical Christians believe that the Bible, as originally written down, is without error and fully inspired by God's Holy Spirit. Not surprisingly, this is the area where we have the most disagreements with other groups and individuals. But sometimes we need to understand where the problem lies. Some people seem to find it easy to believe every word in the Bible. Personally, I'm always a bit skeptical about how genuine this is. "Oh, God's word, it's so wonderful; it ministers to me every day." Christians are always so positive about the Bible.

Nobody ever wants to admit that they have any problems with the Bible; maybe because they don't want to be thought heretics. But I want to tell you that I have had a lifetime's struggle with it, especially with many passages in the Old Testament. It would be so much easier not to believe that it was inspired by God. Now in fact I do believe that the Bible is God's inerrant word, but I can't say that I've arrived at that belief without a struggle, or without many, many questions and doubts over passages in both the Old and New Testaments.

I have tried to run back to agnosticism, I'm not a natural Christian; I'm a natural backslider. I don't believe things easily. I've wrestled with the doctrine of hell every year since my conversion, trying to reject it, so that I wouldn't have to believe that all these non-believers were lost. It would relieve a lot of spiritual pain, a lot of pressure, to believe that somehow all these good people will make it to God some other way than by hearing and responding to the gospel of Christ.

I have been very greatly helped in this whole area by Dr. Francis Schaeffer. Years ago I listened to a series of tapes by Dr. Schaeffer on this and similar subjects,[2] which I found incredibly helpful. There *are* problems for those of us who believe the Bible is God's word. But I believe the problems are much greater for the man who does not believe the Bible is God's word.

And once you accept that the whole of the Bible is God's word, then you need to look at every passage on a particular subject, in context, before you can see what God is saying to us on that subject. You cannot simply base your life on one or two verses on any one subject, taken out of context. And if you take the whole of the word of God, and let one verse balance out another verse, as we discussed in the last chapter, then I believe you will end up in the land of the open-hearted. You will see that God works in different people in different ways and in different situations in different ways. I am aware, of course, that you can also take certain passages and promote a narrow-minded viewpoint. But to do that you have to take some verses and leave out other verses. Let's take the whole of the word of God and enlarge our vision of what God is doing today.

The Holy Spirit

The second large area of disagreement and narrow-mindedness among Christians is over the work of the Holy Spirit in our lives. This is particularly ironical since the Holy Spirit was given to the church so that we could be united and so that we could love one another; so that we might have power to witness; so that we might have a Teacher and a Guide. Perhaps when you look at things from the devil's point of view, it is not surprising that he has used this issue to divide and confuse Christian people.

It is essential to understand that many of our present divisions over the work of the Holy Spirit have arisen from deep, historical differences in theology between the different branches of the Protestant church. Now this is not the time or the place to go into these different theologies, although if this is troubling you, you could write to me care of the publishers, and I will send you a booklist. All that you need to understand here is that some churches emphasize very strongly the sovereignty of God, and therefore that when people become Christians, they are baptized with the Holy Spirit at that point and are then saved for eternity. They are filled with the Holy Spirit day by day if they are walking with God and learning to do his will.

The churches that emphasize this point of view tend to be those known as "reformed" and include many Presbyterian, Baptist, and Free Evangelical churches.

Other churches (including the Methodist and Holiness churches) emphasize much more man's free will and believe that once a person becomes a Christian, it is then necessary to seek the "second blessing" or filling or baptism of the Holy Spirit (here these terms are taken to mean the same thing) as a separate experience. They believe that Christians have the Holy Spirit at conversion, but that they must be filled with the Spirit to receive power to work for God, and that if they turn away from *God*, their salvation may even be lost. Historically, Pentecostal and charismatic Christians have followed on from this line of theology, but they emphasize the "baptism of the Spirit" as a much more dramatic experience, usually involving speaking in tongues. They also tend to emphasize the other supernatural gifts of the Spirit, such as healing, more than other churches.

Where it gets complicated is that, in these days, charismatic churches have arisen from all sorts of denominations, so that you may get charismatic Methodists, charismatic Baptists, or charismatic Anglicans, as well as the "house churches" and "community churches." Most of these groups are very strongly evangelical, and are similar to the Pentecostal churches on their views of the Holy Spirit, although their teaching on other issues, such as church government, is usually quite different. Of course there are many, many variations between all the different groups, between different individual churches, so we must be careful not to generalize about any individual's beliefs.

All evangelical believers agree that the essential thing is that we must be born again. Now some people have tremendously emotional conversions; others have quiet conversion experiences; others are not even sure when they were born again. Are people from the first group going to say that the others have never been born again? Of course not! We can see clearly that God sometimes works like a mighty rushing wind and sometimes like a still, small voice. But in both cases, the important thing is to remember that God is working in different ways in different people.

I believe that the same is true of the rest of the Christian life. God works in different people in different ways. God can fill you with his Spirit, if you are from the reformed tradition, like me, day by day as you walk with him. Or he can fill you dramatically in what some would call a "crisis experience." Billy Graham says of the filling of the Holy Spirit, "I don't care how you get it: just get it!" Today we are spending a lot of time arguing about words, about the language we use to describe how the Holy Spirit works in other people's lives, instead of getting on and letting him work in *our* lives.

Does God only use people from one stream of theology? No, of course not. You only have to read any history of missions to see that some of the greatest men and women of God have come out of one or the other of these schools of thought. And they all lived lives in the power of the Spirit.

In fact if you read some of the biographies of these great men of God, you will soon see that the lives of the one group were as powerful as that of the other group. Wesley, the founder of Methodism, was completely opposite in his theology of the Holy Spirit to Whitefield, the great preacher, and yet God used them both in the great Evangelical Revival in Britain. I wish we had a few men like this now, whatever they believed about sanctification. I wouldn't bother asking a Wesley or a Whitefield what he believed about the work of the Holy Spirit before I decided whether I could work with him. I can work with anyone who has such spiritual reality in his life.

Fruit and Gifts

I believe we need to make an important distinction between the fruit of the Spirit and the gifts of the Spirit. The fruit of the Spirit is produced in all Christians as they yield to the Holy Spirit, as we saw in the first chapter. I believe that once a Christian has been truly filled with the Holy Spirit, however that filling has come about, the fruit of the Spirit will be seen in his or her life:

> The fruit of the Spirit is love, joy, peace, patience, kindness, good-
> ness, faithfulness, gentleness and self-control. (Galatians 5:22–23)

This is why I am not that concerned whether you have had a thunderbolt experience of the Holy Spirit or a "still, small voice" experience. I am convinced that the important thing is what you are *today* in terms of holiness. Is the fruit of the Spirit present in your life each day and in increasing power?

The fruit of the Spirit should be produced in every Christian as he or she yields to the Holy Spirit. But the gifts are given accord-ing to the will of God. He may give one to one person and half a dozen to another! He may even give different gifts to different people at different times in their lives!

I do not believe that we should try to tie God down and insist that unless Christians have the gift of tongues or prophecy or healing or whatever, that they are not filled with the Holy Spirit. It seems to me that to be so dogmatic about what gifts individual Christians should have, and to try to impose those ideas on others from different backgrounds and different traditions, is not biblical and, indeed, undermines the sovereignty of God in our lives.

> Are all apostles? Are all prophets? Are all teachers? Do all work
> miracles? Do all have gifts of healing? Do all speak in tongues?
> Do all interpret? But eagerly desire the greater gifts. (1 Corinthians
> 12:29–31)

What are these greater gifts? Love is the greatest gift of the Holy Spirit, as Paul goes on to show us in 1 Corinthians 13.

Extremism

Going on from divisions among Christians over the work of the Holy Spirit leads us on to look at the position of extremists in the church. Among extremists I include those from all streams of theology, whose beliefs, if carried to extremes, may become dangerous heresies.

For example, Christians may believe in the sovereignty of God.

But if they start to take that belief to the extreme and to believe in the sovereignty of God to such an extent that they take away completely the free will of man, they will deny any need to tell people about the good news of Jesus Christ! "If God wants to save the heathen," they will say, "he will save them. Don't you get excited about it. The whole world is in his hands!"

Other Christians may believe strongly in the need to be "baptized in the Spirit" to give power to witness. But if they are not careful, they may become extreme about the need for "spiritual experience" or "revival" and spend all their time in emotionally-charged meetings rather than getting on with the work for which the Spirit was sent.

I have met some Christians who seem to see demons everywhere and may end up getting themselves into situations they are unable to handle. Every time they see a sick person they think, "Demons!" Now if you see someone who is truly demon-possessed, the thing to do is to fast and pray and to ask the advice of a more mature Christian or Christian leader. Please do not think that you personally must rescue every person with deep problems.

Some Christians become extreme over the question of healing. Now, I know that God can heal the sick. I know that he can raise the dead! I believe God can do anything! I personally have seen sick people raised back to health after praying for them. But that does not mean that we should be so taken up with prayer that we forget to call in a properly qualified medical person, whose gifts of healing also come from God.

Sometimes I meet people who get "guidance" from God through visions and dreams. Now, God's method of guidance is his Word, the Bible. I don't doubt that in some cases he may give a vision to someone, but that vision *must* be in accordance with the word of God. I am also very hesitant about putting a lot of emphasis on God speaking to us through dreams—although I know that in the Middle East we have seen God use dreams very powerfully to turn Muslims to Christ.

How important it is to realize that when we start taking verses out of context we can defend almost anything! No matter what you are doing, you are in trouble when you begin to trust only in your feelings, and then try to justify those feelings from the Scriptures. God says that we are to love him with all our heart, soul, mind, and strength. This includes the emotions, of course, but it also includes our reason and our common sense.

I believe that it is nothing less than a miracle, the way young people in OM from many, many churches and backgrounds have worked together in unity for all these years, with almost no serious division. Truly, only the Holy Spirit of God working in people's hearts could have done the impossible!

But Satan will try to take any Christian organization, even OM, and make it extreme on some point or other. I tell you, *anything*, no matter how good, taken to an extreme, becomes a snare. And if we become unloving and narrow-minded and start to judge and condemn each other, then we are going to grieve the Spirit of God.

But when we learn to open our hearts to God to be filled with his Spirit—whether we have an emotional experience or a quiet, daily infilling—*then* the world is going to shake! It is this that will bring people into a realistic experience of Jesus Christ.

Dogmatism

It is truly amazing what Christian people can find to disagree on. I have been to public seminars where you sit and listen to two Christian speakers arguing with each other quite strongly; sometimes on an important issue, but other times on completely trivial matters.

One Christian leader in America has decided that all televisions are idols, just as there were idols in the Old Testament. And this group of Christians took their "idols" into the back yard, they took out their guns (I don't know what they were doing as Christians carrying guns, that seems to be quite acceptable in America), and they blew up their televisions. Militant Christianity! Yet another leader has declared that all contemporary Christian music, particularly if it has a beat (I don't know how you decide whether or not it has a beat) comes from the pit of Satan.

In his book *Love Covers,* Billheimer talks about the tremendous divisions that arose between the old Holiness Christians and the new charismatic Christians. He found it very difficult, as an old Holiness man, to accept these American charismatics as Christians, when he saw the way they dressed and the way the women used make-up. The old Holiness Christians believed make-up was from Satan! These issues divided families and split churches down the middle. And to this day, churches are splitting over things like this, and best friends are turning on each other.

I have run into storms in this area myself. Once, when I was very young and very ignorant, I showed a set of slides about our evangelistic campaigns in Mexico in a very strong Holiness church. One of them was a slide of my aunt's house, and she had a pair of shorts on. So I said, "Oh, on the way to Mexico for our campaign, we stayed with these Christian people," (I didn't want to say my aunt) "and we had fellowship with them." That was the end of my fellowship with that church! The pastor took me into a corner afterwards, and he said, "I have been fighting shorts for over five years, and you have come in here and in twenty minutes undone what I have tried to do for five years." I was just a young Christian. I didn't know shorts were of the devil!

When. I was younger, one of my areas of very great dogmatism concerned drinking, as a believer, any form of alcoholic beverage. I had a message against alcohol when I was only seventeen that was considered right out of the prohibition era. People compared me with Billy Sunday, who used to smash bottles of whisky in the pulpit during his sermons. And I was convinced that a dedicated believer and a teetotaller were the same.

Then I came to Europe, to Spain. And I was longing to see some of the Spanish Christians moving into full-time Christian work because there was so much for them to do. I was very excited when God answered our prayers and delighted when one of these Spanish disciples came to me and invited me over to his house for lunch. And there they were, pouring out into glasses. . . *wine*!

Of course, I soon discovered that even the most committed

Spanish believers have wine at their tables, and they regard it as a really minor issue. But to me it was not minor! I wrestled with this issue to the point of torture! But in the end I had to accept that people from different backgrounds could have different beliefs and still work together in love.

Separation

One of the biggest issues at present in the American fundamentalist church is that of separation. Many of the American separatist Christians have turned against Billy Graham, and they have also turned against us in OM because they regard us as being part of the ecumenical movement, which is part of the movement of Antichrist.

Now I believe in separation: from apostasy, from heresy, from sin! But what we're talking about here are double-separated Christians; that is, people who believe in secondary separation. This means that if I were to have lunch with a Christian friend (even though I may not agree fully with all his views), and he in turn has shaken hands with a theologian who once denied the Virgin Birth, then I would also be tarnished by that theologian's views, so if you were a true double-separated believer you would not be able to have fellowship with me.

Now you may not have heard of this issue before; you may think this is something quite small and unimportant. But this is one of the biggest issues in the American church, without any question. There was one Christian who was one of the most outspoken voices of this particular brand of Christianity, who conducted city-wide evangelistic campaigns with only double-separated Christians. But after many years of conducting these campaigns, God showed him how unloving, how narrow-minded and rigid he had been, and he decided that he had to leave.

He then wrote an article explaining why he was leaving, which hit the fundamentalist world in America like an atomic bomb. And because he had been so involved he was able to expose all the bickering and the negative criticism that took place in these supposedly super-separated Christians. Indeed, he compared it to a KGB operation in which people and organizations are listed and black-listed according to whether they can be considered truly separated or not.

This issue has caused a lot of hurt and a lot of pain. And that has been felt even out on the mission field. I thank God that the heart of that Christian leader was opened, and that he has written letters of apology to many of the people that he had previously spoken against. I believe that God was able to bring him out of that cul-de-sac of rigidity because of his great love of the word of God. He had memorized so much of the Bible that the Holy Spirit did indeed lead him back to the truth and to a more open heart.

Organizations

Yet another area that divides Christians is the tension between the local church and other Christian organizations, often described as "para-church." This affects us in OM because some people who would benefit both themselves and others by working with us for a time do not come because they or their churches "don't believe in para-church organizations." They believe that all missions should be carried out by the local church. When it comes to sending people overseas, of course, the local churches generally do not have the experience or structures necessary to do this—and so often very little results.

The work of God is bigger than any fellowship or organization. Often, to get a particular job done, God has raised up organizations or mission societies. They have been brought into being to meet a specific need. We don't worship the organization, we don't get uptight because we don't agree with every single thing in that organization. We need to think about the picture of the Body in 1 Corinthians 12:

> The eye cannot say to the hand, "I don't need you!" And the head cannot say to the feet, "I don't need you!" (verse 21)

God has brought into being movements like OM as a response to a specific need. We have a planet of five billion people, with huge churches around America and Europe, and many young people in these churches, at least when we began our work, were sitting around doing nothing. So God said, "These people need to move!" And by his mercy he raised up a movement that had expertise and gifts in mobilizing and training and recruiting people. Now those people (over forty thousand young people have now had training in OM) are working with almost every mission society in the world today.

But still some churches and groups believe that all para-church organizations (such as SERVE, OM, YWAM, or TEAR Fund) are not really of God or are somehow God's second best. They believe (as we do) that God works through the local church. But they seem to see para-church agencies as somehow in opposition to or competition with the local church; whereas, we believe that they should be subject to the local church. Recently we have seen signs that this attitude is changing, and we look forward to the time when we will be able to work with all these churches as an overseas agency to carry out the work of evangelism for and with the local church. We believe that one of the greatest keys to the evangelism of the world is partnership, and we long for that to increase.

Let's stop bickering and judging and criticizing the way things are done in this movement or that organization. Let's praise God for the work that all these different agencies are doing: those that specialize in relief work, those that specialize in outreach, those that specialize in long-term mission, and those that specialize in short-term training. As we thrust ourselves into reaching many, many people around the world who have never yet responded to the gospel, I believe we're going to need one another; we're going to need unity. And I believe that as we become more united, we'll be able to pray together in spiritual power; and as we pray together in spiritual power, then we'll be able to tear down the strongholds of the enemy.

An Open Heart

So I want to plead with you, on the basis of these passages we have considered, and on the basis of many, many other passages throughout the Bible, to have a wide-open heart. Work with all of God's people. Learn to love them. And when someone initially turns you off, go back to your room and say, "Jesus, I believe you're going to do a work in my heart towards that person." And sometimes the greatest fellowship you have will be with people who are very, very different from you.

You may even be surprised and end up marrying someone who's very different from you! I can tell you, there's nothing like discovering, as a hard-line fundamentalist from a good reformed background, several years after your marriage, that your wife is praying privately in tongues in another room! And I am convinced that through unity and through love we don't have to sacrifice basic truth; we don't have to compromise our deep personal convictions. But through love we can operate and live and function in a way that will provide less scandal for the outside community and bring more glory to God.

> *Lord, we pray that unity may increase in your Body, and that we would have enlarged vision, more open hearts, more open minds; not to bring in error, but to keep things in their right perspective by the power of your Holy Spirit.*
>
> *Grant us this as we go forward together, often struggling with very many basic issues in life, but students of your Word and committed to world evangelism.*
>
> *Amen.*

4

real PEOPLE, *real* POWER

HOW REAL IS YOUR CHRISTIANITY? Is it the sort of disciple-ship that Jesus talked about when he said,

> If anyone would come after me, he must deny himself and take up his cross daily and follow me. For whoever wants to save his life will lose it, but whoever loses his life for me will save it. (Luke 9:23–24)

Or are we, in the words of A.W. Tozer, that great man of God whom many called a twentieth-century prophet, simply "serving our own interests under a disguise of godliness"?[3] Instead of belonging to the local sports club or social club, we belong to the church. There we find meetings with like-minded people at regular times (but not too often or there will be complaints), pleasant and uplifting music and even rewarding times of helping others.

But the Christian life is not first about more meetings or more songs. The Christian life is about justice and peace and righteousness and godliness and purity. It's reaching out to your neighbor at convenient times and inconvenient times. It's helping him when his tire is punctured. It's helping him when he needs to get to the hospital. It's not first about giving money; it's about giving chunks of your life. And until we start practicing that, we know very little of what Jesus meant when he talked about being a disciple.

Being A Disciple

What does Jesus mean in these verses by denying ourselves and taking up a cross? It is clear that he is not talking simply about giving up chocolate for Lent or even a "hunger lunch" where money saved on food goes to the starving. He is talking about a continual, daily process.

When Jesus died on the cross for us, he paid the price for the sin of our own hearts. It was that sin which had enslaved and corrupted us. And so, to follow him into deliverance, we need to be saved from ourselves, from our sinful nature and self-centeredness. Only as we deny self daily are we freed from its domination.

So it is our own selves, our own nature, that we are to deny and put to death. For the cross Jesus is talking about here is not some golden ornament to decorate our churches, but an instrument of death. Only as we take up that cross daily, identifying ourselves with Jesus' death to all that is opposed to the will of God, will we be delivered from ourselves.

Now you may say that all this talk of denial and death is old-fashioned and negative. But it is only through that denial and daily death that true life begins. True, the cross is the end of a life of sin and slavery, but it is also the beginning of a life of holiness and spiritual revolution. When Jesus says, "Follow me," he is not calling us to a narrow, negative existence, but to the most exciting and beautiful fellowship you could ever dream of.

The Crucified Life

I believe that God is calling every Christian to this life of self-denial and commitment. Jesus said,

> Anyone who does not carry his cross and follow me cannot be my disciple. (Luke 14:27)

To carry a cross and follow your Lord does not make you into some kind of religious freak. I believe that we can all have a deeper commitment, that we can be filled with the Holy Spirit, and that Christ can be Lord of every area of our lives, yet that this can happen in a very sane, down-to-earth, balanced, and God-glorifying way. I believe that it is possible for us to be genuine and sincere in our Christian lives without becoming overly emotional or introspective.

Why is it that so often, when Christians talk about the need for repentance and the good news of Jesus Christ, they are ignored by the world around? There are many reasons, but I am sorry to say that one of the commonest reasons is that we do not live what we preach. We preach a gospel of love, and yet we do not love each other. We preach a gospel of commitment, and yet we ourselves are not committed. And the man or woman in the street is not deceived by our fine words and religious phrases. It is only when the people around us see the evidence of a changed life that they will begin to take what we say seriously.

The key to reaching people with the gospel is not evangelism at home or abroad, not serving others in the church or in the community (although all these things are part of the gospel), but the changed hearts of Christians. The key is for Christians to allow God to take over their lives, putting self to death and letting Jesus rule instead. We may spend all the hours we like in evangelism and service, but unless our hearts have changed, we will be doing it for ourselves and not truly serving God.

To change the whole direction of our lives in this way may hurt at the time. A man of God once said, "In the Christian life there'll be no gain without pain." No wonder so few are really going on for God today! We are the generation that has run away from pain more than any other generation; we've got every medicine in the world, every kind of painkiller you can imagine. But there's no painkiller you can take that's going to take away the pain of spiritual growth.

Roy Hession in his book *Calvary Road*[4] talks about the need for brokenness before God, the need for coming to a place where we realize that our lives without him are totally worthless, and that we are dependent on him for everything. These ideas are not very popular today. But when God begins to break down the hard core of pride, selfishness, and arrogance in your heart, it's going to hurt. Are you prepared for that? Can you really sing, "Break me, melt me, mold me, fill me" and mean it? Because God will answer your prayer, if you mean it from the heart.

Let's look now at four very practical ways in which we can make sure that Jesus is really Lord of our lives.

Letting Jesus be Lord of Our Relationships

Have you had any really good messages in your church lately on sex? There are over five or six hundred verses in the Bible on the subject of sex that we almost never preach on; but you can be sure that if anyone gets into sexual sin, they will be gossiped about, they will be looked down upon, and they will have a rough time among all the nice respectable Christians.

When we see people fall into sin who are part of the church, we should realize that part of the responsibility is ours. Because we have not taught on this subject, we have not taught our young people how to have healthy relationships with the opposite sex; we have not taught them how to withstand temptation and have a realistic view of sex and marriage. Instead we watch more romantic films, and we read more romance books than any other generation in history, and we're paying an awesome price for it in broken marriages and broken families, as people find that their expectations of married life do not add up to the reality. I'm not saying there's no place for romance, but I'm saying that the whole thing has got out of control.

Billy Graham said that if you don't win this battle against impurity, you lose the biggest battle in the Christian life. And I know there are people all over the world, though they may be leaders, though they may love Jesus, who are walking in sin in the area of impurity. Every time I've ever spoken in a conference, people have come up to me for prayer, or they have written to me and they've confessed sex before marriage or other kinds of immorality or pornography that's been tearing them apart and turning them into a spiritual split personality.

Two thousand years ago, Paul wrote to Timothy and he said "Flee the evil desires of youth" (2 Timothy 2:22). In other words, if you are young and you have a girlfriend or a boyfriend, you don't drive off in your parents' car to watch the sunset alone together on a hot summer evening, and then pray that God will make your thoughts pure. If you take your girlfriend or your boyfriend, however many years either of you have been Christians, and you go alone into the dark corners, the college bedrooms, or the back of a car, you are asking for trouble. No—instead you "flee the evil desires of youth." You keep in the company of others, you take advantage of social events and sporting events, and you build up a friendship and a spiritual relationship that will keep you following God together in the years to come.

In the middle of all the news recently about the immorality going on among Christian leaders, my daughter came to me one day and said, "Dad, I want to know whether you have been faithful to Mother for all the time you have been married." Now I have battled with lust all my life; even before my conversion at the age of sixteen, I was addicted to pornography and had already had over a dozen girlfriends (fortunately that was in the age of romance rather than permissive sex). So it was one of the greatest joys in my life to be able to tell my daughter that by God's grace and by denying self and taking up my cross daily to follow Jesus, I had indeed been faithful to my wife for all of these twenty-eight years.

I am hesitant to tell that story, but I think that it's important to realize that the media generally like to report only the negative things. And for every Christian leader who falls, there are dozens and dozens who learn the basic principles of discipleship, who learn the disciplined life, the crucified life, who know how to stand against temptation, and who are therefore running the race with Jesus day by day.

Letting Jesus be Lord of Our Words

Is your tongue controlled by the Spirit of God? The Psalmist was so conscious of his need for control that he said,

> Set a guard over my mouth, O Lord;
> keep watch over the door of my lips. (Psalm 141:3)

Uncontrolled words have destroyed more churches and more families, I believe, than immorality, crime, or lying. Destructive gossip is one of the most potent forces for evil in the Christian world today. Because every time you repeat a rumor, every time you spread a little titbit of negative comment about a fellow

Christian or Christian group, you are dividing and hurting the Body of Christ. And this has been one of Satan's most effective strategies in recent years.

There is a place for talking on a trivial level, particularly with neighbors and non-Christian friends. Let us beware of becoming so superspiritual that we can only reply with a Bible verse when a neighbor makes some comment on the weather. Our neighbors need to know that we are real, sane people, and that we too are concerned with what concerns them.

And there is a place for constructive criticism, preferably made to the person concerned, face to face. But so often what most of us do is to gossip. We are afraid to confront people who have irritated us, people who have hurt us, people whom we believe are behaving wrongly. So instead of going to them and, in love, telling them how we feel, we let all our bitterness and anger out to our friends. And they pass it on to their friends, who pass it on to their friends. Eventually, of course, it gets back to the original people concerned, but by then it is so exaggerated and negative that they find it very, very difficult to forgive. And so you get division and bitterness arising in the church.

Now unless you have learned, as a spiritually mature person, to have some control in this area, then you are not ready to use your tongue to tell people even in your own culture about the gospel, let alone launch out into cross-cultural evangelism, because the potential for misunderstandings in other languages and cultures is very, very great. The work of God can be put back for years or even decades in a sensitive situation by someone with an uncontrolled and undisciplined tongue.

Learn to think before you speak. Learn to know what Jesus would have said to that person in that situation. Whatever the temptation to seem right, clever, or simply to have the last word, it is our determination to deny self and follow the Lord in this area that will make the difference.

Letting Jesus be Lord of Our Time

Time, it is often said, is our most precious asset. Not one of us knows how much of it we have left, or what will be God's plan for the rest of our lives. Yet when we let Jesus have true control of our lives, we will not necessarily end up doing more. Many of us spend far too much time already in religious activity. We seem to be convinced that the more time we spend, the better our service for the Lord must be. So we rush around like whirlwinds, blissfully unaware that we are victims of our own undisciplined and disorganized lives. We are always "too busy," and yet actually we accomplish very little.

Many years ago I was in danger of becoming a little extreme on this particular issue. I felt I should always get up in the morning by 6:30, and if I slept later than this, even if I had been late to bed the night before, I felt that I should somehow work harder to make up for the lost time. Also, I personally did not feel that I had the time to relax or play sports, because the demands were so overwhelming. God had to show me that he was in control, and that occasionally a little extra time sleeping, a couple of hours playing golf, or even an evening to take my wife to a movie could all be included in his plan.

Tozer says, "Working for Christ has today been accepted as the ultimate test of godliness among all but a few evangelical Christians. Christ has become a project to be promoted or a cause to be served instead of a Lord to be obeyed. . . . The result is an army of men who will run without being sent and speak without being commanded."[5]

Let us make Jesus truly Lord of our time, thinking about the priorities of what we have to do from his perspective, not ours (and that may bring about some changes that will surprise us) and organizing our time for maximum efficiency and speed. Let us keep calm and relaxed, knowing that he is always in control and that no so-called last-minute crisis is beyond his power and grace.

Letting Jesus be Lord of Our Finances

"Any of you who does not give up everything he has," said Jesus, "cannot be my disciple" (Luke 14:33). This is not a popular verse today. For many people, financial security is an important and overriding ambition. We have already seen the absolute importance of surrendering everything we possess to God. Now let us think about letting him be Lord of every aspect of our finances.

For instance, should your choice of career be motivated by the financial security it will bring? Or is your security in the Lord of heaven and earth? This is not to say that he may not guide you into a well-paid career. The rich have greater responsibilities in the kingdom of God. We will see in the last chapter how great is the need for more senders, more supporters, in world mission today. A lack of finance is limiting the work of God today in every place I have ever visited.

Is Jesus Lord of all your possessions? Have you laid them at his feet, asking him which you truly need and which you should sell or give away? Many Christians today seem to follow unquestioningly the materialist idea that every year they should own more and more. But this is not God's way. God supplies according to our needs, and if you no longer need what God once gave you, I believe you should think seriously about whether you should still keep it. Equally, we must learn not to hanker after things simply because our neighbors have them. Our priority should be to glorify God, not to keep up with those next door.

Most Christians today know very little about trusting God for their everyday needs. In the nineteenth century George Müller supported not only himself and his family but hundreds of orphans on the answers to prayer alone. He said that if we want great faith we must begin to use the little faith we already have. Dare today to trust God for something small and ordinary, and next week or next year you may be able to trust him for answers bordering on the miraculous. Many people who have come on Operation Mobilization campaigns over the years have found that having to trust God for day-to-day finances has transformed their attitude to money and possessions. If he is really Lord of all we have, we need not feel guilty about what he has given us, but can use it wisely and sacrificially in his work.

A Deeper Commitment

"If any man would come after me," said Jesus; and in this one phrase he put before us the choice that has divided the world ever since. Do we really want to follow him or is the cost too great? If we really want to become followers of Christ we must become personally involved in his death and resurrection through repentance, prayer, self-denial, humility, obedience, and sacrificial love. That is why it is easier to talk about commitment than to experience it.

The cost of true commitment is indeed great. But the rewards are even greater. It is only when we take Jesus' words seriously and act upon them that his power breaks through into our lives.

Let's realize that the crucified life is for everyone. The lordship of Christ is for everyone. We are all called to purity, to reality. We are all to be keen to spread God's word. Is it wrong for me to think that every Christian should be excited about Jesus, the Son of the living God? He is living in our hearts, making us kings and priests and heirs of his kingdom.

It's because I believe that God has called every Christian to a life of deeper commitment and true discipleship that I am involved in a training program like OM. If you come on OM, you won't study for a degree or spend all your time in books or essays or debates, although there will be opportunity for all those things. Instead our programs have been patterned on the methods that Jesus Christ used. Jesus' training was on the job. His disciples were doers, not just hearers. And they learned as much by their mistakes as by their successes.

In OM we expect young people to move out in evangelism, in prayer, and in team living. And quite soon they start to find out what the crucified life is all about. Because there's nothing like a few real problems of insufficient finance or food you don't like or simply the team member you can't get on with to bring out the areas in your life which are not yet controlled by the Holy Spirit.

Now, I'm not saying that spiritual growth is going to happen overnight. And I want to make it clear that we are learners, and we are stragglers. We are like the learner drivers in Britain with their "L" plates displayed for everyone to see. And yet it's as we are willing to learn that God leads us on to a deeper commitment and a Spirit-filled life.

Pray your own prayer of surrender. Pray a prayer of repentance, come to Jesus in faith, and breathe in that forgiveness and that grace and renewal that the Holy Spirit can give. And determine to be a spiritual fighter, a spiritual runner, a disciple of Jesus Christ.

Let the Holy Spirit fill you. Trust God's word; "God has not given us a spirit of fear but of love and power and a calm mind." Some of us need to understand more of what it is to take a deep drink of the grace of God. I need the grace of God, the forgiveness of God, and the mercy of God every day. And I have found that often God meets us in the moment of weakness, rather than strength. He doesn't always wait until we feel spiritual, he doesn't always wrap life up in a nice little present with a bow on the top. The life of discipleship, the life of deeper commitment includes ongoing battle and ongoing struggles. It will include fear and worry and anxiety at times. But Jesus is always there.

I believe God is waiting for you to make the greatest, deepest commitment and surrender of your life to Christ, his word, and his cause, that you have ever made. I believe he's waiting for you to put your hands on the plough and determine you're not going back, whether he leads you to Hong Kong, Pakistan, or Birmingham, whether he leads you into "full-time" ministry, or whether he leads you to be a hard-working sender supplying the desperately-needed finance.

Do you love Jesus? Do you love Jesus with all your heart, soul, mind, and strength? Have you put your life on the altar as we're told to do in Romans 12:1: "I urge you, brothers, in view of God's mercy, to offer your bodies as living sacrifices"?

Yes, this is a lifetime challenge. You may say it is too much. But I want to say on the authority of God's word that it's not too much. Because God gives grace. He forgives when you fall down. He lifts you up. He cleanses, he renews, he forgives. He knows all about you. And he loves you still. And it's that love that should motivate us to give our lives more fully to him in total commitment and surrender and be the real people that God would have us to be.

Commitment is part of a process; if you're not willing to deny self daily, take up the cross, and follow Jesus; if you're not willing to put into practice the principles of the crucified life, then the initial commitment, even if made for a second or third time in your life, will be of little value. Praise God for the experience that you may have as the Holy Spirit works in your life and blesses you and fills you; but if that crisis is not followed by a process, it will become an abscess.

I believe many people are ready for God's process. I believe the Holy Spirit is preparing many people for steps forward in their Christian lives. He may even have prepared you, if you want to say with all your heart, "I am crucified with Christ. I will surrender everything to him. I'll go where he wants me to go and do what he wants me to do."

Living God, by your Spirit, convict us of areas where we're fooling around. Convict us of areas of laziness. Convict us of the barriers we've built up around ourselves. May self be crucified; may you be magnified, as we consider the challenge before us, as we consider the spiritual harvest fields. We, O Lord, want to be real people. We thank you for real power, the power of your Holy Spirit, who lives and remains in us. We thank you for the power of the gospel, which is your power, O God, for salvation. We thank you, Lord, for the day you saved us and set us free. We thank you for this great gift of salvation.

O Lord, we hunger and thirst for reality, that what we say we believe will be a burning fire in our hearts and in our lives. May we take steps of faith to be your men, to be your women, to go where you want us to go and to do what you want us to do. We thank you, Lord, for your forgiveness and your grace that can make all of this possible.

In Jesus' name,
Amen.

5

accepting **YOURSELF** *and* **OTHERS**

JESUS SAID, "Love your neighbor as yourself." If you have never learned to love yourself you will find it very difficult to love others as Jesus commanded. Accepting yourself is not a once-for-all experience, but something you will learn gradually, often through struggles and failures.

You were created in God's image. And part of his creation was your particular personality, your appearance, and even your background, all those things that you cannot change and that make you into the individual you are. God does not make mistakes. He knew you even before you were born:

> My frame was not hidden from you
>   when I was made in the secret place.
> When I was woven together in the depths of the earth,
>   your eyes saw my unformed body.
> All the days ordained for me
>   were written in your book
>   before one of them came to be. (Psalm 139:15–16)

So God knows how he can work in you and through you and with you. To doubt that God can use you is to doubt his power. Believing that God made you as you are is the first step to self-acceptance.

God's purpose for your life is not to destroy your personality; instead, he wants to enrich it. Being filled with God's Spirit doesn't mean you can't enjoy a sunset any more; it doesn't mean you won't get excited about music or pizza; it doesn't mean that you won't fall in love, that your heart won't pound or your eyes pop when that someone special comes into view. But it does mean that a very powerful degree of self-control will come into your life, so that you will be able to sort out the priorities, the difference between your God-given personality and your selfish nature, so that you will be able to say "no" to self and "yes" to Jesus. It took me a long time before I slowly, gradually, began to accept myself as God had made me. I had this image of what a really spiritual person should be like—very quiet and yet powerful—and I just did not fit that image at all. I even went as far as trying to dress in a way that I felt people expected, in a dark suit and tie. But gradually I realized that God could use me as I am.

You may find that your particular personality means that you don't feel comfortable with certain churches or groups or organizations. You may appreciate them; you may agree fully with what they are doing, but you feel you will never fit in with them. This is not a matter of spirituality but of personality. Sometimes God may ask you to work with them despite that, and sometimes it will be agreed by everyone that it would be better if you worked with another group.

I am very aware that Operation Mobilization is not everybody's cup of tea. God has raised us up as a unique fellowship, to carry on a unique task. We have to train people in a specific way. When I was in Pakistan, I met some of our men and women in OM Pakistan who are learning Urdu. That takes extra discipline. That takes perhaps a degree of soldiering and perseverance that working in Britain may not necessarily demand; here you probably have other problems, for which you need other qualities. We're all different. We all have different amounts of energy; we all have different gifts. Be yourself; don't try to be somebody else.

God's Purpose

It is important to understand why God has created us as we are, with our own particular personality, appearance, and background. He has something planned for our lives which can only be done by someone with that particular combination of characteristics.

His plan for your life cannot be fulfilled by any other individual on this earth.

Many of us may feel that we are too weak for God to use us. But it is through these weaknesses that God's power is revealed in our lives. The apostle Paul was told clearly by God:

> My grace is sufficient for you, for my power is made perfect in weakness. (2 Corinthians 12:9)

We all need to learn this principle. Often in Christian work, we look for the attractive person or the clever person to be in our group. We need to learn to work with the weak, the unattractive, the slow, for this is how God works.

Remember also that God has not yet finished his work in you. However long you have been a Christian, whatever sort of training you have been through, God has only just started in his lifetime process of making you more like Jesus Christ. Let us learn to look forward to what God is going to do in our lives, rather than always looking back.

Think of your outward appearance as a picture frame that shows off the inner qualities and Christlikeness that God is developing in your life. Your inner self, the picture of your personality developed in fellowship with God, is the greatest advertisement possible for the gospel of Jesus Christ. Jesus said:

> Let your light shine before men, that they may see your good deeds and praise your Father in heaven. (Matthew 5:16)

If you are allowing God to develop genuine qualities of love and humility in your life, even though you may not feel he has got very far yet, these will be recognized by unbelievers.

If you find it difficult to accept yourself as you are, or if you find in your heart bitterness or resentment against God for your background or the way you are, ask God to forgive you and help you. Some people have more problems in this area than others. Those who have come from difficult or unloving homes can have real problems relating to God as a loving heavenly Father.

The Human Factor

If we believe that God has made our personality, then we need to allow room for the development of that personality in our lives. This is something that is often overlooked in Christian circles. We must allow for the human factor, or, no matter how "spiritual" we become, we will not survive the tests and challenges ahead of us.

Some of the greatest men and women of God in history have had problems in just this area. One of my favorites is Elijah. In 1 Kings, chapter 18, we read that the people of Israel had been turning away from the Lord to follow the false god Baal. So Elijah summoned the prophets of Baal and all the people and the king to Mount Carmel, and challenged them to a contest. Two bulls were placed on wood ready to be sacrificed. Then Elijah told the prophets of Baal to pray:

> You call on the name of your god, and I will call on the name of the LORD. The god who answers by fire—he is God. (1 Kings 18:24)

Elijah asked God for a miracle, and God answered him. He prayed, the fire fell, and the people were awestruck. He triumphed over the false prophets, made absolute fools of them; and he became the great hero of Israel. But what did he do next?

> Elijah was afraid and ran for his life. When he came to Beersheba in Judah, he left his servant there, while he himself went a day's journey into the desert. He came to a broom tree, sat down under it and prayed that he might die. "I have had enough, LORD," he said. "Take my life; I am no better than my ancestors." Then he lay down under the tree and fell asleep. (1 Kings 19:3–5)

So here is the great prophet, under a tree, thoroughly depressed. I find this story very moving because I see many Christians suffering from depression, and sometimes they don't seem to have heard about the examples that we see in the Bible in these stories of the great men and women of God. Sometimes we always think that these things can be answered by the right Bible verse or someone coming up with the right spiritual prescription, and our pride keeps us from actually seeking the help we need.

I praise God that I have seen people effectively treated, medically treated, for some forms of depression. And so I believe that we need to discern when the problem is emotional or spiritual or when it may be something physical that will need medical help.

Discouragement is a normal part of the Christian life. It is part of our human nature. Some people get discouraged more easily than others, and some get depressed more seriously than others. But if you are active for God, allowing God's word to challenge you; and you're being used even a little by God, then sooner or later you will go through times of discouragement. And it seems to me that if discouragement is a normal part of human experience, then, as Christians, the important thing is to know how to handle it.

I believe that discouragement is the most common strategy that Satan uses to reduce the effectiveness of Christians today. And part of the battle against discouragement is won when we realize that this is something that many, many Christians and Christian leaders have been through before us.

I have treated the subject of discouragement more thoroughly in my book *No Turning Back*. Basically, I believe that learning to handle discouragement is part of normal spiritual growth. We should not expect some sort of supernatural deliverance or emotional experience to wipe out all our negative feelings. God has given us his word, the Bible; we should be feeding on it and learning the promises of God. He has given us his Son, the Lord Jesus, and put within us the Holy Spirit. It's as we learn to draw upon what we already have in Christ by his Holy Spirit that we will be able to come through discouragement.

Look at God's strategy for discouragement in the story of Elijah. First of all he makes sure that Elijah has had a good sleep. Much discouragement can be put down to sheer physical tiredness. Then an angel brings him food, not once but twice, so that he is fully refreshed and strengthened for what is to come. After all this Elijah is ready to go on in the work of God.

I have found this story tremendously helpful. I have always had the potential to become extreme on a number of issues, and some years ago I began to think that it was wrong for me to spend any time just relaxing and being myself. I looked at the number of people in the world who didn't know Christ, and I looked at the need for prayer and the need for evangelism, and I thought that anything else was a waste of time. I was trying to deny the human factor. And God took this verse and showed me that I had to allow time for my own personality if he was going to go on to use me.

I believe that as we learn to trust God more and give ourselves time to relax, we will be able to go on in the Christian life far more effectively. Let us think of God's race as a marathon rather than a sprint; maybe even an "ultra" marathon where people run for as many as a thousand miles at a time. If you started a race like that as a sprint you would not get very far. It is the ones who have trained hard and rested well, and who allow enough time to stop to sleep and to eat who can survive that sort of race.

Forgiving Ourselves

Just as we cannot love others if we do not love ourselves, we will find it difficult to forgive others if there is something in our lives for which we have never forgiven ourselves. We may have confessed it to God and been forgiven. But instead of then forgiving ourselves, we feel we must suffer for the sin, whatever it is, and try to work it out in a sort of self-imposed purgatory.

If you know there is something in your life that you have never forgiven yourself for, first make sure that you have asked for God's forgiveness. Then make sure that you have made things right with the other people involved. For instance, if you have stolen money, even if it is a very small amount, it is not enough to ask God's forgiveness. You must also return the money.

Many of us will go to almost any lengths to avoid going to someone and asking forgiveness. It is amazing what excuses our pride can find for just this simple step. Probably the best thing is to go straight away, as soon as we realize that it is necessary, without thinking too much about it. However, do take care to be sensitive and not to make things worse by speaking in the wrong way.

Sometimes Christians seem to feel that they should not apologize or admit past sins to non-Christians. In fact this is one of the most powerful messages a Christian can bring. Non-Christian people do not like apologizing either, and they will realize that your faith must mean a lot to you if you are prepared to bury your pride and admit you have been wrong.

Accepting Others

The very process of learning to accept ourselves will take us some way towards accepting others, as we recognize some of the struggles they may be going through. However, there are bound to be some times of conflict when we feel another Christian has hurt us, and this can lead to deep-seated resentment and bitterness if we do not react in a Christ-like way.

If you feel that someone has hurt you, keep calm and rational. Try to understand the situation and what caused it. Could you have prevented it? How do the other people involved feel? Try to concentrate on kindness and love for them, rather than your own hurt.

Make sure that you have forgiven anyone who has hurt you. Then leave the hurt alone for it to heal. Do not dwell on it and the way you have been wronged, or bitterness and self-pity will fill you. Do not withdraw from other Christians, even the one who has hurt you, and accept apologies if they are offered.

Forgiving Others

We should forgive others as we have been forgiven by God:

> Peter came to Jesus and asked, "Lord, how many times shall I forgive my brother when he sins against me? Up to seven times?"
>
> Jesus answered, "I tell you, not seven times, but seventy-seven times." (Matthew 18:21–22)

Forgiveness is as basic to our Christian living as the cross of Jesus Christ is to the plan of salvation. Forgiving others means that we believe that God is in control. He is the one who should judge and punish, if necessary, not us.

A lack of forgiveness can lead to many problems in our lives.

Bitterness may result in tension, inability to sleep, and even psy-
chosomatic illness. It will stop our spiritual growth, causing an
inability to love God, doubts about our own salvation, and a bad
witness to others. It is not surprising that depression may be the
end result.

> If anyone says, "I love God," yet hates his brother, he is a liar. For
> anyone who does not love his brother, whom he has seen, cannot
> love God, whom he has not seen. (1 John 4:20)

If you find it difficult to forgive some people, realize that all the
hurt you have experienced may be God's way of pointing out their
need. They may have deep-seated problems that they are unable to
deal with, and that have caused them to hurt others. God may now
be leading you to do what you can to help. Pray for them, help
them, be friendly, and if you have hurt them ask their forgiveness.
This may help them to realize that they also need to ask your forgiveness. Paul wrote to the Christians in Rome:

> Do not repay anyone evil for evil. . . . If it is possible, as far as it
> depends on you, live at peace with everyone. Do not take revenge,
> my friends, but leave room for God's wrath, for it is written: "It is
> mine to avenge; I will repay," says the Lord. On the contrary:
>
> "If your enemy is hungry, feed him;
> if he is thirsty, give him something to drink.
>
> In doing this, you will heap burning coals on his head."
>
> Do not be overcome by evil, but overcome evil with good.
> (Romans 12:17–21)

So let us make these principles a reality in our hearts. Let us learn
to accept ourselves and others in all the complexity that God has
created, listening to God and waiting for his voice. Let us learn to
thank God for what he has already done in our lives and for what
he is going to do, allowing him to fill us afresh each day with his
Holy Spirit, so that we can go where he wants us to go and do
what he wants us to do.

> *Lord, you know all about us, and you love us still. We thank you*

that we have been accepted by you, and that is the basis of our acceptance of ourselves. You love us with an everlasting love; if we were the only one on the planet, you still would have sent your Son to die on the cross for us. We thank you that your arms reach out to embrace us. Draw us in. Deliver us, Lord, from lack of self-acceptance. Deliver us from living in unbelief. We yield ourselves to you, and we believe that you can and will do a new thing in our hearts, in our lives, in our churches, as we move forward by faith, learning to love ourselves and others as you love us, that in the years to come we may still be running, still be praying, still be praising, still be learning.

In Jesus' name,

Amen.

6

new **GENERATION—** **UNFINISHED** *task*

WHAT PART ARE YOU PLAYING in God's plan for the world?

God's plan for the world did not finish with the crucifixion and the resurrection. It is now carried on through his Church, as we are indwelt with the Holy Spirit on a day-by-day basis. It will lead to nothing less than the birth of the living Church in every nation and people group. It will also lead to healing and God-centered change on every level of society.

This task of world evangelism and spiritual revolution has been committed to all of us who know him and are his disciples. There are no spectators. We are all to be in the battlefield and a part of the action.

Before he left this earth, Jesus told us of the task we are to complete and gave us a promise to take with us:

> All authority in heaven and on earth has been given to me. Therefore go and make disciples of all nations, baptizing them in the name of the Father and of the Son and of the Holy Spirit, and teaching them to obey everything I have commanded you. And surely I am with you always, to the very end of the age. (Matthew 28:18–20)

This task that Jesus gave us is not some afterthought of his ministry but is the logical outcome and culmination of the whole of his life and work. Its emphasis is not just on preaching but on making disciples and on teaching obedience. And his command to make disciples of all nations is to all of us. It is not just to a few who feel "called" or to Christian leaders or Bible college graduates.

We all have a part to play in God's plan of reconciliation. And his promise to be with us always is to be claimed as we go forward in faith to obey his commands.

The Task

Patrick Johnstone, in his prayer handbook *Operation World*,[7] estimates the size of the task that lies before us. First of all, we have to think of those who have never even heard the gospel. Out of the approximately five billion people who made up the world's population in 1986, there were between one and two billion who had never heard about the need for repentance and the good news of Jesus Christ. There were also between three and four thousand people groups who had no church or Christian fellowship of their own, and these groups range from small minorities to quite large nations.

You may have heard in the news about the Kurds, one of the largest unreached people groups in the world. There are approximately twenty million Kurds who no longer have their own political nation; instead they are split up mostly between the nations of Iran, Iraq, and Turkey. They were very badly affected by the chemical warfare in the Iran/Iraq war. They are just one of dozens of other unreached people groups I could tell you about; all of these are covered in the prayer requests in *Operation World*.

Patrick Johnstone also reminds us that each new generation must be evangelized afresh: God has no grandchildren. Each person, whether they come from a Christian family or not, must respond to the message of Christ. This means that the whole task facing us is enormous. So how can anyone say that the day of world missions is past?

To get the job done, if we are serious about following the commands of Christ, there must be an increase in the Church's witness worldwide that is at least in line with the increase in world population. This is the task we are facing. Jesus' words have never been more relevant, "The harvest is plentiful but the workers are few" (Matthew 9:37). In many, many areas of the world people are crying out for a Christian witness, and we must ask ourselves why they have none.

Now I am not convinced that it is the will of God for so many people groups to have no witness. And it follows, therefore, that some or many of us are not playing our part in God's plan; we are not carrying out God's complete will, whether it be to pray or to send or to go. We cannot blame it all on God any more than William Carey, the first Baptist missionary to India, could when people told him so many years ago, "If God wants the heathen to be saved, then he will take care of it without the likes of you." It is God's plan as revealed in his word that these people hear the gospel, that they receive a witness.

The challenge of world evangelism is as great today as it ever was. We can use any number of missionaries if they are Spirit-controlled and Spirit-guided, committed men and women. As we see the opportunities that are before us, I believe that there are unlimited possibilities for long-term and short-term service.

The Methods: Long-term

Our objective is to witness to the whole world, whether people respond to the message or not. Obviously we must constantly re-evaluate what we are doing and always try to improve the way we communicate to people and also pray strongly that they will respond. But we must not give up and go home just because people in some areas are slow to understand the message and follow Christ.

We must understand that there may be many reasons why people do not respond. This is why Operation Mobilization has been able to tackle the evangelism of Muslims, where there has been very little response, because we have men and women who stick to the task. In some cases our missionaries have been working in Turkey, which is a mainly Muslim country, for almost twenty-five years. And still, after years of patient and sensitive evangelism, there are less than a thousand indigenous believers in Turkey (and most of these are from minority ethnic groups).

Jesus said, "My food is to do the will of him who sent me and to finish his work" (John 4:34). Our first objective must be not to see how many we can convert, but to obey God. I believe we need to learn about stickability. Paul says in the letter to the Corinthians, "Stand firm. Let nothing move you. Always give yourselves fully to the work of the Lord, because you know that your labor in the Lord is not in vain" (1 Corinthians 15:58). And in the letter to the Galatians he backs that up: "Let us not become weary in doing good, for at the proper time we will reap a harvest if we do not give up" (Galatians 6:9).

Now in that sort of situation, where it's not possible to turn the leadership of the mission over to the national church because there is no national church, and it may take several years to learn the language and the culture, we need long-term missionaries. We need people who are prepared to make cross-cultural communication their career, to study it and work at it for many years. We need people who can remember that they are servants and that their objective is not ultimately to lead the nationals but to make it possible for the nationals to lead themselves.

Such people are rare, and we treasure every one of them. In many specialized missions, such as hospitals, schools, and those which concentrate on pastoral training and teaching, long-term missionaries are also needed. They provide continuity, language and communication skills, and much-needed experience and spiritual maturity.

The Methods: Short-term

However, many Christians seem to have got the idea that these long-term missionaries, with their high levels of gift and grace and training, are the only sort of missionaries that are needed. I read a book recently saying that if we had more short-term missionaries they would only get in the way of the career missionaries and the national church. Some Christian leaders have written off all short-term missionary work as "superficial."

Now this seems to me to be limiting God. Many people who may not have the grace and the gift to be a long-term career missionary learning Urdu or Arabic could probably still make a major contribution by giving two years of their lives to being God's soldiers in an overseas spiritual war zone, particularly in areas where there is no other mission and there is no other church.

Young, short-term workers (and those whose families have grown up) are a practical answer to many of the problems of world missions today. They are able to go out to needy countries at a time of life when they may not have received much training, but neither are they tied down by the family responsibilities of young children or elderly parents. They are also much cheaper to support. These days, the support of a missionary family is beyond the resources of many average-sized churches. So it makes sense to send out young people to gain experience or test a missionary call before they commit themselves to a lifetime overseas.

The short-term worker, whatever his training or lack of it, can play a vital role working under the leadership of the longer-term missionaries and the local church. Literature is still a vital way to get the gospel out; you don't need a Ph.D. or a theological education to distribute powerful gospel literature written for the mind and the mentality of the target audience. We can now use films, videos, and audio-cassettes, but you need people to drive the vehicle, to run the projector, to cook the food.

We live in a highly technical world. It's not any longer a matter of just getting Bible teachers and theological graduates; they are also needed, but they may be limited in their work without mechanics, engineers, and maintenance experts. We need dedicated arms and dedicated eyes.

The big teaching in Britain, the USA, and some other countries now seems to be to go through university, get as many qualifications as you can, get a good job, make money, and then, when you are all settled down, if the Lord leads, you can go to the mission field. Now this sounds fine, but in fact it does not work. Some people do manage it; but most of us, once we are married and settled down with our children, are stuck for life.

It is understandable that with all the changes and pressures that a growing family brings, we are unwilling to take on yet more change and yet more unknowns. And those that do go overseas at this phase of life are usually the ones who have already got involved as short-term missionaries when they were younger. We should be encouraging our young people to make the most of their flexibility when they have it, so that they can then make informed decisions about where the Lord is leading them and their families later on.

It's about time that we understood the difference between reality and geography. Of course, we call people to lifetime commitment. But to give the idea that people who serve for two years and then return haven't made a lifetime commitment to Jesus Christ is false. Their commitment to Christ is not affected by the country in which they are living.

Of course, we need people with a lifetime commitment to serve the Lord overseas. But we shouldn't force people into such a commitment if they're not ready for it, or if their health won't stand it, or those "lifetime" missionaries will be back home in a year or so anyway. Many of the pioneer-missionaries of the last century died within the first few years of their overseas work, but we would hardly write their work off as superficial.

I would like every young (and not-so-young) Christian to consider the possibility, both for their own spiritual growth and in obedience to Scripture, of two years of cross-cultural communication on the spiritual battlefronts around the world today. Let us not be afraid that we're going where we are not wanted. Church leaders are coming to me almost daily, from every area of the world where we are working and asking, pleading for more workers.

We should take note of the fact that the Mormons have twenty or thirty thousand men on their short-term overseas mission program. They have made over a hundred thousand converts in Britain alone. Is that superficial? They let nationals take over the leadership of their groups and continue the teaching they have started. When the short-term missionaries return to America, they send another thirty thousand to take their place.

I believe the Church of Jesus Christ should have at least, at any one time (as well as the long-term missionary force), a hundred thousand men and women on a one-year or two-year program. They would not get in the way of each other, or of the national church, if they were trained in a few-basic rules of the game like submitting to the national church leadership, working alongside people, not lording it over them but learning from them, and making sure that the leadership of any mission or missionary project was transferred to the leadership of the national church as quickly as possible.

The People

What is a missionary? Some people have a vision of a tall white colonial figure in a pith helmet carrying a big black Bible, marching through the jungle, attacking venomous snakes with one blow of his machete, catching hordes of cockroaches with his bare hands and dashing them to the ground. Others imagine an elderly, humorless spinster with a piano accordion teaching little black children to sing "Jesus Loves Me."

If this picture of a missionary was ever true (which I doubt), it certainly isn't true today. Modern missionaries may be Bible teachers, evangelists, or translators, or they may be doctors, nurses, agriculturalists, accountants, or craft workers. Or they may be mechanics, cooks, secretaries, bookkeepers, electronic engineers, or people who are willing to go anywhere and do anything. They must be prepared to go as learners and servants of Jesus Christ and the national church, being what Patrick Johnstone calls "self-effacing spiritual giants."[8]

If you don't feel you're a missionary type, take heart. I don't feel I'm one either. I sometimes think that I must have been the most reluctant missionary in the whole world. But the lady who prayed for me for three years prayed that I would not only become a Christian but also a missionary, so I didn't really stand a chance. In fact, there is room for every type of personality in mission work.

Many people are frightened by the idea that God might want them to serve overseas, even for a year. Their ideas of missionary work seem to be full of horrible insects and eating all kinds of strange food and suffering in extreme climates. But when they begin to understand the depth of God's love for them and move by faith, many of them discover that they actually enjoy it when they get to these countries.

The true missionary is not some kind of ascetic, who is perpetu-
ally pining for his home comforts and his McDonald's hamburg-
ers. In any case, McDonald's are now getting there faster than
we are! I have proved myself that on the mission field, in Spain,
Belgium, Holland, and then India, in the midst of the battle there
are many wonderful and enjoyable aspects of missionary life. It
is one of the fullest, most challenging occupations anyone could
ever get into.

But don't missionaries have to have a *special* call from God? I
don't believe so. I think we're far too inclined to live by feelings
rather than faith. A lot of "missionary calls" are just that—feelings.
Now God may at some point give you an experience which may be
a turning point in your life. God is working in different people in
different ways. Some people have very emotional missionary calls.
They can tell you the moment and the hour they were called.

But many of you are never going to get that kind of emotional
call, so you might as well stop looking for it. If you still feel you
must have it, just write to me. I will send one of my colleagues
around to your house, and we will show you some slides and play
you some inspiring music all evening, and the next morning you
will be ready to go. I can assure you that you will probably not get
very far! Because those feelings are not going to last. Come the
first set of discouragements or the first two years with no apparent
results, that great emotional experience is going to wear a bit thin
or may be replaced by an equally strong feeling that you ought to
drop the whole idea!

It is my experience that many of the people who are doing the
greatest work in missions around the world have never had a *special*
call. Instead, they have realized that Jesus' command to witness
to every nation applies to all of us. They knew that they had some
part to play in God's plan for the world, and they began to ask
themselves what it could be. Gradually, through reading the Bible,
listening to the advice of mature Christian friends, and talking to
mission organizations, they discovered that they themselves were
needed overseas—maybe for a year, two years, or even a lifetime.

The trouble with expecting a special "missionary call" from

God is that those who do not experience it tend to assume that God does not want them to be involved with missions. And those who do experience it sometimes tend to see themselves as God's gift to that country, rather than as learners and strugglers, until they learn better. Maybe when we all realize that we have our part to play, and that those who send are at least as important as those who go, we will be able to work together in partnership with each other and with the national church.

God Can Use You

If you're willing to play a part in God's great plan for this world, you must be ready to count the cost. Before God can use you to your full potential, you need to learn the basics of discipleship, commitment, the revolution of love, and all the other things we have talked about in this book. That involves discipline; it involves having your daily "quiet time," memorizing Scripture, reading good Christian books, and listening to good Christian tapes. It involves being committed to your local church. But it also involves leaving room for your own personality to develop, as we discussed in the last chapter. Super-spiritual people do not survive under pressure.

If you spend two years overseas there's a high chance you're never going to be the same once you come back. You'll have seen how God answers prayer and how the Holy Spirit changes lives, and you'll have caught a glimpse of what God is doing around the world. When people in the church mention mission programs and different countries for prayer, they'll be talking about real people and friends that you have all over the world. You'll have seen the value of Bible study, memorization, praying for the world, surrendering everything to God, and depending on him for your everyday needs.

Of course, living for God is a day-by-day walk, and going on OM or any other program doesn't guarantee that you're going to walk with God all your life; in fact, it may mean that you become a greater target of Satan's strategies. So you must know how to withstand his temptations.

Making your life available to God to use for his purposes does
not end with reading one book, going to one conference, or going on a training program for one year. When Jesus spoke about
counting the cost of discipleship, he emphasized the need for
stickability, telling the story of a man who began to build a tower
and did not have the money to finish it:

> Everyone who sees it will ridicule him, saying, "This fellow began
> to build and was not able to finish." (Luke 14:29–30)

Now if you are going to be able to finish God's marathon race,
you will have to learn God's pace for your life. God does not want
sprinters who go incredibly fast but are exhausted after a hundred
meters, but marathon runners who can go on and on. Many young
people are impatient to know God's will for their life, when it may
well be that it is not God's time for them to find out. There may be
things you have to learn and experiences you have to go through
before you are ready to hear God's call.

The important thing is to go forward in obedience and faith and
not feel you have to force the pace, or you will burn out before
you have developed your full potential. It's not what you do in the
next ten minutes that counts that's important, but it's what you do
tomorrow and next week and next year that really counts. Learn
God's pace for your own life. Don't try to run it at someone else's
pace.

The Call: To Pray

If we really believe that God answers prayer, if we really believe
that God wants us to be involved in reconciling the nations to himself, then praying for different countries and the work of missions
around the world will become a natural part of our lives. Patrick
Johnstone says, "Without prayer God's plan for the world cannot
be achieved."[9]

I find it astonishing that whole churches do not seem to have
heard of the idea of interceding for the different countries of the
world. How can we gather Sunday after Sunday in our churches,
with some of the liveliest, largest church movements in the world,

and yet not pray for those nations, those people groups, where the church doesn't exist at all?

I heard about a prayer meeting in an English city recently where 15,000 people came, yet we are crying out for more workers to go and work with needy churches overseas. If you can have a prayer meeting with 15,000 people, you should be able to send out 1,500 overseas workers within the next year or two, or something is wrong with the praying.

It is completely unscriptural to pray only for ourselves and for our own country. We need the whole word of God. We've got churches that can praise the Lord, and sing choruses; they can have all kinds of wonderful fellowship times. If you call for an hour of intercession, they look at you as if you were some kind of dinosaur.

Often we simply do not have the time in our church meetings for intercession. The space allotted to prayer is so short; even in a prayer meeting we have so much singing and "sharing" that by the time we get ready to pray it is almost time to go home.

How many churches devote a whole day or a whole evening just to pray? Do we really believe God is listening? Or is it simply that we have never learned how to pray? As a teenager I started the habit of having half days with God, then days with God; I often went into the hills or the mountains just to pray. We need to be careful, of course, that we're not trying to clock up the hours or the number of countries prayed for so that we can feel "spiritual'; that would be the height of hypocrisy.

My early attempts at getting alone with God weren't all success. I remember once going for a time of prayer in Spain. I had decided that if the Lord Jesus could pray through the night alone, I was going to pray through the night alone. I'd been in nights of prayer with other people, but there you get somebody else praying and it helps keep you awake. So in great boldness I went outside the city of Madrid for this night of prayer. I'd also decided to fast, so I brought a piece of bread with me that I thought I would eat in the morning when I'd finished breaking through Satan's strongholds and claiming Spain for Christ (this was under Franco, and we needed a lot of prayer, I can tell you).

But it didn't work. About two o'clock in the morning I fell asleep out there by the river. Of course it's very hot in the day in Spain, but it got very cold at night and I wasn't dressed for it, having not really understood this. So eventually I woke up, freezing cold, and decided I was going to eat. I looked round for my bread, but it was gone. To this day I don't know what happened. I think perhaps a wild animal came along, looked at me, didn't see much meat, and took the bread instead!

Don't be discouraged because you fail in your prayer life. Don't be discouraged because your mind wanders. Beware of becoming impatient with your spiritual growth rate. Don't feel you're an extra evil person because in a prayer meeting some amazing young woman or man walks in and blows all your circuits.

Some people think that that kind of experience just happens to the young carnal Christian, but I can tell you from personal experience that it can happen to anybody. A beautiful girl walked into a prayer meeting in Switzerland a few years ago, and I could not think straight, let alone pray. Eventually, though, the Lord helped me to bring my mind under control in that prayer meeting, and now I can't even remember what she looked like.

The Call: To Send

When God called the leaders of the church in Antioch of Syria to send out the apostle Paul and Barnabas as missionaries overseas (Acts 13:2–3), he gave them an important task. They laid their hands on Barnabas and Paul and sent them off, but they were not forgotten. They prayed for their missionaries, sent them all the financial support they could spare, and, most importantly, they continued to support Paul and Barnabas as part of their church family. When the two missionaries returned after several years, the eager reception shown by the Christians in Antioch vividly demonstrated their love for each other (Acts 14:26–28).

Was the role of the Christians who stayed in Antioch less important, in spiritual terms, than that of their two missionaries overseas? It may have been less dramatic, less in the public eye. But their role was no less vital to the work of the mission because, without their support, it is doubtful if it would have succeeded. If they had not recognized their responsibilities, the whole of history might have been different. Christians, even the apostle Paul, are not meant to work in isolation, but as part of the Body of Christ.

Our aim as senders is simple: to accept responsibility for those we send out and to love and support them as members of our own spiritual family. That means loving them as we love ourselves; thinking when they need a letter, when they need prayer, when they need warm clothes or new shoes for their children; when they need a birthday card or a little extra money for a special treat. When we send missionaries out, whether or not we knew them personally before they went out, we take on a partnership with them in the work of God. It is up to us to keep our side of the bargain.

Financial support is, of course, essential. Put simply, if ten Christians give one-tenth of their income to missionary work, they will probably be able to support one missionary. But many church members simply cannot afford to give one-tenth; others do not see the need. Missionaries have families, and the work itself is expensive. So less and less workers can be sent out.

It is not easy to be a dedicated sender in today's affluent society. When all around us are living only for pleasure, it takes courage to be different and to persevere in playing our part in God's plan. Yet that part has never been more essential.

In a world where millions are starving, where tens of millions have no homes, where evangelists in India are praying that they might have a bicycle (and some have been praying for years), we Christians in the affluent society have, I believe, failed to understand Christ's demands upon our lives. Luke 14:33 is very clear: "In the same way, any of you who does not give up everything he has cannot be my disciple."

Those who support and love and pray are not "second-class missionaries"; indeed, if there is going to be a powerful missionary outflow, there must be a return to the revolutionary standards of Jesus Christ and of the New Testament church.

Maybe you feel that God wants you to be a sender but you

don't know anyone who wants to be sent. Don't worry. Write to any mission society, particularly short-term organizations like OM or the less "glamorous" areas like the home bases, and I guarantee you will find people who are trying to obey God's call to go out but are being hindered by lack of support.

I believe that if you let God have his way in your life, if you follow the Spirit of God day by day through difficulty, through trials, and through discouragement, then you will be part of God's great plan to reach the nations, of God's great plan to build his kingdom around the world.

The Call: To Go

Are you willing to respond to God's call to go? If God began to show you that your part in his plan was to leave your comfortable home and church and career for the unknown, even if just for a few weeks or a year, would you be willing to go?

Why are we afraid of God's direction for our lives? When the government of Britain called for men to go into the army for the Second World War and the Falklands war, there were plenty of volunteers, and people counted it a privilege to be in the army.

People were not afraid in Iran in the recent Iran/Iraq war when hundreds and thousands of men and women volunteered to be martyrs, and eleven-year-olds were sent across the minefields to personally blow up the mines with their feet. Their mothers danced at the funerals because they had given another son to Allah, so great is the fanaticism of modern-day Islam.

I wonder if there are some today who would be willing to go out across the devil's minefields, spiritually speaking; maybe risk your future or that lovely retirement program you've already been thinking about; maybe risk even your life or your health, that one more nation might hear the gospel, that one more unreached people group might have a Christian witness, that one more soul might be with God in eternity.

If we believe in the word of God, the ministry of the Lord Jesus, and the power of the Holy Spirit, let us commit ourselves to reach the unreached, to take the gospel to every nation and every people group and to every individual. Let us commit ourselves to be his witness in these places, and also through prayer and faith to see living churches born in each one of these people groups that can multiply and reach the rest of that people group with the word of God.

If you go out even for only two years and disciple a few nationals who know the language already and carry on in that country for twenty or thirty years planting churches, then you will know the joy of working together with God.

Will anybody remember your name in some far off land twenty years from now? Will there be one Christian, one church, that's following Jesus because you obeyed, because you were willing to make the sacrifice, because you were willing to take God at his word? Maybe one day, when you reach eternity, you will discover that one of the people you told about the gospel or prayed for became a believer. And he or she in turn obeyed God and told the gospel to another person. And that person also became a Christian, then brought to Jesus someone who became a great evangelist and brought thousands of people to Jesus.

It's the ricochet effect, the multiplication effect, the teamwork principle, the domino effect with the Holy Spirit pushing the dominoes. It's one of the most exciting principles you can ever get involved in. Will you do that? Will you begin to take some steps of faith? Will you be honest about where you really are spiritually and learn to repent of those things that are holding you back, so that as you pray with others you may begin to go forward with God?

I challenge you to be a marathon runner for God in this great task of world evangelism. And when you're knocked down, just get up, and get back in the race and start running. When you fail, when you fall, get up! As soon as you feel your hand touch the ground, get up! And you'll discover that some day, twenty or thirty years from now, just like me, you'll be still running the race; weary sometimes, wounded sometimes, but still pressing on for Jesus Christ. Let's press on together for the kingdom of God and world evangelism.

O Lord, as we come to you, we ask you to make this great vision of reaching all people with the gospel real to us. Lord, we believe by faith that it can come to pass. We realize that we have a part to play in your great plan for the world. We know that the final decision is ours; that you will take us so far, lovingly pushing and drawing us, but that the ultimate step to be a doer instead of a hearer must always be ours.

Help us to take it.

Amen.

Recommended Reading

Love Covers by P. Billheimer, Christian Literature Crusade, 1981

The Calvary Road/Be Filled Now by R. Hession, Christian Literature Crusade, 1988 (new combined edition)

Operation World by P. Johnstone, STL Books/WEC Publications, 1986

A Living Reality by R. Steer, (Life of George Müller) Hodder & Stoughton/STL Books, 1985

The Set of the Sail by A.W. Tozer, STL Books / Kingsway Publications, 1986

No *Turning Back* by George Verwer, Hodder & Stoughton/ STL Books, 1983

no **TURNING** *back*

Pursuing the Path of
Christian Discipleship

DEDICATION

I would like to dedicate this book to the army of people in Operation Mobilization, many of whom have stood with my wife Drena and me for over fifteen or twenty years, and especially to Jonathan and Margit McRostie. This past year Jonathan was seriously injured in a car crash and is now paralyzed from the chest down. He is one of many whom I have watched live the kind of life spoken about in this book . . . yes, even now from his wheelchair. He recently spoke to 7,000 young people at Mission 83 in Switzerland, and over 700 made deeper commitments to Christ and to the great task of telling the whole world about him.

CONTENTS

INTRODUCTION: PLAYING AT SOLDIERS

THE WORLD IS GOING CRAZY over short cuts.

America is particularly gadget-mad. The silliest example that has come my way recently has been the electric toothbrush. It is clearly too much to expect of any grown man that he should move his arm up and down; shortly, I imagine, a device will descend from the ceiling while you doze in bed with your mouth open, and hey, presto! Your gleaming dentures will be ready to face the world.

When, however, it comes to reaching the world for Christ, or producing a man of God, there are no short cuts. When the Apostle Paul said goodbye to the Ephesian elders on his way to Jerusalem, he commented, "I consider my life worth nothing to me, if only I may finish the race and complete the task the Lord Jesus has given me—the task of testifying to the gospel of God's grace. . . . So be on your guard! Remember that for three years I never stopped warning each of you night and day with tears" (Acts 20:24,31).

Whenever I read these verses I can almost feel the throb of Paul's leadership. Paul led the way in world evangelism, and those who follow in his steps will not be travelling an easy road. Jesus is looking for those who are ready to enroll full time in the service of the King of Kings. You can't become a soldier for a summer. In the United States army, there is a system known as short-term enlistment whereby you can serve for three or four years. The service of Christ is not like that. Jesus asks for a lifetime's commitment to the armies of the Lord: you serve until you die.

This attitude was plain in Paul's dedication. Now Christians use military terms very glibly, but we frequently know very little about the military life, preferring the easy and soft path of the holy huddle. I have been much attracted by the history of Britain during the First and Second World Wars, and in particular by the nature of Winston Churchill and some of the other leaders of that era. They seemed to have astonishing stamina, iron in their souls. Churchill promised sweat, toil, and tears to those who went forward, yet they flocked to volunteer. I strongly recommend to anyone who has ambitions to be a disciple of Jesus Christ that they should read one of the books on the invasion of France—how the men came back from Dunkirk, recovered, and invaded on D-Day. They were floated across on immense barges, and seasick, landed on the French beaches to offer their lives for their countries and the principles they held dear.

When you read the history books it seems shocking, unreal, despite all the war films. Yet it really did happen. My wife's father was scooped up in a bucket and sent back to a nondescript grave in the USA. Maybe some of those who read this book will have lost fathers in that same conflict. It was horrific.

In the Mediterranean world of the first century AD, soldiers and military installations were everywhere. Paul would undoubtedly have had a clear understanding of what it meant to be a soldier and was himself no stranger to physical suffering. Yet he can write to Timothy: "Endure hardship with us like a good soldier of Christ Jesus" (2 Timothy 2:3). Paul was not using words loosely. The choice that faces every professed Christian is this: are you truly concerned to be a trained soldier in the armies of the Lord, or are you secretly wishing you could be up in the grandstand, waving your handkerchief as the troops march by? To train and go forward as a soldier is the most demanding (and yet the most fulfilling) experience you will ever go through.

When I first set out as an evangelist, shortly after I was converted, my primary aim was to get people to make decisions for Christ. All my prayers were directed to this end. Nowadays I pray for and seek out soldiers: unless we get soldiers and mobilize our forces we shall never reach the world for Christ. The reason that most of the world's trained Christian workers serve amongst 10 percent of the world's population (in the UK, USA, Canada and New Zealand) is that we lack soldiers and have forgotten our battle plans.

You are probably wedded to certain customs, to a particular language and food and style of dress. You may prefer a particular climate and culture. Most people do. This is why the missionary societies often will not accept older candidates, since they find them too set in their ways to adjust. (Changes are now taking place in this policy.) It is very easy to exist in a Christian climate, singing hymns in church, praying and going to meetings, and generally breathing the air of the Christian sub-culture. You may be considered a fine evangelical Christian, full of good theology and fine phrases.

And yet—there is little militancy, little conquering spirit, little thirst for risk, adventure, and suffering. Do you think it is part of God's plan that the Jehovah's Witnesses out-distribute, out-evangelize, out-shine the Christians in just about every way? We don't like to admit it—nor to admit that the Mormon Church in Salt Lake City sends out more missionaries than all the Christian churches in the UK, Canada, Australia, and New Zealand put together. They have 24,000 young men on the march today. Each of those men is responsible for the baptism of two new converts each year. Each convert, so they estimate, takes 500 hours of door to door visitation.

The Mormon Church is the fastest-growing cult in the British Isles. I remember a schoolgirl of sixteen I met in the West Country who spent four hours per day in evangelism. She came into one of the Operation Mobilization meetings collecting names and addresses of possible contacts, and on her dress she had a badge with a big question mark. If you asked her what it meant, she would say, "That is just so that you can ask me why I am wearing it, and then I can tell you that I am a member of the Church of Latter Day Saints and invite you to discuss this with me." She was only sixteen, and yet she knew the Book of Mormon backwards, and much of the Bible too. What is the average evangelical girl doing at sixteen or twenty-one? Ask the average evangelical boy.

Most people I meet have a stale Christianity. It simply fails to excite them. If you are young in the Christian faith, then be particularly careful to guard against creeping flabbiness. The middle-aged spiritual spread is a miserable sight. When I was converted in Madison Square Garden, many years ago, I got excited about Jesus Christ, and I've been excited ever since. Yet when you go to many a good evangelical church — of whatever denomination — on a Sunday morning, you sit there and feel at the end of an hour that you've just made a short trip to the North Pole and back. There is so little joy, as if we had been saved to sorrow, but in fact we have been saved to serve. Such service is perfect freedom, a freedom which is fresh and alive.

I believe that the reason many Christians are so dull and lifeless in their faith is because they are not in the battle, not using their weapons, not advancing against the enemy. Young Christians often seem like peacetime soldiers, sitting around, getting out of condition, playing cards, chatting idly. So many Christians act as though they were on a conveyor belt to heaven at the least possible cost. Yet God did not create us to live this life at a minimum cost. What was his purpose? Not just that we should be saved and thus get back to where we ought to have started, but rather that we should go on to conquest and worship and joy and life in abundance. "I have come," said Jesus, "that they may have life, and have it to the full" (John 10:10). It is my prayer for the readers of this book that they should close it feeling that they can echo Paul's words: "For me to live is Christ, to die is gain."

The picture of the church is not all gloom. Here and there across the world I have come across groups of young people whose desire was that at any cost the sleeping giant should be roused, that an army should be raised up for the service of Christ, that the commandments of Christ should be obeyed. This is what it all hinges on. In John 14:21 we read, "Whoever has my commands and obeys them, he is the one who loves me. He who loves me will be loved by my Father, and I too will love him and show myself to him." Yet most people I know think that if they go to church twice on Sunday they are getting rather spiritual, and if they go to a mid-week prayer meeting as well, they are getting super-dedicated. Christians are commanded to pray, yet prayer is regularly pushed to the closing minutes of the meeting. We have lots of messages and books and meetings and films but few real prayer warriors. This deficiency hurts the missionary effort of the church; it hurts the cause of Christ; prayer is a part of soldiering.

We must not play at soldiers. My prayer for this book is that it should call you to effective service and show you some of the disciple's weapons, that it should teach you how to press on when the going gets tough, and that it should help you to live a life of love—a life worthy of the Lord you serve.

PART I

The Call To Be A Disciple

1

DISCIPLESHIP *in an age of* TENSION *and* FEAR

IN TALKING TO YOUNG CHRISTIANS I sometimes end the conversation with a sense of confusion, a lack of focus. It happens especially when I have been listening to plans for evangelism, or when I have attended a prayer meeting which was long on enthusiasm and short on understanding. Christians are often from stable and comfortably-off homes, reasonably well educated, to some extent isolated from what they read in the papers. While they remain within the protected circle of their Christian friends, they are secure enough, but once they decide to deepen their commitment as believers they become vulnerable.

Modern society is not kind to those who seek to serve with practical love and in purity of body and mind. It is a fallacy to suppose that Christians are immune to emotional and mental breakdown: mental illness affects one person in ten in Britain at some point during their lives. But it is also quite wrong to think that if you do suffer a "nervous breakdown" (which is a very inexact term) you are only fit for the rubbish heap. Perhaps God is trying to teach you something you can learn in no other way; perhaps he is giving you insights so that you can help others. The point is that Christians have to acknowledge real problems; you can't pretend that you are immune to immorality or alcoholism. If you are serious about your commitment as a Christian then you are in the firing line, and you will encounter the powers of darkness and their effect on a lonely and disordered world. Remember this when you meet other Christians who have fallen in some way. It is extremely easy to be unfair to those with emotional problems and to push your own under the carpet in a totally insincere attempt to appear whiter than white. It is very easy to lie.

One frustration, which is a cause of much despair, is simply the scale of the task of reaching people for Christ. Not only is Western society extremely complicated, but there are more people in Britain today than there were in the whole known world of the Apostle Paul. What do you do with seven million refugees? With one thousand million people in China? If we allow our imaginations to range over the numbers yet unreached by the gospel, we will hang our heads in defeat, yet we cannot simply ignore the facts and concentrate on the local needs. The Lord is constantly pushing men and women forward into new channels of action.

The solution to these pressures lies in the *rest of faith*. The writer to the Hebrews comments, "There remains, then, a Sabbath-rest for the people of God; for anyone who enters God's rest also rests from his own work, just as God did from his" (Hebrews 4:9–10). We are told to cease from our own works: to know that we are able to pass all our concerns over to the Lord, in the certainty that he can bear them far better than we can. In Luke's Gospel it is recorded that Jesus advised his disciples, "Consider how the lilies grow. They do not labor or spin. Yet I tell you, not even Solomon in all his splendor was dressed like one of these. If that is how God clothes the grass of the field, which is here today, and tomorrow is thrown into the fire, how much more will he clothe you, O you of little faith!" (Luke 12:27–28). Yet a high proportion of emotional problems affecting Christians are a direct result of their refusal to cease from their own works, to stop worrying.

Peter tells us to "cast all our care upon him." This is a key principle to grasp right at the start of training to be a disciple. It is not something just for Sundays, but a daily practice which you must adopt to survive. If you cast your cares upon the Lord, and as you pray they come rushing back, then cast them up again. You may find it useful to keep a pen and paper beside you as you pray: as concerns for the day ahead crowd into your mind, write them down. You can offer them to the Lord and go on praying without fear of forgetting whatever it was that occurred to you. I lay such stress upon this point because I am a fearful worrier and suffer daily from anxiety and fear and a sense of failure. My greatest help in Christ is that moment by moment I can pass my distress over to him. This is not a point you should agree with and skip over, but a discipline to appropriate for yourself. Without it, you will find yourself avoiding prayer and ultimately service, as too painful and burdensome.

In dealing with Operation Mobilization business, I frequently work very long hours. I could never do so if I didn't know the rest of faith. When I do not let Christ shoulder my worries I soon flag, but when I do release them I can work longer and harder with much less effort. Here is an answer to the frustration and despair which can floor us as Christians, since in doing so we become far more effective—and can lay down our burdens at the end of each day. Deal with worry as soon as you can, before it ruins your health, your life, your home, and your family.

We are not immune to the lifestyle around us. Have you ever stood at a station on a commuter line around 6:30 p.m. and watched the drawn, strained, defensive faces stream past? The latest killer disease of the Western world is workaholism. There is no special virtue in working a twelve-hour day. We do not boast of being lazy, why should we boast of being over-active? Yet you hear people speak of their long hours as if they were badges of merit. One of the most advanced societies in the world is Japan, but along with their astonishing industrial record come records in other fields—nervous exhaustion, suicides, pollution. An article a few years ago described how wives would watch to see whose husband came home earliest from work, for it was regarded as virtuous to come home particularly late!

Christians are especially prone to workaholism. The Puritan tradition of work as valuable in its own right has been etched so deeply into our minds that we drive ourselves harder and harder. To work well is a good witness to our non-Christian colleagues, indeed, but we are very quickly in danger of working simply for the rewards of prosperity and promotion—and our lifestyle as Christians is soon identical with that of the people around us.

But there is a further danger. The pace of Western civilization has invaded our spiritual lives. The more busy we are, the more spiritual we must be, and so we fill our spare time with meetings. Bible studies, prayer meetings, and committees can become a cancer upon the church. They are usually good in themselves, but they can so easily conceal from our Christian friends and from ourselves the emptiness of our faith. Sunday is designed as a day of rest, but for many church members it is the busiest day of the week. (If that is really the case, and you simply cannot avoid being busy on Sunday, then you should make sure that you take off at least half a day at another point in the week to relax and enjoy yourself.)

Frequently we hear the expression, "I want to burn out for Christ." In one way this is right: all we have is Christ's, and we are to serve with all our heart, soul, mind, and strength. But there is a difference between petrol and coal, and I should prefer to be coal—to go on burning for a long time, slowly, steadily. Give me plodders, as William Carey put it. Michael Griffiths, Principal of London Bible College, considers that phlegmatics make better missionaries than cholerics.

Workaholism can stem from fear of failure, too. As Christians we can be sure that God loves us, each one of us individually, and we can find our sense of identity and value in this fact. Yet so often we feel that we have to prove ourselves, earn our salvation, and in this way, too, we show that we have swallowed wholesale the false values of our culture. Yet we all fail, and the more we attempt the more frequently we will fail. If we have been given a position of leadership, we will fail very often. All the great men of history have made their blunders: Winston Churchill tried to whip the Turks and got fired when the plan came unstuck. At several points I was ready to abandon the project for M.V. *Logos*[1] as a total write-off, and though I had faith, I was still ready for God to blow the whole thing up and make me look an utter nitwit. Failures are not all bad: you learn far more by them than by your successes. They are a springboard—as a source of theory they are far richer than victories. Oscar Wilde said that the man who succeeds is the one who learns to survive failure.

There is a further point to remember. Failures for the believer are always temporary. God loves you and me so much that he will allow almost any failure if the end result is that we become more like Jesus. Unless you see the hand of God in the ridiculous, the confusing, you may one day find yourself on the shelf. The Devil wants you reprobate, a cold, shrunken, Christ-denying figure. Christ's message is one of grace for sinners, not of tonic for successful salesmen.

Please believe that I write this with compassion. I have failed far too often as a disciple of Jesus to be other than sympathetic. I have seen far too many enthusiastic young Christians get hurt when they tried to live in a truly committed way. Most of those who will read this book have, to some extent, led sheltered lives. In other parts of the world the pressure is far greater: how would you like to work in a refugee camp with dying children around you day and night? Yet even though our own problems seem so much smaller than those we hear on the radio, or see on television, God is still interested in ministering to us and helping us to find the way of peace and victory.

We can only ask ourselves to carry the light of Christ into the world because Jesus is constantly with us. He is at our side, ministering to us, offering us rest and comfort and love, totally forgiving us, building us up, calming us down, warming our hearts. If we want to live as his disciples amidst fear, tension, frustration, despair, loneliness, then we need again and again to acknowledge the presence of Christ. We need to tell him what we are facing moment by moment, to practice the presence of Jesus.

2

GETTING *out of the* FOG

WE HAVE CONSIDERED SOME of the pressures that can hamper us when we resolve to live as disciples of Jesus. But there are more: the pressures that come from within. Many of the would-be disciples I meet seem to have drifted along for years, usually in the wrong direction, apparently powerless to make their lives count. In fact most of us need a turning point at some stage. Somehow we have missed real, revolutionary, dynamic Christianity. Pious words are cheap and easy to use and get bandied around a great deal in Christian circles — and often disguise the fact that much of our zeal is borrowed and stops at the fine phrases. If we have been raised in a Christian environment in particular, we are likely to know little of spiritual revolution. It has been well said that "God has no grandchildren." Our faith cannot be second-hand and survive. We suffer from the fog of spiritual unreality.

I believe real Christianity is genuinely a revolution, a revolution of love. This is what we have somehow missed: what the love of Christ can do when it begins to move through our lives and when we allow it to have complete control. It both gives a great deal and demands a great deal. We just do not appreciate this. Many of us are so deep in the fog of unreality that we can hear a thousand messages, read a thousand books, and yet never change.

Such a change does not take place overnight. It takes a lot more than prayers such as, "Lord Jesus, I give myself to you," or "It's just you and me, Jesus, and I can't do anything." Prayers like this may be sincere enough, but they soon become commonplace. It is easy to pick up the lingo without picking up the light. Too often we want all that Jesus has to offer without letting go of anything of ourselves.

Yet there is plenty of negative teaching in the Bible. We may love to focus on verses which speak of pardon and wholeness, yet we should not skip over verses which read, "If anyone would come after me, he must deny himself and take up his cross and follow me" (Matt. 16:24). Or, "Any of you who does not give up everything he has cannot be my disciple" (Luke 14:33). Most Christians want all of the privileges and none of the responsibilities. The Book of Hebrews speaks of the Lord as a "consuming fire," and if we live the way the Bible teaches, we are going to be ignited. This is not a comfortable process, but if we allow it to take place within us we will become a hot, sharp, burning revolutionary instrument in the hands of God. This is not the abnormal, but the normal Christian life.

You may feel by now that I am being unreal. Perhaps you have stumbled along the Christian path for years. You have heard all the revolutionary talk before and cynicism has set in. But what I am saying applies particularly to people like you. You are lost in the fog of unreality because your picture of the Lord is unreal. As J. B. Phillips put it, "Your God is too small."

To put it another way, many of us have a tendency to undervalue ourselves. This is really to insult God because he made us, we are his, and hence we are of real worth. We are not willing to accept ourselves as we are. We may look in the mirror and wince, "What happened when they gave out faces!" Yet if you are a quiet, shy, withdrawn person, God is not going to turn you into the local loudmouth or the town extrovert. He is not going to turn you into me, and you can rejoice at that! God may indeed break and mold you, but your basic temperament will remain the same. A book by Tim LaHaye called *The Spirit-Controlled Temperament* is well worth reading on this point: it helps us to get past the pattern of thinking that "I wish I were him." (It is this kind of thinking that turns us into evangelical hero-worshippers. Because we undervalue ourselves, because our Christian lives aren't getting anywhere, because we don't think God can do anything with us, we turn to the big names. It is the Church's version of the worship of film and rock stars.)

If we desire to be disciples, we must take this basic step of accepting ourselves. If we don't, then we are not dealing with ourselves as real people. Most of us know that we are not supermen, but quite a lot of us are convinced we are failures. Even the Apostle Paul had to come to terms with his own weaknesses. In 2 Corinthians 12:9–10 he writes of a "thorn in my flesh" which the Lord refused to remove from him. "But he said to me, 'My grace is sufficient for you, for my power is made perfect in weakness.' Therefore I will boast all the more gladly about my weaknesses, so that Christ's power may rest on me. . . . For when I am weak, then I am strong." Here Paul is saying that recognition of your own weakness is an essential condition of service.

Again and again I have discovered how true this is. Each day I find I have to look at my problems in front of me and say—with relief—"Lord, I am passing this over to you." But it took me a long time to learn this lesson and to admit my own weakness.

I am very, very skinny. One day—when I was still a teenager, before my conversion—I was reading a magazine and saw an advert with a picture of a pretty girl on a beach with a skinny young lad beside her. The ad was for some expensive method of putting on weight and building muscles. The next illustration showed a big hulking character with bulging muscles coming along. He shoves the skinny bloke out of the way and walks off with the girl. This shook me up badly, as I was particularly interested in girls at that point, and I immediately wrote off for the kit. When everyone else was out of the house, there I would be, standing in the living room in my bathing trunks, straining to stretch the springs of the muscle-builder. After many months of effort I had gained scarcely a pound, was more frustrated than ever, and felt desperately inferior!

I used to put on a big act. I would go to all the dances, but all the time I would feel terribly inferior inside, especially in front of the girls. Then when I became a follower of Jesus Christ on March 5, 1955, in Madison Square Garden—Billy Graham was preaching—I discovered a whole new way of life. I found that God loved me. I found that he accepted me, all 124 pounds of me. I found that he could use me, not by crushing my temperament, or showing me up for the wretch I was, but rather by offering me love and working through me by his Holy Spirit.

This kind of revolutionary Christianity does work, and it will free us from many of our hangups. This is the real revolution, not running down the street with an armful of tracts or sailing off to Indonesia. It is not a question of working harder and more radically, but of being transformed by the accepting, healing love of God. The revolution begins in your own heart.

A Christian can be compared to a mirror. He has no light of his own but seeks rather to reflect the light of the Lord. His ability to reflect light can be reduced by the fog of unreality, an unreal view of God, or an unreal view of himself. But there are other "fogs," most obviously the fog of sin.

So many young people lead a double life. The Devil is no respecter of persons. Once a Bible College student came up to me after a meeting and confessed that every weekend he would sneak away and visit a prostitute. Most of us know secret pride in some area. Probably our sins are quite sophisticated: we used to gossip, but now we simply share prayer requests about other people rather freely. We bring a kind of evangelical aroma to our irritability and envy.

Envy is particularly prevalent in Christian circles. It is so easy to be jealous of another's talents. Someone else is asked to stand up and give their testimony, and you are asked to clean out the toilets. A Christian psychiatrist in India wrote to tell me that he believed that 30 percent of people's problems stemmed from bitterness and envy in their hearts. Perhaps we resent a friend or our marriage partner or our parents. Until we are willing—and it is a question of the will—to let the blood and love and forgiveness of Christ wash it clean out of our hearts, we shall be crippled by it.

It is most unpopular to speak of sin today. We would much rather hear messages about inner healing. Yet it is featured on almost every page of the Bible! One of the main reasons we don't shake ourselves free of sin, but instead go on playing about with it, is that we simply do not hate it enough. Let me give a few examples.

We are snared by our materialism. We are extremely reluctant to pay attention to Jesus's teaching on this point. We will not face up to the fact that we have blinded ourselves to our affluence, to the cushy society we are living in. This love for material things is not easily eradicated: it takes a tremendous struggle. Tozer puts it this way:

> There is no doubt that the possessive clinging to things is one of the most harmful habits in life. Because it is so natural, it is rarely recognized for the evil that it is. But its outworkings are tragic. This ancient curse will not go out painlessly. The tough old miser within us will not lie down and die obedient to our command. He must be torn out, torn out of our hearts like a plant from the soil, he must be extracted in blood and agony like a tooth from the jaw. He must be expelled from our souls in violence as Christ expelled the money changers from the temple.

The British and North Americans and Western Europeans represent the rich young rulers of the world (See Matt. 19:16). The poorest members of our societies are in the rich young ruler class by comparison with the rest of the world. Things we regard as dire necessities, such as clean water and medical facilities, are prized luxuries elsewhere. This is of course one major reason why European and North American missionaries have frequently been ineffective. Remember 1 John 3:16–17: "This is how we know what love is: Jesus Christ laid down his life for us. And we ought to lay down our lives for our brothers. If anyone has material possessions and sees his brother in need but has no pity on him, how can the love of God be in him?" This kind of statement is so revolutionary that it makes a Marxist look as if he's going backwards on a conveyor belt. I have heard Communists admit it. Yet most of the people who read this book will be drifting in the fog of materialistic society. I believe that God today is desperately trying to speak to the Church through books like John White's *The Golden*

Cow, but so often we are not even willing to take the time to read such a book.

God looks at the heart. You may be very poor. Your poverty will not release you from materialism—if anything it will increase your desire for wealth. Yet, if you accept it willingly, it can become a treasured freedom. Most evangelicals have swallowed wholesale the competitive accumulation of possessions which is the value system of Western society. This is simple hypocrisy. We may attend conferences and read books and discuss the deeper life, but until our words get put into practice and turn our lives upside down and change our attitudes towards one another, Communism will be more dynamic, and the world will view it as such.

We are also snared by our impurity. You can fool your parents; you can fool your teachers; you can fool your very roommates; you can have pornography stashed away and be feeding your mind on filth. I would not make such comments if it were not for the dozens of people who come to me after meetings to confess such sins.

Billy Graham has called this generation a generation of sex gluttons. So many of us, for a few moments of pleasure, repeatedly throw away the prospect of a lifetime of spiritual growth and power. Yet, if you really desire to stay pure, then by the grace of God you can. Like most young men I lived for girls, for the next date—though, thank the Lord, I never did commit immorality, as I was saved at the age of seventeen, just in time. It would not have been very long before I fell to this temptation, as it was all there in my mind. Jesus taught very clearly that the sins of the mind are as unacceptable to God as the sins of the flesh.

We neglect or distort so much of God's teaching on the subject of sex. This is not the place to give details of God's plan for this most important area of our lives, but there are a number of good books available, such as John White's *Eros Defiled.* Whatever your depth of understanding, don't shove the issue under the carpet. Many evangelical young people have got hold of the idea that sex is dirty, something to be giggled over furtively, or suppressed as best as may be. Many Christians have developed all kinds of hangups. There have been some tragic instances on the mission field, partially as a result of inadequate teaching. I know of several cases of homosexuality or lesbianism among missionaries: and in most instances a lot of the blame can be laid at the door of the whole Church for refusing to face issues squarely. If you repress your sexual urges, whatever they are, and refuse to talk about them, then you are making a rod for your own back. It *is* possible to be freed from sexual problems, whether lust or perversion, and yet so many of us are caught up in this particular fog. In consequence, we shall never serve Christ effectively and may end up bringing disgrace to the work of God.

The right time to sort out this aspect of your lives is now, especially if you are still young. Roy Hession, author of *The Calvary Road,* told me once, "If you think this is a big problem among young people, let me tell you that from the counselling I have done all over the world, it is a far greater problem among those who are married with kids and in their mid-forties." Simply getting married doesn't solve the problem of sexual temptation: it can make it worse. The Devil has no borders, and the marriage border presents no more of a barrier to him than any other.

The answer is not to rush into marriage, but rather to open ourselves to the Christian revolution of love and self-discipline, of living in the light with one another, of being ready to face repentance. I know many who have been released from problems in the area of sex simply by opening their hearts and minds to someone else of the same sex, preferably someone a bit older than themselves, and praying with that person that the Lord will take them through. You will never get through by yourself.

I realize that this goes against the whole way we live our lives. We all prefer to hide behind the stiff upper lip (in the States it is sometimes called the "John Wayne syndrome") and pretend that all is well. "How are you today?"—"Oh, fine!" But this attitude is very close to pride. In Galatians 6:2 Paul writes: "Carry each other's burdens, and in this way you will fulfill the law of Christ." I know that this is very sound advice. I would have left Operation Mobilization years ago if it were not for the fact that practically everyone I have known who has been willing to share their burdens in this way has come through victorious. Learn to pray together. Seek to support one another and care for one another. This is a basic principle, and not just a once-off matter: nor does it only apply to sexual issues. We are part of the body of Christ and operate best in partnership with others. If you don't have someone with whom you pray regularly and share deeply—someone of the same sex—then see what you can do to find such a person. It is a great means to power in Christ.

God can indeed keep you out of the fog of impurity. If you do fall, he will help you to get up again. This is one of the marvellous things about God's love: you know that by the love and grace offered to us in Christ you can be forgiven and made whole once more. It is most unlikely that you will get through the battle without a wound. When you see wounds—inconsistencies—in other people, do not be amazed or censorious, but rather watch to note which parts of your own Christian life bear scars.

It is not a quick process to reach even a small degree of spiritual maturity. It can take five or fifteen or twenty years of yielding yourself to righteousness, of reckoning yourself as dead. Pray to be hungry for Christian growth! You will discover that unless you first face up to those areas of your life where the Devil has control, you will have great difficulty in taking them to the cross and making your repentance have real meaning. We are very good at confessing in general, but it is extremely hard to be specific to ourselves or anyone else. Yet I do know from my own experience that the Lord can free us from the fog of impurity, and, that without the freedom that he offers, there is no hope of spiritual victory and growth.

Emotional problems are often a direct result of impurity. You simply cannot play with sin in any form without it affecting your mind. This especially applies to those who have been reared in evangelical homes or who have spent years in evangelical circles, as the damage is compounded by rebellion and guilt. You may have had such a rigid standard set for you by your parents or church that you utterly reject it as too legalistic. You may have had your ears so pounded with Bible verses that you have a deep aversion to even walking into a church. Perhaps you are sick of a religion that seems to consist largely of big cars, clean shirts, and moralizing. (Of course a man's faith has nothing to do with the length of his hair or the style of his dress. At one Billy Graham rally in Minneapolis, two long-haired men wandered down the aisle to take seats at the front and were promptly ejected by the conservatively suited ushers. Billy Graham disagreed: "I won't be preaching tonight until the two men in the audience who look most like Jesus Christ are invited back in.") Yet even if you have grown up in the smart-suit environment and turned right against it, you may still be completely healed of emotional problems.

For years my wife suffered severely in this area, with back-aches, migraines, headaches, and heart murmurs which were a direct result of emotional upset. Her own father was killed in the war and her step-father did not get on with her. Consequently, she grew up deprived of love. When we met and fell in love, she was still suffering from this early lack and was frequently prostrated by pain. Then one day she came across a book which helped her to understand that the compassion of Christ could reach into her and heal her, and this realization led to healing where all the pills and therapies had failed. This is quite often the case. God will bring us to the point where we are willing to admit that he is sufficient. Our faith is not Jesus plus anything—plus a job or a husband or this or that spiritual practice—but Jesus alone. So my wife simply surrendered her life to the Lord and said, "Jesus, I believe and I trust you." She went to sleep, and the next morning the aches were gone. She still occasionally suffers from past hurts, but now knows that she can be healed.

This is just one example of how the power of Christ reached into a person's life and restored them deep down. Do not reject this kind of healing as superficial. Doctors in England have suggested that as many as 50 percent of the patients attending their surgeries complain of illnesses resulting directly from their mental condition. There are a number of books on the subject: I recommend *Healing for Damaged Emotions* by David A Seamands.

Jesus redeems the whole person. Just as sin affects every part of our being, so the love and death of Christ are effective in clearing away deep wounds, resentment, and jealousy, our failures to love ourselves as we should. With Christ beside us, we can walk taller and hold our heads high, not because we are proud of what we have made of ourselves, but because we are proud to be made in his image. Whatever form our "fog" takes, we can be free of it.

So often we are ready to speak of the great blessing we received five years ago. But what about the blessing we received this morning? As you open yourself daily to Jesus, he will daily fill you, making you ready for daily communion, repentance, combat. With grace and forgiveness nothing can stop us.

3

FRUITFULNESS

WE HAVE LOOKED AT SOME of the factors which hold us back as we try to make our lives count as soldiers of Jesus. As we take our first wavering steps towards fuller commitment, we can be hampered by sin or by an unreal view of ourselves or of God, by deep-rooted emotional problems, by the pressures and false values of secular society. I will assume for the moment that you recognize the major difficulties you face and that you still want to go on. You believe that God will help you find the necessary courage and humility. You are anxious that, as in the parable of the sower, you should produce thirty-, or sixty-, or a hundred-fold: that you should be fruitful. (In the context of this chapter, by "fruitfulness" I mean the making of new Christians.)

I want you to stop at this point and read the first six chapters of the Book of Acts. Please do so before you go on.

What was your reaction as you read? Probably you were stirred, and you marvelled at what God did in Jerusalem in those early days. Did you feel that it would have been wonderful to live then and to see God so mightily at work?

Let me assure you that such things can happen today. If you live in Britain or parts of Europe or the United States, you will find it easy to think that the Spirit of God is no longer very active in drawing men to himself. Yet in other parts of the world, much more dramatic events than those recorded in the Book of Acts are taking place. In 1978, according to the Information Service of the Lausanne Committee for World Evangelisation (June 1979), 6,052,800 new Christians were added to the Church in Africa alone.[3] The growth in Latin America and Asia is equally startling. Fruitful indeed!

It is clear that God does not operate the same way all the time in every land. Some places can only be categorized as "hard." It is very tempting to send missionaries to those areas where great revivals are taking place and to ignore such parts as the Arab countries of the Mediterranean and the Persian Gulf. Yet God has not told us to miss out the hard bits, rather, to "go into all the world." This may mean the fruit will not come as quickly as some of us desire, but it will certainly come if you and I are willing and ready to lead the kind of lives and be the kind of people that God can use.

If you look at the ministry of the apostles, you will see that it is characterized by reckless faith. They were not daunted by flogging or threats or social ostracism. The truth in their hearts burned so joyfully bright that nothing else mattered.

Equally, I believe, God is seeking men and women of reckless faith today. He is in need of those who are ready to have faith that he will save the toughest cases—those who refuse to take no for an answer, those who refuse to be sidetracked into professionalism and bureaucracy and too much social emphasis. It is so easy to lose the vision for souls. No matter what form your ministry takes, if you have no passion for souls, you are in danger of missing out on the essential urgency of the Christian message. If you have no time to drop your important job and tell someone about Christ, then you are too busy. It is a *sin* to be too busy. If you don't have the time or the energy to visit the local hospital and offer a little comfort or to talk with the man next door, then you are too busy.

The first symptom of creeping busyness is often a cut-down in your prayer life. The prayer meeting becomes a discussion session or a fellowship hour—and soon you are losing spiritual power and drive as you seek to do things in your own strength. Prayer is the Christian's vital breath: without it you can't move.

The apostles were aware of the problem. They knew that it would be very easy for them to get sidetracked into the administration of the young Christian community and realized that their first priority was the job they had been called to do: "Prayer, and the ministry of the word" (see Acts 6:1–7). How many Christian leaders today are bogged down with paperwork when they should be out teaching, and guiding, and *leading?* The busy life is frequently barren. To be reckless in your faith does not mean to be unthinking, but the reverse—concentrated, single-minded in your concern that God should be glorified and souls won. Don't kid yourself and don't kid others by the amount you do.

I don't have as much boldness as I used to. Perhaps I am wiser now and do not embarrass people so much. Yet I frequently think that I'm in danger of getting too careful and tactful, and failing to rock the boat when that is exactly what is needed. I haven't given out tracts on an airplane, but Arthur Blessit has. He certainly annoys people, but who has won as many souls for Christ as that reckless warrior? His kind of boldness would have fitted well into the pages of Acts.

I am not advocating loudmouthed, discourteous evangelism. Apart from giving a bad impression, it does not work. Nor am I suggesting that you should be bold in witness without an adequate knowledge of the word of God. Nor am I suggesting that you confuse the energy of the flesh with the power of the Spirit. Yet there is a time for speaking out to cut across shallow politeness and you must be sure that you are not using extra study as an excuse for avoiding your duty to bear witness and you must indeed bend all your talents and capabilities to the task. If this sounds complex, remember that God can use even our blunders. The history of the Christian church is filled with instances where God has made use of acts of foolishness in the world's eyes to save men.

Without Holy Spirit boldness, the world will remain unevangelized. We may hand everyone we meet a tract and a Bible with it, but until we get involved in the foolishness of personally preaching the word, we are not going to see very many saved. There can never be a substitute for the power of the Spirit working through willing men and women, and that power will bring boldness—not noise, but guts to speak and discernment to know when to speak.

Compassion is an essential ingredient in this boldness. If you are giving out tracts or dropping hints about your faith just because you feel it is the right thing to do, then be careful because your evangelism is a forced growth, a hothouse plant. Under such conditions we need to get down on our faces and ask the Lord to give us the compassion we need. If our evangelism is mechanical rather than natural, we are likely to be acting out of our own resources, and little fruit will result. Of ourselves we cannot make converts: only God in his sovereignty knows how to mix man's Spirit-led action with his grace. Paul puts it this way in 1 Corinthians 3:6, "I planted the seed, Apollos watered it, but God made it grow."

Allied to compassion, we need discipline. I shall be saying more about discipline in a later chapter, but for the present let me remind you that Jesus said, "If you love me, keep my commandments." Discipline is not a god, and Christianity is a religion of grace not law, but discipline is unquestionably a means to an end. Take letter writing, for instance. Perhaps you are in touch with someone who has shown a lot of interest in Christian matters. That letter which you never quite got around to writing might well have encouraged them to take the final step—but now you seem to have lost their address. Such little things count. Tracts have limited effectiveness, but do not neglect them. Always carry a few with you and keep some in your car so that you can give one to any hitch-hiker you pick up. Be careful to obtain those which you find the most attractive and persuasive; your local Christian bookshop should be able to supply you or give you addresses of organizations that will be able to help. My little book *Literature Evangelism* may also be helpful. These may seem minor matters to you, but just wonder: what if the person who led you to the Lord had also considered it, a minor matter to strike up a conversation with you?

To illustrate the need for faithfulness even in tract distribution, let me tell you of a man I heard about recently who was going from door to door giving out tracts. At one house he had to wait some time before the door opened to his knock. The houseowner took the tract and slammed the door in his face. Later on, he called at the house again, and this time the man invited him in. He took him upstairs and showed him a box in the attic, and a rope above it: he had been just about to hang himself when the visitor had called previously. As a result of the tract, instead of hanging himself he knelt down by the box and gave his life to Jesus Christ.

Fruitfulness is not an optional extra for Christians. Suppose that a man in some Indian, French, or Turkish village knew that you have the secret of eternal life. What kind of letter would he write to you? "Dear Christian brother, I understand that you have many calls on your time. Your own needs are acute, and I would not want you to put yourself out. But if at some point you could possibly drift this way and share the message of the gospel with me and my neighbors, we would be most grateful—but please do not lose any sleep or miss any meals on our account . . ." No! Rather he would send a telegram— "COME AT ONCE STOP WE NEED YOUR HELP DESPERATELY STOP WE ARE ON THE ROAD TO HELL AND YOU ARE OUR ONLY HOPE STOP."

Christ can make us fruitful if we are prepared to surrender ourselves to him. The more he has of us the more he can do. You have probably realized that it is quite possible to read such a book as this and yet never to surrender the larger part of our lives. As we die to ourselves, to our failures and jealousies and hatreds and lusts, we can turn our eyes away from our own sordid tangles to the glory and beauty and wholeness of Jesus. We will find that the lives we have abandoned to him are given back to us abundantly and with joy, both now and in the life to come. We are accepted not as soul-winners but as sinners. We are the grain of wheat that falls into the ground and dies, so that it may produce thirty-, sixty-, a hundred-fold.

PART II

Biblical Principles of Discipleship and Victory

4

LOVE: *the hallmark of a christian*

WE HAVE THOUGHT OVER some of the challenges that Christ offers to his disciples, and some of the drawbacks that threaten to snare us as we seek to serve. This second section will, I hope, provide you with some guidance in crucial aspects of Christian conduct.

It is tragically true that a major cause of failure and bitterness in many missionary societies, including Operation Mobilization, is the break-down of personal relations between members of the mission team. I am afraid that you are likely to know from your own experience that this is also true of churches at home. The minister or pastor is a favorite target for scorn and backbiting.

In view of our overwhelming needs in this area, it is perhaps surprising that we get very little teaching today on the theme of love. Yet many chapters in the New Testament are devoted entirely to this subject, and it is clear from even a quick survey of Jesus's instructions to his disciples that whatever we do or think must be built on a foundation of love, first for God and then for the brethren. Look at John 13:34–35: "A new commandment I give you: Love one another. As I have loved you, so you must love one another. By this all men will know that you are my disciples, if you love one another." And in John 15: 9 he says, "As the Father has loved me, so have I loved you. Now remain in my love." What an amazing truth this is! It is precisely because we are loved and know ourselves to be loved that we are able to love one another. As we love each other, we show that we are disciples of Jesus: we are offering a picture in miniature of Jesus's love for us, so that the world may understand. (This is another aspect of the gossip and jealousy which eat at the Christian Church—we are giving a very poor reflection of the love Jesus bears for men.)

Love is the hallmark of the true disciple. If however we think that love will come easily into our lives, we are making a serious mistake. There are two extreme views which are both common: that love is a product of extensive training and discipline, and that love is a natural result of a deep encounter with the Spirit. The second view is very widespread: yet as we grow in Christian maturity, we must expect to go through "dry patches." These are valuable times, for they allow us to learn for ourselves that Christian truth is bigger than our own feelings. Speaking of this initial wave of love and enthusiasm, H. A. Hodges writes in *The Unseen Warfare*:

> This fervour is especially characteristic of beginners. Its drying up should be welcomed as a sign that we are getting beyond the first stage. To try to retain it or to long for its return in the midst of dryness is to refuse to grow up: it is to refuse the cost. By our steady adherence to God when the affections are dried up and nothing is left but the naked will clinging blindly to him, the soul is purged of self regard and cleaned in pure love.[4]

I have thought long and hard over this. Of course, new joys and insights which move the heart do come and are welcome. But there is no point in bemoaning the initial zeal and love of twenty years ago—today we must deny ourselves and take up our cross and follow Christ, knowing that we are his, abiding in the Vine; for if we abide in the Vine, fruit will come, with or without a great amount of emotion. We have already looked at one major aspect of being fruitful in the last chapter, but there are others. You cannot separate love from showing that you love: and if you show that you are loving, then you are in the Vine, and you are going to bear fruit. These aspects are all bound up together.

Do not be led astray by the popular way of thinking that if you feel it to be right, then it is right. For years now hit records and romantic films and novels have been saying, in effect, that while the feeling lasts, everything is fine, but as soon as the feeling dies then it is time to move on. The Christian faith certainly offers plenty of joy and love and deep satisfaction, but it works from the other way round: do what is right, and your heart will follow.

There is another problem here that we need to be aware of. Some Christians find it very tempting to be so very certain about what is right that they start laying down the law. Often it is difficult to be both firm and loving. A. W. Tozer put it this way:

> It requires great care, and a true knowledge of ourselves, to distinguish a spiritual burden from a religious irritation. Often acts done in a spirit of religious irritation have consequences far beyond what we could have guessed. It is more important that we maintain a right spirit toward the others than that we bring them to our way of thinking, even if our way is right. Satan cares little whether we go astray after false doctrine or merely turn sour. Either way, he wins.[5]

Do you know what Tozer means by "sour" Christians? Often they have a good grasp of doctrine and a clear analysis of the situation, but seem to lack gentleness and peace. Any follower of religion can have a religious irritation. I remember an early meeting on board M.V. *Logos* when someone jumped up and began to yell objections to what was taking place. It seemed when I talked with him afterwards that someone had touched his "holy cow." It is very easy to be right in the wrong way. The Apostle James faced this issue directly:

> Who is wise and understanding among you? Let him show it by his good life, by deeds done in the humility that comes from wisdom. But if you harbor bitter envy and selfish ambition in your hearts, do not boast about it or deny the truth. Such "wisdom" does not come down from heaven but is earthly, unspiritual, of the devil. For where you have envy and selfish ambition, there you find disorder and every evil practice.
>
> But the wisdom that comes from heaven is first of all pure; then peace-loving, considerate, submissive, full of mercy and good fruit, impartial and sincere. (James 3:13–17)

Just as it is easy to judge others, so it is easy to be cynical. We look around at our fellow Christians and see all too clearly how far they are falling short of the standards they profess. Unless we are abiding in Christ—trusting in him, praying, worshipping, reading his word, opening ourselves to his love—we are likely to fall into the trap of cynicism. We read the Sermon on the Mount; we study Christ's teaching on love; then we turn to our local church and see so clearly the lust disguised as censorship, the veiled ambition in leading members, the dominant manner to conceal envy and insecurity—oh yes, it's all there to find. It is very simple to see people's inconsistencies and to mock them, forgetting that communication is an art and not everyone is a perfect thinker with the gift of self-expression. God looks at the heart when people pray, no matter how clumsy their prayers may be. Cheap jibes are just that—cheap.

Please beware of a cynical spirit in any area. Don't be cynical for any reason. Don't be cynical even towards yourself. For every Christian who is troubled by pride, I suspect there is another whose opinion of himself is so low that it hinders him from seeing that God is bigger than his faults.

Tozer offers some good sense on the subject:

> In this world of corruption there is real danger that the earnest Christian may overreact in his resistance to evil and become a victim of the religious occupational disease, cynicism. The constant need to go counter to popular trend may easily develop in him a sour habit of fault-finding and turn him into a critic of other men's manners, without charity and without love. What makes this cynical spirit particularly dangerous is that the cynic is usually right. His analyses are accurate, his judgements are correct, yet for all that he is wrong, frightfully, pathetically wrong. As a cure for the sour, fault-finding attitude, I recommend the cultivation of the habit of thanksgiving. Thanksgiving has great curative powers, and a thankful heart cannot be cynical.[6]

An essential part of love is generous service, the kind that is concerned not for your own status but for the "welfare of another. Jesus gave a vivid illustration of this kind of love at the

Last Supper—an occasion when every word and gesture would have been savored and memorized by the apostles. After giving the bread and the cup, he got up, took off his outer clothing and wrapped a towel round his waist. Then he poured water into a basin and began to wash his disciples' feet. This was the kind of task that would normally be performed by a household servant or slave. Luke records that at the Supper the disciples had begun bickering over which of them was the greatest, and Jesus told them, "The greatest among you should be like the youngest, and the one who rules like the one who serves" (Luke 22:26). So, as a servant, he went round the disciples, but when he came to Simon Peter, Simon refused . . . until Jesus explained that unless he was prepared to accept, he could not be one with him. Then Simon was glad to accept Christ's service.

I think that Simon Peter refused because of his pride. Jesus was challenging all his assumptions about honor and position by the task he was performing. Such things just weren't done, in Simon's eyes. He knew himself to have the kind of personality that others would follow, and he looked forward to receiving the status and respect of the world as Jesus's right-hand man. But his pride went deeper than that. It takes a certain amount of humility to allow others to do things for you: and perhaps in refusing to let his feet be washed he was betraying that he felt he didn't need Christ. This is one of the frequent stumbling blocks for those who are close to the kingdom: to admit a need of salvation seems like a recognition of failure—as of course it is. It is so easy to be stiffly formal and to conceal our needs from the world. Sometimes we will offer our help but die before we will admit we need help.

What I particularly want to stress, however, is the kind of service that Christ teaches us. Most churches today have the bread and the cup, but unless we also have the towel, our worship is likely to be a mockery of the presence of Jesus. If we go to the Lord's table remembering the Lord's death but not willing to serve one another, love one another, and give ourselves to one another, then something has gone wrong. I am not talking about the sort of service that wins you recognition and respect, such as the Pharisees used to perform, but rather the sort that God alone knows about and honors.

The Holy Spirit will give us compassion and imagination as we open ourselves to him to see what needs to be done. But our obedience to the Spirit's promptings is a matter for the will. You may feel, "Aha! I knew this was coming. This is where it gets hard." In a way I agree: there are many different avenues for grace, and among them are training and self-discipline. But in this our human nature plays a part, for we are creatures of habit. You will know this to your cost if you have ever seriously tried to rid yourself of some practice which shamed you, like impure thinking. It is possible however with the indwelling power of the Spirit, to cultivate attitudes of generosity and selflessness. The first few times it will be very hard: gradually it gets somewhat easier. As you seek to love those who are to you unlovely, you will certainly fail at first and be tempted to discouragement. Then you will start to see dignity where you had only seen foolishness, or integrity where you had only seen dishonesty. Equally, if you turn up early to put out the chairs for a meeting, it will at first be difficult not to hint that it was you who did so. After a while it becomes—most of the time—your regular practice "to give without counting the cost," in some areas at least.

Love expressed in such generous service will really help to bring about unity among believers. The jobs get done, the lonely and misfits are made to feel wanted, the minister or pastor and other leaders feel secure and valued. The whole church becomes more open-hearted and ready to praise and worship. Paul puts it this way, "Let no debt remain outstanding, except the continuing debt to love one another, for he who loves his fellowman has fulfilled the law" (Romans 13:8).

By contrast, sourness and legalism will swiftly divide a fellowship. I believe that legalism is one of the greatest plagues of the church today. Don't do this or that, especially on a Sunday; more young believers, I suspect, have been destroyed by legalism than anything else. Of course there have to be rules and principles in church life, but if we judge others to be unspiritual because they don't follow our particular set of rules, then we are making a great mistake. Love *fulfills* the law. Once you seek to keep all the laws of the Old Testament, you are heading for extremes. Most of the false cults have taken their policies and regulations, out of context, from the Old Testament, failing to grasp that the keynote should be love. Once we start following all the laws of the Old Testament, then we ought to adopt such practices as the Year of Jubilee, by which those of us who own land would have to return it to its former owners when the Year came round. By the same token, quite a number of us would have to be stoned to death! We should rather appreciate that the law of the Old Testament is to be summed up in the New Testament teaching on love. (Please note that I am not suggesting that the Old Testament can be neglected: it is the record of God's dealing with his people; Jesus quoted from it extensively, and you will not get a full understanding of the New Testament without seeing it as the fulfillment of the Old.)

The love we should show to one another should extend to tolerance of different religious practices and emphases. When Operation Mobilization teams move into various church contexts, they do their utmost to respect the customs of each church. We see it as really important not to be some kind of stumbling block to our Christian brothers. For example, I have been on teams in Scotland, which is a very conservative area and where there are many fine believers, where it has been regarded as highly wrong to sell books on the Lord's day. Naturally we accept this while we are there. Yet such a view would just not be acceptable in India, where people come to the churches on a Sunday from villages many miles around. On Sunday many hundreds of Bibles are sold, for it is the only chance these villagers have to buy Bibles. Another thing I have noticed in other churches is the tremendous emphasis they place upon regular attendance at the Lord's Table every Sunday morning. I visited one church where you are given a little pin to wear in your lapel signifying that you haven't missed a Sunday's attendance in ten years. I really respect the dedication and consistency this shows: wouldn't it be great if we could put the same devotion into loving our neighbors as these brethren put into attendance at the Lord's Table?

For love is long term. When there are new Christians in the church, we nurture them and give them our special care and love. But when someone has been part of the fellowship for twelve or fifteen years, we seem to think that because they have been walking with the Lord for so long they will not be offended so quickly if we ignore them or make cutting remarks about them or make unreasonable requests of them. Their faith is surely so strong that they will be quick to praise God when they are not appreciated and their gifts go unnoticed. People do not grow less vulnerable as they grow older, however, and may indeed become more prone to despair or depression. Sometimes, too, you will need years and years of patient loving and acceptance before you can really build trust and a sense of worth in somebody who has been crushed by past rejection or failure.

Many of these thoughts are to be found in concentrated form in I Corinthians 13, the Mount Everest of this principle of love. Every Christian should memorize this chapter. Please keep it open beside you as you read the rest of this section. It deserves a great deal of study with the aid of a good, thorough commentary, but for the moment look at the following:

> *Love is patient.* This can be deeply impressive to non-Christians, as well as being an essential part of the whole nature of love. It is easy to love for half an hour. The home is an area where the patience of love is essential: those of you who are mothers will know how much grace it takes to live with children and husbands. (My wife has a great deal of such grace—I am a very untidy person!)

> *Love is kind.* Simple kindness and gentleness are in very short supply these days. When we first set up the operation for M.V. *Logos,* we found this was a real problem: we had to teach people how to treat one another with courtesy and consideration. Kindness is not just going around with a goofy smile on your face; rather it is the exercise of the imagination God gave you to see how others are feeling and to work out

what they are likely to need.

People often come up to me after a meeting and ask how they can get further into the spiritual life. One method is by memorizing Scripture—getting steeped in the word of God. Another is by having good, close fellowship and talking matters over. Such fellowship means, among other things, giving freely, being quick to apologize, and forgetting righteous indignation. If difficulties arise between you and another Christian, then keep your mind on the primacy of love and unity: if a major matter of morality or spiritual principle is involved, then love and unity are all the more necessary. This is one area of life where we do need brainwashing—love, love, love all the way. Love is my aim. I know that I need many other gifts in my Christian life, but my primary goal is love.

5

FOUNDATIONS *for*
spiritual GROWTH

AT THE CLOSE OF HIS SECOND LETTER, the Apostle Peter encouraged his readers to "grow in the grace and knowledge of our Lord and Savior Jesus Christ."

If love is the dominant characteristic of the Christian's relationship to his fellow men, then growing in grace—growth towards spiritual maturity—is the chief element of his inner spiritual life. The two are linked: as you get to know God better, so you find yourself able to love more generously; and as you seek to love more freely, you find yourself searching harder for God and his strength.

To grow as Christians, we have to recommit ourselves to Jesus each and every day. True commitment is continuous, a fresh dedication of ourselves in the different situations and pressures we encounter, even hour by hour. At present I am the father of two teenagers and one twenty-two-year-old son. That is very different from being the father of three young children, or of three babies, and different again from the experience of being married but without a family. In each of these contexts, I have had to discover afresh just what it means to be a committed disciple of Jesus. The kind of commitment that I had at college would not have carried me through the years that followed.

We could talk of a *habit* of recommitment. The way I trust myself to Jesus and offer myself to his service is based on all the other acts of trusting that I have made over the years. It is helpful to try to see your life in the long term, to build up habits of this kind. One of my greatest burdens for young Christians in particu-

lar is to encourage them in continuity and consistency of life. I am
not interested in seeing people following Christ just for one year.

Yet, unless you get a firm footing to your Christianity, a good
strong foundation, that is exactly what is likely to happen. Even
if you do doggedly continue, without a strong footing you will be
just a house built on sand. Short-term Christians are terribly common in the fast pace of the industrialized world. In Singapore, for
example, where there are large numbers of young people in the
churches, the drop-out rate can be as high as 75 percent. Once they
get married, develop a career and start a family, they don't darken
the doors of the church any more. (The problem is not confined
to Singapore.) Christians are needed who will stick at it year after
year, realizing that the Devil changes his tactics, and that each day
presents a new challenge.

Let us go over some of the basic foundation stones.

First of all, be sure that you *are God's child*. "I write these
things to you who believe in the name of the Son of God so that
you may know that you have eternal life" (1 John 5:13). If you are
going to grow, you need to be completely sure that you are born
again, that your sins are forgiven. Perhaps this seems obvious, but
in much of the counselling that I have been involved with, I have
found that many people are not really sure of their own salvation. They've had failure in their lives; they've not seen the fruit
they hoped for, either in terms of evangelizing others or in their
own characters; they've wrestled with their own ugly emotions;
they've heard arguments against the Christian faith "without
thinking them through; and all these things have led them to doubt
their salvation.

We badly need to re-emphasize the doctrine of justification
by faith. This is the answer: no amount of failure or stormy emotion can take us away from Jesus—he knows all too well that
we are failures! But some pride within us is always reluctant to
accept that grace is utterly free, and again and again you find
churches which have lost sight of this truth. For so many people
it is justification by faith plus works, rules, church attendance,
or baptism. This is a major error which denies the whole basis

of our faith. It is the subject of the whole of Paul's letter to the Galatians.

I think it is quite normal for all of us to wonder from time to time whether we are really saved. Billy Graham said once that some years ago he went off by himself into the mountains for a few days to make sure of this very point: that he really knew Jesus Christ as his personal Lord and Savior. If Billy Graham, who has led so many tens of thousands of people to the Lord, feels at times the need to search his heart, then perhaps we should not be too worried if we also sometimes feel the need to search our own.

When this happens we should always go straight back to the word of God, and to its clear, simple teaching that salvation is by faith alone. Now this faith is bound to be tested, and doubts will come. In one way these are to be welcomed, for deep faith is not produced in the absence of doubt, but rather as we battle through our doubts. Not only will you probably doubt (if you haven't already) your own salvation, but you are also likely to doubt whether any of this Christianity business is true—God, the Bible, salvation, everything. If you have a brain and are using it, then doubts will come, especially if you have something to do with psychology, philosophy, or history as it is often taught. This is precisely why I think it is good for Christians to be involved in all these areas, so that there are no no-go areas of intellectual activity.

In this context I would like to recommend two books by Josh MacDowell entitled *Evidence that Demands a Verdict* and *More Evidence that Demands a Verdict*.[7] These set out to present good intellectual grounds for faith in Christ. Josh MacDowell has led not only many, many students but also quite a few professors and liberal pastors to the Lord. The second volume deals with some issues raised by "higher criticism" that has damaged the faith of theology students. Intellectual doubts can be answered—though we should be aware that a lot of our so-called intellectual doubts are simply big emotional struggles in disguise.

Often simple obedience is at the root of the matter. Once we begin to really obey God and hence to see fruit in our lives, then we gain a greater assurance. In one way, God does not allow us to have all the assurance we would like if we are living a defeated, disobedient life. If there are areas where we are clearly conscious of disobedience, then we just don't deserve to have complete assurance, and it would not be a kindness on the Lord's part to give it to us. We deserve rather to be somewhat on edge about things, and that will drive us back to him and to the cross. Use your doubts, then. Don't take to your heels.

Secondly, be sure that *the Bible is God's Word.* "All Scripture is God-breathed and is useful for teaching, rebuking, correcting and training in righteousness, so that the man of God may be thoroughly equipped for every good work" (2 Timothy 3:16,17). The two books by Josh MacDowell give a lot of good grounds as to why we can know that the Bible is true. There are certainly plenty of problems for the man who decides to accept Jesus's own view of the Old Testament—that it was fully inspired—and we would be foolish and unrealistic to pretend otherwise. It is a matter of great controversy. Yet there is a good deal of archaeological evidence that has come to light in the past thirty years that enables us to say with confidence that the Old Testament relates real history. I remember hearing Dr. Francis Schaeffer speak about the problems that arise for the man who *doesn't* believe in the Bible, and I think these are far greater, intellectually and in every other way.

There have been low points in my life when I have been tempted to throw the whole Christian business in and go back to the world, but each time I have realized I just couldn't do it. It would be like running into a brick wall. I knew the truth of God and the intellectual facts concerning the faith; and though there were some problems, in particular some passages in the Old Testament that I found hard to swallow, the problems were far greater if I tried to say that this is not God's world or that a personal God does not exist.

I frequently ask at meetings how many people have read the Bible through from Genesis to Revelation. As a rule the answer is less than 10 percent. Yet you find people saying quite confidently that the Bible is not truly inspired, and when you question them, they admit that they have not read it in anything like such detail. Before you reach a verdict, you should examine the evidence. If you have not yet done so, may I encourage you to read the Bible right through, so as to get an overall view of God's purposes and acts in history? It is a remarkable boost to your faith: you will wonder when you have done so why ever you did not do it before.

The truth of the Bible was my great area of struggle during my first year at college. I was at a college where some of the teachers were agnostics, and they took a particular delight in tearing apart anyone who believed in the Bible. I was a very young Christian, and I had to wrestle hard to find out what I believed. In the process I realized that the truths that it contained, if they were true, were so great—heaven, hell, Jesus, the Second Coming—that I would have to commit myself to them heart, mind, and soul. When, in due course, I reached the conclusion that the Bible was indeed to be trusted, I had no choice but to go ahead and make that commitment.

Without this conviction about the Bible, there would be no Operation Mobilization. It is a conviction that leads us and many a missionary to do things that we would not otherwise choose to do. Some seem to think that there is such a person as the "missionary type," who wants to live in climates he doesn't like, eating food he can't stand! They seem to believe that we are evangelical masochists. Yet on the basis of the Bible, missionaries have given themselves to the Lord, and he is the one who tells them where they must go and what they must be.

Confidence in the Bible makes radicals of us all. It is this that the churches of Britain and the USA in particular need: there are so many people who give lip service to the authority of Scripture, but do not allow it to dig into their lives. (I have never heard so many people justifying the status quo!) It has been a characteristic of great men of faith in every age that they had a high view of Scripture. Samuel Logan Brengle, an early leader of The Salvation Army and a notable evangelist, wrote of the fire that the Spirit who inspired the Bible lights within us:

> What is fire? It is love, it is faith, it is hope, it is passion, purpose, determination, it is utter devotion, it is divine discontent with formality, ceremonialism, lukewarmness, indifference, sham, noise, parade and spiritual death. It is singleness of eye, and a consecration unto death. It is God the Holy Ghost burning in and through a humble, holy, faithful man.[8]

I feel broken in pieces when I read of the lives of some of the great heroes of faith such as Brengle and see, not only what they said, but how they lived. It can all be traced back to the fact that these men believed that the Bible was God's word.

Billy Graham has told how he once had a deep crisis of faith over the trustworthiness of the Old Testament and went away by himself to think it through. This was in the days before he became well known, and the decision he would reach was to be crucial for the whole of his future work. In the end as he worked through the arguments, he came to a position of trust in the Bible and went back to the preparations for his Los Angeles Crusade which was the beginning of his amazing ministry.

In the end the decision to trust is one of faith, not mental assent. This is important; without faith and love your Christianity will be a hollow thing, no matter what its intellectual credibility.

Without a firm foundation on the Bible, we shall find it impossible to develop sound doctrine. Leading a man to Christ is only the start of the process: we must ensure that that man is grounded in Scripture, loved, and encouraged in the faith. It is essential to care for and cherish those who come to faith so that they may grow: a major part of spiritual growth is precisely a good grasp of doctrine. Without it you will be swayed and confused by each new idea and each one-sided sect. But more than this, sound doctrine is a splendid avenue to a deeper knowledge of God himself, for doctrine concerns the nature and purpose of God and can be a subject which is a joy to study.

The third foundation stone is *a correct view of God himself*. In Isaiah 6, the prophet records how he was called and commissioned by God. Before the Lord could send him out to make a start upon his long and harsh ministry, he needed to give him a deep experience of himself. "In the year that King Uzziah died, I saw the Lord seated on a throne, high and exalted, and the train of his robe filled the temple. . . . 'Woe to me!' I cried. 'I am ruined! For I am a man of unclean lips, and I live among a people of unclean lips, and my eyes have seen the King, the LORD Almighty'" (Isaiah 6:1, 5). This was exactly the right response for Isaiah to make as he faced the holiness of God, and also the right response for us. But Isaiah also met the mercy of God as the coal from the altar touched his mouth and, in consequence, was able to say, "Here am I. Send me!"

We too need to encounter both God's holiness and God's mercy. Many people, young and old alike, seem to have a concept of God as a stern father figure up there with a big stick, ready to hit them as soon as they do anything wrong. Sometimes this can be traced back to a bad relationship with their own fathers, or to the fact that they have had little contact with their fathers in this world of soaring divorce rates. Under such conditions it takes time and profound healing to get free of false ideas about God. It is very easy to stress the "thou shalt nots" of this Christian faith and to forget that the Lord who made you and saved you also loves you. If you reduce your spiritual understanding to rules and regulations, then you have become a legalist. Legalism is one of the chief enemies of the spiritual life, a key weapon which Satan the accuser uses to load us down with guilt. It will probably stay this way until Jesus comes.

The legalism that results from a false view of God creates pressures on people to pretend. Thus they constantly try to give the impression that they are up, up, up, when really they are down, down, down. Therefore they grow unwilling to share their problems, even with themselves, and the drain that results upon their personality and emotions puts an end to any hope of spiritual growth and health.

A sound view of God develops as a result of steady reading in his word, with attendant thought and prayer. There are many good books to help you to organize and develop your understanding. I would particularly recommend J. I. Packer's *Knowing God*. But the subject demands a lifetime's study: fortunately the Holy Spirit is a good teacher.

Our fourth foundation is a *correct view of ourselves*. This is exceedingly important, but as I have dealt with the matter at some length in chapters one and two, I will only touch on it briefly now. Some people think more highly of themselves than they really should, and pride in all its forms can be dangerous in the spiritual life. But there are others, I think the majority of us, who are suffering rather from a very low image of themselves.

As a result they are afraid to witness and to launch out into doing new things for God. Jesus told us to love our neighbors as ourselves—but how can you do this without loving yourself? If you do not like or respect yourself, then you will be hampered in trying to like and respect others. A lot of people are unable to relate to those around them because they are unable to relate to themselves. Years ago the Devil's primary tactic seemed to be to kill Christians in the arenas, through persecution, on the mission field. Today he seems concerned to maim and disable. The amount of depression, self-rejection, and mental illness there is today among both Christians and non-Christians is unbelievable.

Now, I get scared when anyone starts coming up with simple easy answers when the world's best medical and pastoral brains have not solved the problem. However, I do know that prevention is better than cure. Every Christian can learn how to rest in the Lord and to cast every burden upon him, to deal as seriously and as radically with worry as you would deal with fornication. I regard worry in some ways as a greater evil today than lust. Whether it is worry over legitimate matters or worry over shadows, it can still break you mentally. Our academic systems are so rough on people, and can instill such a sense of failure, that some of the best brains we have are rusting on the shelves of mental hospitals.

If you are obsessed with worry and failure, then you are leaving God out of the picture, and that is very much a wrong view of yourself. If God has given you a good mind, use it, but don't sacrifice your emotional and spiritual life in the process. It is not worth it. Better the most menial occupation you can imagine, if it preserves in you a healthy mind. "For God did not give us a spirit of timidity, but a spirit of power, of love and of self-discipline" (2 Timothy 1:7).

The fifth foundation is a very practical one: simply *allowing time*—time for studying God's word, for prayer, for witness, and for fellowship. All four are essential if you are going to maintain a spiritual life. Like taking a leg off a chair, your spiritual life will keel over if you neglect any one area. If you look at the picture of the early church in Acts, you can see these principles very clearly. "They devoted themselves to the apostles' teaching and to the fellowship, to the breaking of bread and to prayer" (Acts 2:42). And soon they were moving out into the whole region, witnessing. These are basic means of grace.

I would like to stress again the value of memorizing Scripture. The psalmist said, "I have hidden your word in my heart that I might not sin against you" (Psalm 119:11). When I was first converted, I had enormous problems, especially in the areas of lust and impatience, and felt at times that I was bound to blow my whole faith sky high. The thing that helped me the most on a practical level was intense memorization of the word of God. The Navigators have emphasized this, as have many other Christian groups, but if you ask the average Christian today what he does for his quiet time, he will tell you that he reads a page from *Daily Light,* perhaps reads a bit of a psalm and goes off to work. That is not Jesus's way. When tempted in the wilderness, he rebuked the Devil using the words of Scripture, and his teaching shows clearly how thoroughly he knew the Old Testament. A well-stocked memory is a powerful weapon, both in defence against temptation and in witnessing.

If you are going to set aside time, you will have to make a special effort. For some it will mean getting to bed a little earlier, so that you can rise at six or six-thirty to read and pray. It is so easy for us, especially the activist types, to put our relationship with people ahead of our relationship with God. If you are of a more mystical nature, you may find it easier to hide in your cupboard with a flashlight and a Bible! The average person is a more social animal, and time for God means disciplined living, saying no to the body and yes to God. Alan Redpath has said that the greatest challenge to Christians is blanket victory—getting the blankets off in the morning.

Sixth and last is *accepting God's pattern for your life*. Paul wrote to the Philippians, "In all my prayers for all of you, I always pray with joy because of your partnership in the gospel from the first day until now, being confident of this, that he who began a good work in you will carry it on to completion until the day of Christ Jesus" (Philippians 1:4–6).

That "good work" goes forward at the Lord's own pace. Moreover, it is a matter between ourselves and God. We can never know how far another person has progressed spiritually, and it is futile to try and make such judgments. Never assume you know another person's spiritual status, for good or ill: I have seen far too many bright Christian stars who have suddenly fallen, with their lives in a mess and their marriages ending in the divorce courts.

Some people throw away their faith because they do not seek to discover God's pattern and are too impatient to wait until it is revealed to them. They aim so high and demand extraordinary things of themselves, and when they don't get there in one year, they turn away in disgust, convinced that Christianity doesn't work. You will come across people who have tried all the techniques, have had hands laid on them, have tried all the different churches, and yet have rejected their faith after one or two years because they are still falling into sin in some particular area.

This comes from trying to push God into a corner, telling him how he ought to be working. But perhaps God isn't planning to release you from whatever sin you have right away: perhaps he is trying to teach you that failure is often the back door to success in the long run, that cleansing and forgiveness are a major part of Christian experience. King David had to learn the hard way that restoration is part of God's plan. Let us therefore bounce back when we do sin. By all means fight against sin with every ounce of spiritual energy, but when you do sin, remember the reality of 1 John 2:1,2, "If anybody does sin, we have one who speaks to the

Father in our defence—Jesus Christ, the Righteous One. He is the atoning sacrifice for our sins, and not only for ours but also for the sins of the whole world."

Our ultimate foundation is Jesus. He must take complete precedence in your life: be totally in love with him! He must be in charge of your emotions, your money, and your time. As you give yourself humbly to the Lord and to your fellows, the Spirit will work in and through you. If I hadn't seen the Spirit doing this in thousands of lives over the past twenty-odd years, then I wouldn't preach about it, because I'm interested in *practical* Christian living. I can assure you that it really works.

6

DISCIPLINES *of the* *spiritual* LIFE

ONE GREAT WEAKNESS IN today's Christian world—perhaps particularly in Britain—is that people think and learn without acting upon what they have thought and learned. Evangelical Christians get an enormous amount of good teaching: in the UK there are more people per capita teaching the word of God than in any other country in the world, including America. British Christians have been spoiled and pampered in this respect, and I fear that a special judgment may well fall upon the British, as upon the servant who hid his talent in the ground, because of our lack of response. Northern Ireland is a particular example, for in that country there are an extraordinary number of preachers and churches and conventions. Yet all this wisdom is not getting out into the world. This is not to attack the beautiful believers of Northern Ireland, but it is still a fact that very, very few young people have gone out from there in the past years as missionaries.

Such thoughts may come as a bit of a shock. I can hear people saying, "But how can we send anyone out? We don't have enough pastors and teachers here ourselves." No one ever thinks they have enough teachers. Yet there have never been enough missionaries or pastors in any of the countries that I've ever lived in. In Spain there are whole provinces with only a few gospel churches. In India, in those states where the churches are responding and growing, there is such a need for Bible teachers that when Operation Mobilization has sent in mechanics, who perhaps couldn't even give their testimonies properly, they have been asked to become

Bible teachers—and I get letters saying that they are now teaching the Word of God among the believers.

I have been in churches in Britain where they have had six or eight trained men capable of teaching, yet were not doing so. Maybe they were comparing themselves to one of the outstanding men such as John Stott or Alan Redpath, but there is no point in making comparisons of this kind. The world will not be won for Christ simply through the ministry of a few men especially anointed by God. Such men should be ministering to the ministers!

In the West, we have sermons and Bible teaching from the pulpit, in books, on radio and cassette. Yet in many lands a modern version of the Bible is not available, and there are still over 3000 languages across the world into which no part of the Bible is translated. This is where the great work of the Wycliffe Bible Translators comes in. I believe that encouraging workers to go overseas will actually strengthen the Christian ministry in the West: others will get trained up to fill the gaps, and a church with a vision for missions overseas will usually find a vision for missions at home. We don't want to neglect the work at home, but to encourage both.

If we are going to take advantage of our own wealth of teaching, then we must learn to lead a disciplined life. When people talk about discipline, they mean, as a rule, fasting, regular Bible study, and prayer, and perhaps confession. These things are good and should be a part of every Christian's life; I would strongly recommend a book entitled *Celebration of Discipline* by Richard J. Foster which discusses the use of these disciplines in some detail. But I want to encourage you to think of discipline as an attitude towards the whole of your life. Even the bleakest of moments can be occasions for learning and profit. If you can learn to look for hidden riches and good results during times of challenge and anguish, then you will find that it is a matter of real fact rather than of pious conviction that the Lord is truly in control. This will lead to reality in your prayer and witness, and to power in your service.

The author of the letter to the Hebrews refers to this truth in 12:7–12:

Endure hardship as discipline; God is treating you as sons. For what son is not disciplined by his father? If you are not disciplined (and everyone undergoes discipline), then you are illegitimate children and not true sons. Moreover, we have all had human fathers who disciplined us and we respected them for it. How much more should we submit to the Father of our spirits and live! Our fathers disciplined us for a little while as they thought best; but God disciplines us for our good, that we may share in his holiness. No discipline seems pleasant at the time, but painful. Later on, however, it produces a harvest of righteousness and peace for those who have been trained by it.

Therefore, strengthen your feeble arms and weak knees!

What are these disciplines?

Firstly, the *discipline of disappointment*. God can use disappointment very wonderfully: he has the sovereign ability to use everything that comes into our life. This is not to say that God *sends* everything into our life: that would be to adopt a very masochist theology. We should distinguish between God's permissive will and God's perfect will, between what God allows to happen to us in our fallen world and what God actually wishes to happen to us. We should remember that many of the things that happen to us are the direct result of man's sin. Yet God can use everything. If disappointment comes to us, we should remember that we have not yet resisted sin to "the point of shedding your blood" (Hebrews 12:4). Put all suffering in this perspective. Suffering can be a most valuable means to chasten and discipline us and bring us back to the Lord. Those who suffer rarely find it a real barrier to faith; it is the idea of suffering that causes problems.

Perhaps you look at those who are Christian leaders with a seemingly successful spiritual life and a wide public ministry and feel jealous. That is a big mistake. No one with my kind of personality and with as many goals, burdens, visions and ideas, is likely to be free of disappointment for long; I have had my full share. There are people who have professed conversion and have now fallen away, and I am in correspondence with many of these. One brother came to work with us in Europe for a year, and was very dear to us. But we did not recognize the depth of a social problem he was facing. At the end of that year, he went right away from the Lord. Another young man was a stalwart in the faith for many years but then turned away completely. He came from a very bad home background, and he went right back to his old ways. If you are going to get involved with people—and Christians must be deeply involved, in order to love in truth—then you will be disappointed. Yet this is a chance for you to recognize that you must turn the problem over to God, and to trust that his timing and planning is correct. Remember, through whatever period of darkness that you have to struggle, that God is there, and that he will never leave you nor forsake you. Eventually the light will break upon you.

I recognize that this is not an easy issue. I deal with it in greater detail in a later chapter entitled "Discouragement," so do turn to that now if you want to.

Then there is the *discipline of danger.* It often worries me that the average evangelical Christian does everything he can to avoid danger. But to be a Christian is precisely to be exposed to danger. I can hear you saying, "But what danger is there here, in America or Western Europe? You only meet danger if you paddle up the Amazon or go out as a missionary."

It is a great mistake to put missionaries on a special pedestal. I have met adulterers, fornicators, liars, and embezzlers on the mission field. If this surprises you, read your New Testament. Missionaries are real people, with real problems.

This is why we should be holding missionary prayer meetings and agonizing over the condition of our missionaries. I have heard of missionaries who have gone out to India to witness for Jesus and have ended up by becoming Hindus or Buddhists themselves. Pray for them indeed; we have sent them into danger. And praise God for the majority of missionaries who serve God faithfully!

Do not think, however, that the only danger we will meet at home is the preacher going on too long with his sermon. We are at war. We are exposed and vulnerable and Satan is on the attack.

If you read your Bible, you will see that those who love the Lord are constantly exposed to danger. Yet danger is not something to be avoided, any more than it is something to be sought in foolishness; it will come as we move obediently forward against Satan's territory. I do not refer simply to spiritual danger. Many of our cities are becoming more and more dangerous in ordinary physical terms, and sadly there are not many Christians who are willing to go into these areas for fear that they may be attacked. We have little holy islands in the city, little corner churches, but no one is deceived. We are at war, and everyone who reads this book is either a missionary or a mission field. (Many of us feel we are both.) As the Spirit begins to move, he will send us into danger.

This reluctance to get stuck is false caution. It is perfectly possible to face danger and death in the nicest places. One friend of mine lived in a very pleasant suburb with no obvious dangers, yet his small son was electrocuted in the garden of his house through an overlooked loose wire.

Thousands die from car accidents each year. Children get into the medicine cabinet and drink poison. Many are willing to face danger for money: see how many flock for jobs on the North Sea oil rigs for the high wages paid there. It is far better to be willing to face danger—whether it is a knife in some city alley or the scorn of your workmates—for the sake of the gospel. For Jesus, however, most of us seem to want a no-risk program, and it is very sad.

The right response to danger is daring: the *discipline of daring*. There is a story of two daring men in Numbers 13. The majority of the Israelites were afraid to enter the Promised Land, as the walls were too high, the enemy too numerous, the champions too strong. But there were two faithful scouts, Caleb and Joshua. In verse 30 we find that "Caleb silenced the people before Moses and said, 'We should go up and take possession of the land, for we can certainly do it.'" If we are not willing to dare we will not enter the Promised Land either, or at least we will never know Promised Land living, victorious living. C. T. Studd said, "God is not looking for nibblers of the possible, but for grabbers of the impossible." We must be as willing as Caleb to dare, to gamble, and to trust. You just cannot read the Old or the New Testament without coming across men who were gamblers for God.

Do not get the idea that I am a courageous daredevil for God, ready to go anywhere. Far from it. Down inside me is a deep, deep fear of the unknown. But I do believe that the Spirit of God produces courage in the life of the believer. This is, however, an experience that few of us have had, because so much of our evangelical faith today is little more than words. We have never been truly tested. We think that we are sanctified, that we are ready to go all out for God, but we simply haven't yet had to face the music. I do know for sure that I wouldn't have got anywhere at all in the Christian life if I hadn't been prepared to gamble, to say to the Lord, "Well, I haven't got much faith, and I'm not very strong, and I don't know much, but . . . I'll go. I believe that somehow you'll hold it together."

We nearly *shook* with fear when we realized the dangers of the ship project[9] — an old vessel, no insurance, all those young people aboard with their parents hovering anxiously in the background. I used to have nightmares about the ship going down and would wake up thinking, "Let's keep it in the warmer climates, so that if it does sink at least the kids will have a chance. If you go down in cold seas, there's far less hope." Yet time and time again the word of God has pulled me out of these fears and thrust me again into times of courage, especially the book of Joshua. It would be worth while memorizing the following passage from chapter one where the Lord commissions Joshua to lead the people of Israel into the Promised Land after the death of Moses:

> Be strong and courageous, because you will lead these people to inherit the land I swore to their forefathers to give them. Be strong and very courageous. Be careful to obey all the law my servant Moses gave you; do not turn from it to the right or to the left, that you may be successful wherever you go. Do not let this Book of the Law depart from your mouth; meditate on it day and night, so that you may be careful to do everything written in it. Then you will be prosperous and successful. Have I not commanded you? Be strong

and courageous. Do not be terrified; do not be discouraged, for the LORD your God will be with you wherever you go. (Joshua 1:6–9)

Joshua could well have felt nervous! Like him, one of the ways in which we can become more courageous is by meditating on the word of God day and night.

Many young people and many adults, too, shy away from the thought of going to the mission field for fear that they will not make it. What sort of Christianity do we have in our bellies that we turn away from the mission field in such fear? What about all the promises to be found in the Bible, such as those made to Joshua? The Christian church, for all its supposed emphasis on the laity, is in fact becoming more and more professional. There are more and more people today in the church who do what they are doing, whether they would admit it or not, because they are getting paid. There's a lot of unemployment about! Once I heard a man giving a superb, most powerful sermon. I was very moved, so much so that during it I rededicated my life. I went up to him at the end of the service, and, as I was waiting to speak to him, I looked around at all the church people with their expensive suits and new cars. I asked him whether he really thought they would respond (I was about nineteen at the time). Then I noticed that he too was very well dressed. He looked down at me and said, "See here, young man, I'm an evangelist and this is my living. This is how I make my money, by preaching and doing God's work. What I was speaking about, that was all true, but I doubt if anyone would really live that way, unless perhaps there was a war on." I walked away feeling very shaken.

Please do not misunderstand me. I do not object to ministers and other "full-time" Christian workers (for in one sense we must all be full-time Christians) receiving their due reward; indeed, we often pay them far too little. Parish priests in England are some of the lowest-paid workers in the country. But I tell that anecdote to illustrate how far professionalism can take hold. The Christian faith is far too important to be left in the hands of the professionals. No one can afford to sit back. Moreover, to create and pay a class of professionals is bad stewardship. How can it be that Christians in some countries can earn so many thousands of pounds while evangelists and pastors in other parts of the world cannot afford a bicycle to visit the thousands of people to whom they are taking the word of God? How inconsistent can you get?

There are so many comfortable, biblical, middle-class evangelical churches where, because we do not wish to judge or pry, we are secure from one another. This is well, for if we were to ask awkward questions, we should begin to wonder why we all have the same standard of living, like a flock of well-dressed sheep. I am not saying that all who live this way are lost, simply that they have not appreciated their inconsistency in this area. It takes a very radical and brave person to see his own faults.

Once again, it all comes down to the discipline of daring, of being willing to take risks for God. This is what the life of faith is, by definition. We are so security-conscious. We take out fat insurance policies. We save for retirement. Where is the verse of Scripture that says we should have a nest-egg laid up? Is there nothing we can leave in the hands of God? Must everything be left in the paws of the government or the insurance companies? In gold bricks underneath the bed? We are so controlled, so prudent. I know, of course, of the comforting horror stories, like the one about the young man who went out trusting God and ended up in a ditch eating apples. May I say that I have never found anyone in this category, though I have heard such stories repeatedly used as a justification for keeping things as they are. I *have* heard many missionaries and others praising God for his generous provision.

Are you willing to be under attack, like Caleb and Joshua, to risk danger? This attitude of daring and trust can pervade our whole lives, make our faith a thing of joy and excitement in every little decision we make, as well as the great ones.

There is indeed danger, especially in reaching out to new lands, and I doubt if a summer goes by without one of the members of Operation Mobilization finding themselves in prison. This should not be a surprise. In the Book of Acts, Paul and his companions were constantly in and out of prison. Yet today when the big Bible teacher comes to speak he checks into the local Hilton at $200.00 per night. When Paul was going to a town he would send one of his companions to check out the local jail! Read 2 Corinthians 11: 23–29.

Then comes the *discipline of the declining days*. I believe that one of the very subtle attacks of Satan is to get people lonely, discouraged, and confused during their period of senior citizenship. One of the great strengths and encouragements to me has been to see my father and mother, who are now seventy or more, and who came to Christ during their late forties, serving the Lord quietly and persistently in their own way during what people call the declining years. There is no reason why, despite physical infirmity, you should not know and experience life richly; age can be a great discipline, concentrating the mind on the things that are truly important. Discipline in one area often breeds discipline and brings reward in another, and it takes discipline to run the race to the end—or at least walk to the end. Often the most valuable praying is done by the elderly. It's a great mistake if we think the world is going to be evangelized by youth movements.

I frequently have to take myself to task for neglecting the *discipline of delay*. Impatience is one of my greatest failings, and God has dealt with it to some extent by means of delay. He taught me to wait for six long years while the M.V. *Logos* project got off the ground. I find myself constantly irritated by long waits for planes, trains, and people. Yet God can use this; I believe that he often allows delay as a means of taking us deeper into himself. Quite often our prayers fail to take account of the timing: we become concerned that the Lord is not answering us, but in fact our prayers are bang on target—simply our estimation of the timing is wrong.

One particular area where we need to learn God's patience is in the question of finding a husband or wife. There are quite a number of men and women in the churches who are still waiting, and this can be the cause of a good deal of pain. Some have had to wait until they were thirty-five or forty before God brought along the right man or woman. Many marriages get rushed into and end in disaster. Do not be unduly super-spiritual, since there is a strong need for common sense, particularly in this sensitive area. Do realize, however, that you are men and women under God's authority, like the centurion (Luke 7:8), and that patient obedience is a good teacher: "The testing of your faith develops perseverance. Perseverance must finish its work so that you may be mature and complete, not lacking anything" (James 1:3,4).

Try also to cultivate in yourself the *discipline of dependability.* David was faithful in a small matter—he looked after a few sheep conscientiously—and from these small beginnings he became one of the greatest leaders this world has known. One part of dependability is accuracy, a desire to do things properly, and David was a master on the harp. Not for him, the half-hearted attitude which so many adopt when they buy a guitar, strumming a few chords and giving it up. He became so competent upon the harp that it led him to the palace of the king.

Dependability is a rare virtue. It is simply amazing how often you ask someone to do something and it just doesn't get done. Dependability does not come through an emotional commitment at some meeting or through reading a book. It comes rather by the daily discipline of self, the day-in-day-out denial of self in the service of Jesus.

Another part of dependability is detail. One small mistake can lead to an awful lot of tragedy. One of the things that we try to teach in OM is how to get organized—addresses, papers, time. Christians are working to contact others for Christ; make sure you keep phone numbers of those you speak to. I have known of people saved because of a single phone call or letter. A few seconds of spiritual laziness can trip you up. We are in the spiritual Olympics, where the stakes are far higher than sporting honor: we are going after the souls of men. Detail is very important in working for God's glory—but we must, as we consider this realm of our service, also remember the rest of faith, doing the best we can and then letting go and leaving the problems to God. Please do not make of this a big stick to beat yourself with. Jesus died to set you free from guilt.

I would especially encourage you to take to yourself the *disci-*

pline of discipling men. Look at Paul's instructions to Timothy in 2 Timothy 2:1–2, "You then, my son, be strong in the grace that is in Christ Jesus. And the things you have heard me say in the presence of many witnesses entrust to reliable men who will also be qualified to teach others." This was the method Jesus used—man to man evangelism, one person encouraging and teaching another. This is more expensive in terms of time, but it is infinitely more effective than simply lending one another books or inviting one another along to meetings. Christians have a real duty to encourage one another personally, taking time to explore subjects together and to learn together how to rely on God. It is a strategy which Operation Mobilization adopted many years ago when the movement was just getting under way, and we have found no reason to change it.

Yet discipling is a sadly neglected ministry. We seem to manage to read the gospels without seeing the basic pattern of Christ's education of his disciples. Out he would go into the towns and villages, healing and teaching, and using opportunities as they arose to offer his pupils some new insight. If Christ the Rabbi, the master teacher, could use this system, then it is not for us to neglect it. We throw out messages; we get masses of people flocking to conventions and seminars; but while they do retain some benefit, they remember much less than they should. I am convinced that they would do far better if they got regular encouragement in their own churches, especially if each church made fuller use of talented and informed members within its own ranks to teach the newer and less well instructed.

Many of the young people who come on summer missions with Operation Mobilization have never done any evangelism before. They need to be taken by the hand and shown how. Most of us are not very good at learning such things from books. What is true of evangelism is equally true of pastoral counselling, youth work, leading Bible studies, you name it. By contrast, it seems to me that in most churches the poor pastor has the task of teaching the whole congregation, with all its widely varying needs and fears and ambitions. Any educationalist would tell you that the smaller the ratio of pupils to teachers the better. In consequence, half the congregation knows the subject well, the other half is struggling to keep up.

The biblical principle is very different. While there was (and is) a place for the mass meeting, Paul and his companions were careful to place the responsibility for the oversight of each new congregation in the hands of responsible elders, with the injunction that the chain of teaching should go on from man to man, as we saw in the excerpt above from 2 Timothy. The leaders disciple others, who in turn disciple others, right down to the grass roots of the congregation who as they reach out are in their turn discipling outside the church on an individual grass roots basis, by far the most effective means of spreading the gospel. Jesus did not simply give out a set of instructions; instead, he lived with his disciples, caring, suffering, talking, illustrating from their common life along the road. In our churches today, the modern equivalent is for the pastor to be training the leaders who then train others.

Perhaps you feel this is all quite unrealistic. You are completely incapable of training anyone else; it would be like a fish showing people how to ride a bicycle. Remember that the best way of learning something is to teach it. As you try to explain sticky passages and wrestle with awkward questions, the word of God will become more and more real to you — and it will give you a real impetus to find things out, asking those older than you in the faith and digging into commentaries. Just think what would happen if you could, in the next six months, disciple just one other person, and then in the following six months you could both disciple one other person each, and so on — how the word would spread! Perhaps it seems modest to you as a goal, but such a progression soon mounts up. All too frequently Christians, in aiming at the stars, don't even hit the trees. We become number neurotics. How many people were there at that meeting? A thousand? Praise the Lord! Yet God is more concerned with quality. (And beware also, for those on the front line get attacked. Satan will do all he can to put his oar in when he sees people being won to the Lord: and when he manages to draw any one disciple, he will rejoice because that whole congregation of believers that might have been reached through that one person who may now be cut off.)

A further discipline, a further practice which I would urge you to adopt is what I call the *discipline of distribution*—the distribution of Christian literature. I used to feel faintly embarrassed at taking up good preaching time talking about Christian books, but recently I found moral support from no less a person than John Wesley. Wesley said that the Methodist faith would die out in a generation if the Methodists were not a reading people. He told his preachers that it was necessary for them to spend at least five hours in every twenty-four reading, warning them that one could never be a good preacher without extensive reading, any more than a thorough Christian. He aimed at the education of his followers by editing and publishing some of the great Christian classics. Every preacher was expected to distribute his books, the content of which he expected them to master. Wesley was criticized for pushing his wares from pulpit and platform, but he would not be put off, for he believed that his ministry in print was as important as his preaching. To his preachers he said, "Exert yourselves in this, be not weary, leave no stone unturned, as a travelling preacher is a book steward." The Methodist Conference of the day exhorted them to be more active in distributing books.

Ordinary Christians can and should be more active in distributing Christian literature, including magazines and cassettes. You can take Christian papers from door to door. You can put Christian magazines in waiting rooms and doctors' offices. One of the most effective means of evangelism at the moment is the small house meetings for those who wouldn't go to a church or to a specifically religious gathering. At such times you can have a display of Christian books and during coffee and biscuits, you can explain a little about some of the titles on the stall and perhaps ask someone to talk about how one particular book has affected him or her. It is amazing how good a salesman you can become if you get excited about something! Just look at Tupperware parties and how successful they are. Christian book parties can be just as effective. The vast majority of the people are not in the churches, so we have to go out to where they are and make contact. Yet it does take discipline. Tract distribution is especially hard but can be immensely valuable. You can engage in "spontaneous" distribution by always having some tracts in your pocket and passing them to people on planes, trains, buses—even to the man on the petrol pump. Do you ever leave a tract for your milkman? There are unlimited opportunities if you are prepared to take the initiative.

In the last chapter I discussed the place doubt plays in the Christian life. I should like to make it clear that there is a *discipline of doubt*. You will remember that I suggested that it is quite normal to doubt, and that doubts will come to anyone who has a brain. Please do not do as so many young people feel they should, who get so ashamed of their doubts (as if they indicated a weak and vacillating spirit, rather than an honest mind) that they are unwilling to ask questions, instead suppressing them and all clear thinking at the same time. As a result, when they are discussing matters with a non-Christian and get asked a question they can't answer, they do not come back and say, "I don't know, but I'll see if I can find out." Rather they reply airily, "Well, you have to take these things on faith, brother," and go on to quote John 3:16 and a few other verses they have learnt out of context. Away walks the poor non-Christian in disgust.

It is, rather, a sign of a healthy mental and spiritual state, to doubt when there are so many strange and terrible things happening around the world and so much muddled thinking and wrongheadedness in the churches. But do not hide behind your doubts: use them. Ask questions. Learn to live in faith when you have not yet found a solution to a given problem, for it is amazing how many problems fade away to nothing with a little more time and a cooler brain to consider them. You can glorify Christ in the midst of doubt, living with unreconciled tension and still placing your trust in him. Your faith will be a great deal stronger if you have fought and won than if you have known no conflicts. The Christian who knows no conflicts is ducking the issue, however. If you finish this book determined to be a really valiant soldier of Christ, you will certainly find some fiery darts coming in your direction. Doubt can be a strengthener, but it can be a loophole for Satan if you let it fester.

Doubts change with circumstance. You may have never wondered before whether the "heathen" are truly lost. It is fairly easy to say with certainty that the drunk down the road, who curses whenever Christ's name is mentioned and has spurned him time and again, is not a Christian; it is a different matter to consider the people of China or North India, who have never heard of the gospel, and to ask whether they too are lost. If you end up witnessing in a Hindu or Muslim country, you will discover a whole range of intellectual questions that you have never had to face before. The same applies if the Lord gives you a burden for Muslims in your own country. New initiatives will often produce new tests of faith that you have to battle through.

Having said all of this, and having acknowledged that there are good intellectual grounds for faith, and that some of the world's finest scientists are Christians, we must still recognize that there are some questions without answers. They are usually questions at a philosophical rather than a practical level: the origins of the soul, the relationship between predestination and freewill, the suffering caused by natural disaster. In such instances all we can say finally is that, with St. Paul, we "see through a glass, darkly."

Sometimes I am assailed by great waves of doubt. I think that Jesus Christ was just a man, that it is possible for great masses of people to be deceived, for the whole church down the ages to have been mistaken. At such times I have to battle hard to a place of faith, even though I recognize in such thoughts the prevailing corrosive cynicism of the West. One of the things that helps me is to keep it simple. It is best to put the church and the evangelical doctrines and all the rest to one side, and to simply ask, "Is there a God?" I have never been able to get round the fact that if I deny the existence of God I create for myself far more intellectual, and emotional, problems than if I allow that God exists. The order of the universe points to a creating intelligence. Every human society has given a prominent place to some form of religion: even today in the so-called godless West, every popular newspaper carries a horoscope, and tales of the supernatural fill every bookstall. The arguments are many. What explanation will you choose for the acts of Jesus, for the rapid growth of the church despite persecution? As you wrestle with such questions and contemplate a bleak and godless universe without meaning or purpose, where the tenderest human love is race perpetuation or herd instinct, you find for yourself that doubt is truly a beneficial discipline, for it drives you back to the center of all things. Once God's existence is accepted, I soon find my mind able to believe the other basic doctrines of my biblical faith.

I associate with doubt the *discipline of disillusionment,* for it too drives you back to God, and it is just as common. I have been disillusioned many times, as have we all, with some person or church in whom we place the highest confidence, only to find our trust misplaced and crumbling in confusion and hurt feelings. You find those who come along talking big, full of great ideas, and then things go wrong or turn sour, financial questions raise their heads, and the end is worse than the beginning. Disillusionment then comes upon you like a plague. The discipline comes in your reaction to it.

Consider the story of Joseph, disillusioned with his own brothers. He must have felt so hurt, bouncing up as he did with all his dreams of how they would all bow down to him, all young and excited. "I didn't mean any harm," you can hear him crying as they push him into the cistern. Yet Joseph had his own maturity, and saw in these events the hand of God at work. Rather than wallowing in the injustice of it all, he clung to the insight right through the years in an Egyptian dungeon. Looking beyond the immediate pain, he was able to be the channel of salvation for the whole country. This is so often the Christian path. The bloody, disastrous war in Bangladesh turned out to be the opportunity for the greatest advance of the gospel that land has ever known. God is sovereign over all the states of man, even over man's sin—though that doesn't mean that when we see God overruling that we have been given a retrospective license for having sinned! It is amazing how God can turn a sow's ear into a silk purse. You can marry the wrong person, and God can still work it out. If you think that there is only one girl for you to marry, then your God lives in a match-box. God is great. He can make a go of your mistakes. That does not mean that you should put this book down and go and marry the first good-looking girl that walks down the street. The point to remember is that even in the midst of pain we should keep in mind that he is in control.

During our lives most of us will be disillusioned with our marriage partners or our closest friends, with our parents or our children; leaders with followers, followers with leaders. We are not good at building long-term, lasting relationships that hold when the wind's blowing. In the churches people seem to shift around like pieces on a gigantic chess board. I am convinced that God wants us to stay in unity and build close bonds with one an-other, not asking the impossible of our fallible friends but staying faithful. Otherwise, what do you get? A steady increase in broken relationships, hard feelings, bitterness. An enormous number of missionaries have come home from the field because of poor rela-tionships: it is probably the biggest single cause of failure on the mission field, despite the fact that the Christian faith is a religion of love. We Christians preach a lot about forgiveness, but we are very poor at practicing it. Yet forgiveness is one of the principle antidotes for disillusionment.

Do not nurse your hurt feelings. You may be confused and up-set when you see Christians snapping and snarling at one another, each insisting that their religious practices or doctrines are the right ones. Reach out instead in gentleness of spirit, knowing that the Lord works with the material to hand. Does your own church have no weaknesses? Of course it does—it is full of people like you! Yet the kind of super-idealism that characterizes so many evangelicals makes them unwilling to see that the Lord can use many different means of worship and church administration to serve his ends. Very little in church history has been pure truth. Happily the Lord does *not* say, "I will only accept you after you have got all your doctrines right and your church practices word perfect!"

Fight, too, against disillusionment with yourself, and seek to accept your own humanity. It has been a great struggle for me to accept that I'm not as flexible as I would like to be and sometimes believe myself to be. Although I've lived in Britain for the past twenty years and more, I still think like an American, speak quasi-American, and my favorite food is a hotdog, a hamburger, and a milkshake. I like to think of myself as an extrovert, able to get along with everyone, but I always find it hard to be amongst a great crowd of people. Unfortunately much of my life has been spent in shared accommodation. Often we think of ourselves as able in Christ's strength to love all men, but there are always a few people who really bring a sour taste to our mouth. It is unrealistic to pretend that such tendencies don't exist. Do not think that because you have such reactions the Holy Spirit cannot work in you and through you: that is a sure path to cynicism and depression. Sometimes when people stand up after a meeting to dedicate themselves to the Lord's service, I have to tell them to go away and sit down and accept themselves first. Understand that although the Spirit is within you, you still have to let off steam from time to time.

Face disappointment, disillusionment, delay, and the declining years and realize that they are part of God's means to encourage you to reach out for greater faith and greater compassion, greater reality. Face danger with joyful daring. Use your doubts. Cultivate dependability, that you may disciple men more effectively. Distribute good Christian literature of all kinds, carefully suiting the book or the tract to the man. Acknowledge God's timing, and cultivate patience. Above all, keep in mind that God knows all about us, and knows our lack of discipline and loves us just the same. You don't gain any merit with God by being disciplined: there is nothing to be gained by developing an interesting neurosis on the subject. Your motivation and reward are God's mercy and love.

7

WEAPONS *and* WARFARE

"FALLEN MAN HAS CREATED a perpetual crisis. Until Christ reigns over a new, redeemed, restored world, the earth remains a disaster area," wrote A. W. Tozer.[10] I do not think anyone with a biblical faith would seriously contest this: everywhere the evil things man does are blazoned across newspaper headlines. Even now in a dozen different places around the world, people are being murdered, tortured, and killed in the name of God. Our Lord must weep afresh at the atrocities committed in his name. Sometimes we get so sick that we can take no more and turn off the radio and avoid the papers; but then some fresh thing occurs to remind us of the evil in men's hearts, perhaps within our own family. The point of these bleak reflections is that we will get a lot further, faster, if we recognize and take to heart the fact that Satan has made rack and ruin of this good earth.

Let us look too at the extent of the task. We may feel that the churches are growing strongly in many parts of the world, and so indeed they are, but experts in the field of population movement and growth estimate that the world population will *double* in the next forty years. One million or more are added every month. Probably one in twenty-five of all human beings who have ever lived are alive today.

With these facts in mind, it is not surprising that at least half the people in the world have never heard the gospel. Some missionary magazines and books rather leave one with the impression that worldwide evangelization is only a matter of time. More careful research will show that in densely populated areas the work of evangelism is going backwards rather than forwards. Giving a

man a gospel tract is hardly evangelizing him in the full sense of
the word, but even by this poor definition less than half the world
has had this bare minimum witness.

In view of this our tactics are simply crazy. Perhaps 80 percent
of our efforts for Christ, weak as they often are, are still aimed at
only 20 percent of the world's population. Literally hundreds of
millions of dollars are poured into every kind of Christian project
at home, especially buildings, while a thin trickle goes out to the
"regions beyond." Half-hearted saints feel that by giving just a
few hundred dollars they have done their share. I am not keen to
criticize the efforts of any group that is getting the gospel out but
if we are going to be realistic, we must pray and work towards
stepping up the intensity and purity of the present campaign ten-
fold. Often the very people doing the job do not have a really deep
commitment to the Lord. We have all measured ourselves so long
by the man next to us that we can barely see the standard set by
men like Paul, or by Jesus himself.

During the Second World War, the British showed themselves
capable of astonishing sacrifices (as did many other nations).
They lived on meagre, poor rations. They cut down their railings
and sent them for weapons manufacture. They lived in the most
abstemious conditions. Yet today, in what is more truly a World
War, Christians live as peacetime soldiers. Look at Paul's injunctions to Timothy in 2 Timothy 2:3–4: "Endure hardship with us
like a good soldier of Christ Jesus. No one serving as a soldier gets
involved in civilian affairs—he wants to please his commanding
officer." We seem to have a strange idea of Christian service. We
will buy books, travel miles to hear a speaker on blessing, pay
large sums to listen to a group singing the latest Christian songs,
but we forget that we are soldiers.

Imagine what would happen if someone were to explode a
bomb in your street tonight. Phone calls would go out for doctors
and police; others would be providing hot water and bandages,
sheltering the wounded, searching for further "devices." Anyone
not helping as they could would be branded as a traitor: a man
without compassion. *Satan has exploded bombs today in every*

town and village in the land. Any Christian who is not on the job, rescuing people, is a traitor to the cause of Jesus Christ, no matter what doctrinal banner he may carry.

We do not go empty-handed into battle, for the Lord has given us weapons. "The weapons we fight with are not the weapons of the world. On the contrary, they have divine power to demolish strongholds. We demolish arguments and every pretension that sets itself up against the knowledge of God, and we take captive every thought to make it obedient to Christ" (2 Corinthians 10:4–5). We exercise these weapons on two fronts, the inner war against temptation, doubt, cynicism, and the outer war against the activity of Satan in circumstances and in those we meet, wherever his strongholds may be.

Some of the weapons are listed in that well-loved jewel of a passage, Ephesians 6:10–18. This is one of the sections of the Bible that it is imperative to Christians to have by heart; not least because the sword of the Spirit, with which we advance to attack, is the word of God itself. I have considerable difficulty in memorizing Scripture, but take heart from the story of the man who tried to carry water home from the river in a wicker basket. By the time he had climbed half way up the hill, the basket was empty: he filled it afresh, but the same thing happened again. An onlooker queried the wisdom of the action, and he replied, "No, I don't collect much water, but my basket gets a little cleaner each time." Scripture memorization is also a valuable mental discipline. It is by the word, as we saw when considering the foundations for spiritual growth, that we are fed and grow as Christians. But we must feed ourselves, not endlessly spooning in pap, but disciplining ourselves to chew and digest the real meat of truth. I am in danger of mixing my metaphors here, but the point is clear: the Bible is the source of our knowledge and the guideline by which we judge good conduct; it is the very word of God which has a unique authority in evangelism and pastoral care; it is the best possible refutation of Satan's lies. However, we must seek to keep our sword sharp, ensuring that it is a part of our daily lives and making full use of good commentaries.

With the sword of the Spirit comes the shield of faith, without which none of the teaching this book offers will become real. All these injunctions must be "mixed with faith," or our sense of weakness and inadequacy must overwhelm us. The long record of heroes of faith in Hebrews 11, I believe, is there precisely so that we may know how much God values faith. The Bible is full of examples such as Joshua taking Jericho and Moses on the mountain with his arms raised against the Amalekites. Stories of faith and victory are endless. Perhaps our palates are jaded, perhaps we have heard this kind of exhortation too often for it to have any effect. Perhaps long disobedience has ingrained the habit of listening without doing, so that we are no longer able to obey. There has to be some explanation for why these many examples do not penetrate our hearts—yet if we allowed them to enter, we should become men and women of power, able to tear down the strongholds of the enemy. Our faith is not blind: God has been faithful, is faithful, so he will be faithful.

Worship and praise are other great weapons. Often when we feel the enemy moving within us, we can stand against him through praise. When depression or discouragement nags at you, or you feel spiritually dry, the answer often is to praise the Lord, to thank him for what he has done for you and given you, for who he is, for the magnificence of his creation, for the authority of his word. For each of us the emphasis will be different. As we acknowledge the Lord's authority over even the dark passages in our lives, we find a new and healthier perspective. (I am not suggesting this as the only therapy, especially when clinical depression or deep wounds are concerned, but it is astonishing how often it helps.)

Make time each day just to worship the Lord, for I believe that the highest goal for every believer is not evangelism, but worship. See that it becomes your number one priority. You will find that evangelism and every other Christian activity is easier in consequence. Give worship pride of place above intercessory prayer, and simply enjoy God because he is God. Worship, Tozer comments, is the missing jewel of the evangelical church. If it is lacking in your life, you are probably experiencing a power shortage.

Our motivation as we march into battle is love. As we saw in chapters three and four, unless we have love, our Christian lives are not only dull and painful, but noisy and worthless, "a resounding gong or a clanging cymbal." Yet within ourselves we cannot generate the love we need, for very few of us brim over with charity. This is not a cause for guilt, however, though it may be a sign that we need to repent of the hard feelings we have harbored against one man or all men. We need rather to turn to Christ and ask him to fill us with his love. We have Christ within us — let him out! Don't pray for the Lord to be present, for he is present, in the person of the Holy Spirit. Thank him for his presence. Pray that he will fill you: no matter how filled you are, he can still fill you more, seeking new areas of our lives to move into. We can't take all of God at once, for it would overwhelm us: we need to pray that he will increase our capacity. He is gentle and will give us just as much of himself as we can take. (If we can't hold very much, it is because we haven't taken the lid off!) As he reveals more and more of himself to us, so we become able to love with real heartfelt concern.

This concern will spill out in all kinds of ways. People ask, "What's different about you?" You will find yourself wanting to reach out in all kinds of ways. A crowd of people beside the road? Stop and talk to them, give them some of the literature you keep in your car. The phone rings, and it's a wrong number? "No sir, don't hang up, this is the right number because there's something important you ought to hear."

We have the weapons and the motivation; we have the Spirit within us, but there is no assurance that we will not be wounded in battle. Rather the reverse: if we are fighting, we shall certainly be hurt. Do not let yourself be thrown by past defeats. Don't keep on fretting about things that humiliated or depressed you or feeling guilty once the time of repentance is past. Regret can be one of the most subtle forms of self-love. We don't have to backslide and can go to bed every night free and worshipping the Lord. There is no reason for us to stay filled with hatred or fear. Avoid phrases like "if only . . ." which drain away your strength. Some Christians have exchanged their backbones for wishbones. "Stand firm. Let nothing move you" (1 Corinthians 15:58). If you look at men, you'll be disappointed. If you worry about situations, you'll get discouraged. If you think of yourself, you'll get depressed. Look to Jesus, however, and you'll be able to get up and go on from victory to victory. Keep on keeping on.

War may well demand great sacrifice from the soldier on active service. If there is anything that you value more highly than your Lord, it will have to go; moreover, the Lord may be telling you that there is something about your home that needs to be sold to pay for some aspect of his work. If you have a $4,000 car, perhaps it should be a $2,000 car. (If you belong to Operation Mobilization, perhaps a $200 car!) A year or so ago, someone gave me a beaten up Mini. It wasn't very good, but then I was given a second beaten up Mini. By cannibalism we now have one beaten up but service-able Mini, which has carried us far. Cars are really a god to our society, and Christians are particularly guilty in this respect.

Many Christians are keen to travel to Israel, a kind of pilgrim-age which costs several hundred dollars. Was it well spent? Often you hear the pious comment that if Christ gave so much for us, then by comparison we can give him nothing. That is frequently just what we do. I prefer the argument that if Christ gave all for us, then what can we possibly hold back? God is probably willing for you to keep your car, but what you need to do is say, "Thank you, Lord, for the use of this car. It is yours, so please use it as you see fit." Perhaps you should hold a commitment service. Do you have an insurance policy which would allow other people to use it? Peter said to the beggar, "Silver and gold have I none," but that would be an infrequent testimony today. So often we are blind to the grip material things have upon us, but as we seek to shake it off we see results. Such action will lead to spiritual revolution.

There are four kinds of action for the soldier of Christ. The first is reproduction, which is covered under the heading of discipling men. Second is disciplined action, and that too we have covered. The third is united action. That doesn't mean that we have to be of one mind on every point. We may be talking about divine truth, but it is transmitted through earthen vessels, and I know that anything that comes through George Verwer has quite a lot of earth attached! However, unity is essential, and the New Testament speaks of it at length and in many contexts. It is not easy because anyone who starts living a revolutionary life in the church today is going to find himself out of step with a lot of people. But even if we are out of step, we can still exercise patience and love. If our fellowship is marred by back-biting and irritation, then it will be no fellowship at all, instead of the source of encouragement and strength and love that it can be. The same applies within marriage: you and your husband or wife should be a two-person team, working closely together, not seeking constantly to outdo the other or allowing yourselves to ignore one another for the sake of "Christian" service.

The fourth area of action is world-wide action. The churches should be following the New Testament pattern and asking themselves, "Whom should we be sending?" So frequently it is left to the individual missionary to sense a call from God, whereas the whole church fellowship should be functioning as a commissioning body. They should be sending out their very best people. Read Acts 11–13, and you will see how the fledgling church at Antioch received word from the Holy Spirit to set aside Paul and Barnabas for further missionary work. Paul and Barnabas? But they were the people who had founded the church—they had only been there a year—how could the group possibly survive without them? But there was no such quavering; after fasting and prayer, the church laid hands on them and sent them off. Should you be sending out your own pastor if he can preach and teach and is walking with the Lord? Do not hang on to your best men but seek out whom the Lord needs elsewhere. This kind of thinking would make an enormous difference to the areas being evangelized, and you would find that as you tried to look beyond your own needs, so your own needs would be met. As you prayed for mission elsewhere, mission would be happening at home.

As Christians launch out into the mission field of the whole wide world, as we start living rather than talking, as we begin to give and pray in a truly sacrificial way, as we mobilize, so there will come the counter-attack. I hope that you will put this book down with a sense of calling and encouragement, but you can be sure that discouragement will follow soon enough, making you doubt your commitment and causing you to stumble. The higher you go in the Christian life, the greater your fall: it is the peril of the victorious life. This means that we must work slowly and steadily, build our foundations well, and build in unity. We are not concerned to win skirmishes or even battles, but the war.

PART III

Continuing in the Way

8

REPENTANCE

THE THIRD SECTION OF THIS book is designed to provide some help for day-by-day Christian living. Christians are often willing to start the race, but all too frequently they fall by the wayside. Someone once asked D. L. Moody, "Why do you go on and on about being filled with the Holy Spirit again and again and again?" Moody just looked him in the eye and answered, "Because I leak." May I assure you that I too am a weak and leaky Christian leader—but I have discovered where the refills are! To be filled with the Holy Spirit is the normal Christian life, in Watchman Nee's memorable phrase. As you learn to walk in the Spirit day after day, you grow more teachable and can take in some of the lessons of the New Testament. The Spirit is the provision for every believer.

First of all, I should like to stress the value of repentance. Please put this book down and turn to 2 Samuel 11 and 12, and remind yourself of the story of David, Bathsheba, Uriah, and Nathan. The sins that David committed were several: adultery, murder, dishonesty, self-deception, faithlessness in return for faithful service. His crime was not a momentary lapse, but a long-term refusal to acknowledge that he had done wrong and was doing wrong. How could he be the leader of God's chosen people under such conditions? The Golden King, the figurehead and joy of his people, had shown conclusively that he had feet of clay.

Nathan loved his king, but he loved his Lord more and spoke the words the Lord gave him without caring for possible reprisals. He phrased his accusation so cleverly that David was condemned out of his own mouth and happily retained enough integrity to admit that his sins had found him out. His repentance took just six words: "I have sinned against the Lord."

These six words can revolutionize the life of any believer. David was rewarded with no lengthy sermon, simply with Nathan's assurance, "The Lord has taken away your sin. You are not going to die." The mercy of God was, and is, ready to burst through like a thunderclap. One reason that so many Christians today are living defeated lives is that they have not recognized the truth of instant forgiveness. It seems to me that mercy was almost hovering over David, waiting to fall as soon as he gave the word and confessed that he had sinned. Often we feel beaten down by our failure to live and work as we should for the Lord and horrified by our own false motivations. God does not want us to wallow in self-pity or to make guilt-inducing resolutions and promises, but rather to let him drop his blessing upon us like a cloud. However, the blessing destined for us will be missed if we don't learn to repent at once, more swiftly than David—not least because we have someone greater than Nathan to chide and guide us in the person of the Holy Spirit. Part of the work of the Spirit is to convict of sin.

As you progress in the Christian life and get deeper into the ways of the Lord, you will find more and more that the Spirit shows you your sin. This is good. It is an essential part of the victorious life: without repentance and instant forgiveness, you will go on struggling in self-pity and self-revulsion and will be useless in battle, incapacitated by your own misery. The path ahead is to get down on your knees and say, "Lord God, I have sinned against you. Have mercy on me."

I don't believe in the victorious life. Not at all—if by that is meant the kind of life that is apparently without blemishes, full of prayer and soul-winning. Whenever I have met someone "up there," I have gone away feeling that what they really needed was to get down and confess that they were loaded with pride. I do believe in the victorious life that is constant fellowship with God in Christ, a life of growth being continually cleansed by his blood. Have you repented of anything today? If you have lived right through today without sinning, I would love to get to know you!

Whoever marries you will be very fortunate. It says in 1 John 1:8, "If we claim to be without sin, we deceive ourselves and the truth is not in us." Very few days go by without my needing to repent of something or other. It doesn't have to be a big affair, and you need not even express your repentance verbally. Constantly during the day I have to say, "You were right, Lord. I was wrong. Forgive me." Usually it is not a question of some specific outward act of lust or cruelty or anger, but rather a sin of heart and mind, a willing progression from being tempted to harboring sin.

Forgiveness doesn't mean that there won't be consequences. Nathan told David that the child Bathsheba bore to him would die. David must have felt ghastly, knowing that an innocent child would die because he had sinned. For seven days he fasted and prayed, lying upon his face, but he had to face the results of what he had done. I like this, in a way, terrible though it is because it keeps the balance. God is merciful, but not over-indulgent. In his wisdom, he knew that if David had been let off more lightly then the lesson would not have struck home. The judgment still came. Once a boy and girl came up to me after a meeting and told me with much sorrow how they had slept together and now had come back to the Lord. The Lord accepted them but that didn't stop the birth of the baby or the great suffering that came to them and their families as a result of what they had done.

This then is an additional reason why we should keep short accounts with God. If we do so, we shall never get into the kind of mess that David found himself in; but if we let the sins pile up and our relationship with God grow faint, then we shall regret it bitterly. I know of one Christian youth ministry that was wiped out in one city after another because members of the team sinned as David did. David should have repented upon the roof, not a year later; he reached the stage that no believer should have to reach, where he had to be called forth and publicly rebuked. Essentially he had become a hypocrite. The double life can go very deep: you can be sitting reading this book and know that you are worse off than David was, no matter what your fellow Christians may think of you.

Repentance is a key word in Scripture. The Laodicean church

was guilty, not of drunkenness or immorality, but of a lukewarm heart and of smug satisfaction with their material wealth. Many of us need to repent in these two areas! Look at what the Lord told them: "I counsel you to buy from me gold refined in the fire, so you can become rich; and white clothes to wear. . . . Those whom I love I rebuke and discipline. So be earnest, and repent" (Revelation 3:18,19).

Usually repentance is a purely private affair. If your sin has injured a few, confess to those few. If your sin is a public matter, then often so should your confession be public. Frequently, the hardest thing of all is to confess to your husband or wife. I remember once during the crusade in Italy in 1963 that my wife and I exchanged some particularly hard words, and we went into separate rooms to lick our wounds. "Lord," I said, "if she comes to me and admits she was in the wrong, I'll also apologize for what I said." Next door she was thinking, "Lord, if he comes in here and says he's sorry, I'll be prepared to admit that I was at fault, too." You can spend your whole life like that! I think that my wife and I are still together because neither of us has ever managed more than ten minutes in separate rooms. We've often as not bumped noses in the hall as we've run to put our arms around each other. It's the same in Christian work. When I'm under stress, I get quite intolerable, nervy and silly and snappy. Many's the time I've had to phone some brother long distance to ask forgiveness. Remember, however, you may have to ask forgiveness from your marriage partner or your fellow Christian, but it is against the Lord that you have sinned, and to the Lord you must offer repentance.

Learn the secret of repentance. Then get up, go on, rejoice in God's goodness and grace and love. You're going into front line combat, and it's going to be hot and hard, and sometimes you're going to want out. Remember that his mercy is available to you. Take it.

9

DISCOURAGEMENT

BY THIS TIME YOU WILL HAVE realized that I am deeply concerned that our spiritual life should be realistic in every respect. While we should certainly be God-centered rather than problem-centered, there is little point in hiding from ourselves such problems as we do face. I have already touched on the fact that those who journey forth to war are likely to get hurt. Now I would like to specify some of the ways in which we can get hurt, so that we can be on our guard and also some of the things that I have found helpful. Simple, straightforward discouragement is the biggest drain on our spiritual resources. No one is free of it; many suffer from it acutely. I would reckon that at any one point perhaps 25 percent of the personnel on the Operation Mobilization mission teams are feeling discouraged, and they are a pretty highly motivated bunch. How much more so the pastor whose church is largely empty, the youth club leader who has just had his clubhouse wrecked by vandals, the young idealist who can't come to terms with his own sexuality, or the career man damaging his own prospects by remaining honest in a corrupt system? Discouragement is one of the most subtle and tricky techniques in the Devil's arsenal for stopping the forward movement of the gospel.

This is plainly visible in the great saints of the Old Testament. So often we read Christian biographies which emphasize the strong points of the man or woman of God. But as we make a detailed study of some of the Bible's characters we see discouragement plainly: Elijah after Mount Carmel and Jonah after one of the greatest evangelistic campaigns the Middle East has ever seen. In the New Testament, we find that the disciples of the Lord

Jesus almost specialized in saying stupid things at the wrong time. How embarrassed and confused they must often have felt as they put their foot in their mouth yet again.

Then too, those of us who yearn for higher plateaus in the things of God—who at times read perhaps too much from A. W. Tozer!—also get badly cast down. Why aren't God's people doing more we wonder? Why is there so much disunity? Even in Britain, which is in many ways a cynical and highly secular society, the latest statistics indicate that 11 percent of the population goes to church, which is substantially more than those who go to football games. The church is not small. One recent speaker at Spring Harvest (the spring conference organized each year by *Buzz* and *Family* magazines) suggested that there could be as many as 100,000 cells of Christians in the UK. In the USA and many parts of Asia, Latin America and Africa, the figure would be far higher, and so would the percentage of believers. In view of all this, how can we be other than discouraged at the lack of activity and the under-used potential?

I need to be careful not to make careless generalizations, as they are usually misleading. Christian leaders are very prone to simplify matters, and to say, "We need to pray more, or to be filled with the Spirit more, or to have a greater sense of commitment." This in itself can lead to discouragement. So I do not want to offer superficial answers, but I am pretty sure that I am correct in generalizing about the overall degree of discouragement.

Discouragement breeds discouragement. You get cast down about the quality of your prayer life, so you don't get to the prayer meeting, so your pastor gets discouraged. You are ashamed of your lack of missionary zeal, so you don't attend the missionary's talk, so he gets discouraged.

The lack of reality in my own prayer life is one of the things Satan has used to try to discourage me. Discouragement in fact attacks me almost every day: when you are thrust into the thick of spiritual warfare and face heavy pressures on many different fronts and attempt the impossible so frequently, you are bound to meet discouragement; it is an occupational hazard and does not disappear as you advance in the Christian life.

In all this we badly need one another's support. If your Christian brother seems to be low on prayer power or caught up in some carnal trap or hung up on doubt, then don't shun his company; he needs love and prayer and probably quite a lot of tactful concern. It is all too easy to instill a sense of inadequacy in people. Don't judge, therefore, whether by word or attitude, but *care*. When I was at Bible college God had to take me in hand and rebuke me for my attitude towards so-called non-spiritual people, the ones who didn't show up to prayer meetings and at times made fun of spiritual things. They are often not so dead to the spiritual world as they may appear, but rather feel keenly the need to prick a few bubbles. As such they have a most valuable function. (Having a family is a good ally here. The thing that has brought more balance to my life than any book I've ever read has been having three unique, aggressive, on-the-march, ready-to-have-ago-at-Dad offspring!)

If you are by nature an extrovert and energetic type, then do not get impatient with those of a quieter nature. Different temperaments respond to pressure in different ways. For many years I didn't understand why my wife used to get so discouraged, until I took the time to understand what her temperament, her background, her physical being were asking of her. We are all made differently, and all of us have some areas of vulnerability. Therefore do not judge.

What are some of the specific ways in which discouragement seems to attack God's people? The first, the most obvious, is through *unanswered prayer*. How are we to respond when we pray urgently, with all of our hearts, for something which is in our eyes clearly needed, and then get no response? We shrug it off, perhaps, thinking that we cannot understand all the Lord's ways, and then we hear a sermon on prayer or read one of the more idealistic books available, and a slight cynical streak begins to develop. We are warned in Hebrews 12:15 to see that "no bitter root grows up to cause trouble and defile many." Cynicism is the path to bitterness, especially if you read lots of Christian

biographies and find them full of miraculous answers to prayer or
if you know people who are always full of another joyful story of
God's abundant grace. Now I do believe indeed that miracles happen today, even quite frequently, and that God pours out his grace
upon his church to the full measure that we are able to receive.
Yet unanswered—or seemingly unanswered—prayer is one of the
great altars upon which God makes true men and women. My life
is full of unanswered prayer. Not even 50 percent of my prayers
have been answered over the years, not yet at least. I refuse to be
discouraged by this. I recently returned from a visit to Turkey, a
country for which I have had a deep concern for almost twenty-
five years, and there saw setback after setback in the work of OM.
One of our workers in Turkey some years ago was shot by extremists on his own doorstep. I should have come out totally discouraged, yet somehow I was given the confidence to battle through in
the knowledge that the Lord will do a great work in that land in his
own good time. There is no harvest without sowing.

A second reason for a lot of discouragement is *failure:* in relationships, in the family, with our children. This is a common
problem, and if you are worried about your family, then you are
not alone: the children of many Christian leaders have totally
rejected Jesus. If you do have trouble in this area, then you may
want to pick up John White's remarkable book *Parents in Pain*.
Failure may strike you as you try to witness to your faith. You
hear a good series of sermons, read a book, go through a two-day
training course, and launch out on your campaign of door-to-door
evangelism, only to discover that you have tremendous difficulty
relating to unconverted people. As they blow smoke in your eyes
and you have a coughing fit, you wonder how anyone could ever
win any of these people to the Lord. So you withdraw and decide
it is better to go to the Keswick Convention for your holiday and
to avoid the unsaved as much as possible. I can assure you that it
is ten times as hard to witness to Muslims as to talk to someone in
our own culture.

Third, we get discouraged because of our own *sin*. I found that
I was especially prone to discouragement in this area because I

was hyper-idealistic, and for quite a long time I had false views about the victorious life. I just could not see how the victorious life could include knowing what to do when I sinned—and yet it must. The victorious Christian simply has to know what to do when he does fall, for fall he unquestionably will. Perhaps we get victory in Christ's strength over an area of particular difficulty in our life, and go for weeks or even years without failure. Then one day an unusual temptation arises when we are especially tired or depressed, and we fall in that very area. At once the accuser of the brethren is there, crying, "Ah, you see how weak your will is— you've failed, you're finished. Your basic nature hasn't changed, you're just the same old pathetic rotten creature that you were a couple of years ago." (The danger is of course that he is right—but remember that ours is a religion of grace.) So you get the familiar pattern which causes such depression: every summer little Johnny goes to Bible camp and recommits himself, and every winter back he slides again. Then along comes Mr. Easy-Answer, one of Job's counselors, and rains him further into despair.

Fourth, many get discouraged because of *physical illness*. Most people don't understand this until they get ill themselves. Many illnesses have much longer-term side-effects than we realize in the forms of depression and lethargy. You and your body are one. Yet physical illness can still allow the exercise of spiritual power. I have a dear friend, a prayer partner in Bromley, whose husband, a pastor, died some while ago. She is confined to her bed and is totally deaf: I have to communicate with her by passing little notes on a pad back and forth. Yet that lady has a ministry of intercessory prayer that reaches the ends of the earth. She cannot get to church and often is badly isolated, but she is uplifted by the presence of Jesus.

Fifth, many are discouraged because of the *disunity within the church,* the broken relationships, the suspicions and resentments between denominations, fellowships, and individuals. This too is the result of hyper-idealism, the kind of thinking that argues that when we get the right set of doctrines and the right spiritual blessings and the right songbooks then we shall become angels, more or less. Why have so many left the established churches and gone into house fellowships? Some have gone for legitimate reasons, but many others from a vague sense that if we get into smaller and more intimate groups and really worship the Lord properly (i.e., as he wants), then all will be well. In the process they have caused painful splits and lasting sadness. I am in touch with the leaders of many house churches, and they are going through just the same sort of battles that the big churches are going through. People are people. You put them in a church or a cathedral or a living room and they are still people with problems. Many are now leaving the house churches as they left the main-line denominations earlier, once again discouraged and beaten down. I personally believe that because of God's love and mercy he is working in both.

The answers simply do not lie in human organization. All too often we are seeking something in our church or house group that God has never meant to exist, and that is only found in him. The evangelical Utopia doesn't exist on earth. We live on a cursed planet, filled with lost men, filled with sadness. The Christian is different not because he is immune to these things but because he is rooted and grounded in the love of God. This is our unity.

Let me outline a few basic things that we can do to stand against discouragement, remembering as we saw when examining some of the spiritual disciplines that great faith is forged as we battle through with our eyes upon the Lord.

My first practical defence is a *deeper knowledge of God himself*. I shall explore this topic more fully below. This is why I try to get people to read books by Tozer and Packer, because they have a remarkably clear understanding of our Lord. Our goal is God, and when I am much beset by problems, then my first and most immediate means of relief is to turn away from Christians, who are weak and fallible, and to concentrate on the majesty, love, and awesome splendor of our great Lord. It might help in doing this to turn up your favorite psalm or perhaps David's song of praise in 2 Samuel 22.

Second, *a greater knowledge of God's word*. Simply spend time in the word of God. Memorize, meditate. I strongly recommend the very practical advice in this area given in Ralph Shallis's book *From Now On*.

Third, stress to yourself, stress as a church that there needs to be *more emphasis on faith and less on feeling*. I am a terrible slave to my emotions; in the course of a single day, I can go up and down as much as twenty-five times. If any of those who read this book lean a bit towards a similar instability, then I can tell you that there is still hope: I have found it necessary to be ruthless with my feelings, to dominate my gut-level reactions. It is not easy, but the reward is great.

Fourth, constantly seek a *greater understanding of those around you*. If you are let down by someone, or meet with a lukewarm response to your excited visions for the world, then ask yourself why they are reacting like that. Perhaps they have special griefs and burdens of which you know nothing. Be a good listener by using your imagination and calling on your reserves of sympathy, and try to believe the best about the person concerned. Your opinion of someone is often a self-fulfilling prophecy. If you expect them to react well, then they may surprise themselves by doing so.

Fifth, *keep some kind of spiritual perspective*. Try not to let the incidental encounter or calamity get you down: as you walk with God, try always to see the bigger picture. If you hear a juicy titbit of gossip, refuse to respond to it in isolation. The same applies when you overhear blame or criticism heaped upon yourself, especially if you feel it was unjust; what pressure was the speaker under when he said that? I have learned not to listen to most gossip, which is a cancer on the church, but rather to believe the best and press on. We have a big God, with a big heart, and this is the reality behind the bickering church.

Sixth, *set yourself more realistic goals*. One of the main neuroses in the USA is that Americans set extremely high goals for themselves, linked with an overemphasis on "success." You won't understand Americans unless you see that. Most end up either discouraged or in pretension and hypocrisy. (Read Romans 12:3.) Keep to reasonably attainable targets in your mission work, your prayer life, your church life, unless God specifically directs you otherwise. By all means claim great things from God, but do not try to manipulate him by lofty rhetorical prayers. It is just as well the Lord has a sense of humor! I remember once in Mexico that a girl on our team started praying in a prayer meeting one night for a thousand souls to be saved. At that point hardly anyone had shown any interest. I stopped the meeting and asked, "Did the Lord put that prayer in your heart? Because we haven't seen five yet." Such prayer can be a covert form of boasting: "I've got more faith than you have."

Seventhly, *put more of an emphasis on praise and prayer,* as we discussed in the chapter on weapons. Keep your eyes on the Lord, and avoid overmuch introspection. I am involved in counselling a number of people who seem so quickly to want to put themselves down. This is not the road to humility, but to self-absorption. We are indeed unworthy servants, but we are also Spirit-filled kings, priests, friends of God. As we fix our attention upon our glorious Lord and offer him our worship, we will know the encouragement he offers. It is God's will to work in our lives and to bless us in one way or another.

The eighth point may seem strange, but it is crucial in rising above discouragement: *Learn how to be hurt.* Unless we do so we shall participate in the general back-biting and bitterness which is a part of most church fellowships. Some people have nothing for Sunday lunch but roast pastor! You cannot hope to be effective in the Lord's service if you carry around the burden of the hurts you have been given or received for the rest of your life. Being hurt is a part of living on this planet, and forgiveness is utterly necessary. If you are being honest with yourself, there is almost certainly someone against whom you feel bitter anger, and that person is probably a Christian.

For some time now I have carried around with me a little article I found called "First Aid for Spiritual Emergency." It has a lot of common sense and tells you what to do when a hurt is inflicted on you by a brother or sister in Christ.

1. *Keep calm.* "Be still, and know that I am God." Rushing about trying to correct the injury usually causes greater damage.
2. *Apply direct pressure of understanding to the wound.* What caused the incident? Could you have prevented it? How does the offending party feel? What if things were reversed?
3. *Wash the wound thoroughly with kindness* to remove all hardness and vindictiveness.
4. *Coat liberally with the ointment of love.* This will protect from infections of resentment and bitterness.
5. *Bandage the injury with forgiveness.* This will keep it out of sight until the wound is healed.
6. *Don't take the scab off.* Bringing up the subject will re-open the wound. Serious dangers from infection (see No. 4, above) still exist which could prove fatal spiritually.
7. *Beware of painful and touchy self-pity.* This is often referred to as withdrawal pains, as the symptom is withdrawing from others, especially the one inflicting the injury. The remedy: accept apologies.
8. *Prescription.* Take a generous dose of antibiotics from the word of God several times daily, using prayer each time. This has a soothing effect and is a good painkiller.
9. *Stay in close contact with the great physician at all times.* Depend on his strength, joy, and peace to help you during convalescence.
10. *Full recovery is reached* when the patient is restored to complete fellowship and harmony, especially with the offending party.

My ninth point is a wonderful antidote to discouragement, especially with yourself: *realize that God is easy to live with.* He is a God of love and mercy and forgiveness, ready to note the smallest effort. If a cup of cold water can be a deed worthy of his praise, what shall we say of witnessing, tract distribution, long-term assistance to others, faithful prayer? One of the things that has kept me going over the years has been the sureness that even at moments of utter failure he still loves me and wants me to get up and start running the race again.

Tenth, *learn to refuel,* D. L. Moody was once told, "The world has never seen a totally dedicated man." I believe many have been led into extremes by trying to be someone they were not meant to be. The way God measures dedication and the way Mr. Fellowman measures it are two quite different things. Since you can't achieve perfection, acknowledge the fact and give yourself some time off when you need it. For some it's a walk in the woods or a few days' holiday or just getting away and reading (preferably something non-spiritual). Perhaps a good film.

The Apostle Paul was a master of encouragement. He doesn't mince his hard sayings, and that makes his generous comments all the more valuable. I would like to close this chapter with one of his parting injunctions to the Corinthians, which must have been treasured by them in their tough surroundings: "Therefore, my dear brothers, stand firm. Let nothing move you. Always give yourselves fully to the work of the Lord, because you know that your labor in the Lord is not in vain" (1 Corinthians 15:58).

10

SPIRITUAL *balance*

THERE ARE QUITE A NUMBER of areas where I believe it is important for the Christian to try to maintain balance. We have an enemy. He is not a funny little character with horns and a pitchfork, but a clever—and, from the human point of view, beautiful—being who is seeking to deceive and to bring havoc. We easily get into tangents and extremes if we are ignorant of his devices, not exactly getting into a cult, but developing a cult-like practice in a given area.

Once a person commits his life to Jesus, it seems that Satan does everything he can to lead him off on a tangent so that his Christian life will lose its impact. John Stott, in his excellent little book *Balanced Christianity*,[11] points out how the Devil is concerned to polarize us and to get us into different camps, chopping away at one another rather than working together against him. This is right against the cardinal principle of love which we examined in chapter 4. Tempers rise, people grow upset and start reacting to one another in the flesh. Those who are militantly orthodox can often be unloving: it is not difficult to end up with your doctrines all correctly labelled in the right sort of packages, ready to hit your neighbor over the head! In one Bible college in England not long ago, a student of Calvinistic persuasion and one with an Arminian viewpoint got so excited about their respective positions that they actually came to blows.

The first area, then, where we need to find balance is *between the crisis experience and God's growth process*. Some Christians lay a heavy emphasis on crisis: they make a point of attending different conventions and house parties to find a new peak of awareness and commitment. It is easy to misuse Keswick, Filey, the Dales Bible Week, Greenbelt, or even an OM conference in this way. Often such mountaintop experiences are perfectly legitimate, and we should never despise what the Spirit of the Lord may be doing. But unless that summer crisis is followed by a process, it will become an abscess, generally by December, with predictable guilt and discouragement. The process of growth towards maturity is primarily your responsibility and should be taking place 365 days a year. It is not just a matter of "let go and let God." Love and the fruit of the Spirit are not automatic. God works in different people in different ways, for he does not destroy your individuality: as you give it to him, he returns it to you, straightened and purified, made whole. Compare Colossians 3:16, "Let the word of Christ dwell in you richly," with Ephesians 5:18, "Be filled with the Spirit." We need both, and note that both are imperative. Neither is an optional extra.

We also need balance *between discipline and freedom*. Here, too, the Devil is hard at work polarizing God's people, for you get those who insist on planning everything down to the very last detail and insisting that half an hour's Quiet Time is indispensable for salvation. Then on the other side, you find those who feel that such things are devilish in themselves and a temptation to rely on the flesh rather than the Spirit. I have heard quite a number of (rather bad) sermons where the preacher felt it was unspiritual to prepare. Yet both messages are in the Bible. There is a time to step out in faith that things will work out—and sometimes we have no choice—but there is also a place for using the wits that God gave us. St. Paul writes at length about freedom from the law, but can also say in 1 Corinthians 9:24–27:

> Do you not know that in a race all the runners run, but only one gets the prize? . . . Everyone who competes in the games goes into strict training. They do it to get a crown that will not last; but we do it to get a crown that will last for ever. Therefore I do not run like a man running aimlessly; I do not fight like a man beating the air. No, I beat my body and make it my slave so that after I have preached to others, I myself will not be disqualified for the prize.

Another area is the balance *between zeal and wisdom*. Perhaps you are a young Christian, anxious to smother his neighborhood with gospel tracts. Already you can see your elders at the church shaking their heads and muttering, "Ah yes, we tried that in 1954, and it didn't work then. You'll only put people off." Satan is keen to polarize the old and the young. He must rejoice when he sees churches made up almost exclusively of older people, where the only man under retiring age is the vicar—and will be quite happy, too, when he finds churches full of young madcaps bouncing with energy and sure that anyone who doesn't find Joe Zealot and the Fishbones the best thing since Noah has probably been around since Noah. Youngsters are often keen to condemn the established church. The Children of God called it the "system" and encouraged people to leave it, and rebellious young people did so in great numbers. Ironically, they have ended up probably more regimented than any branch of the Christian church.

The answer here lies not in moderation so much as in both extremes together: we need as much wisdom and as much zeal as we can find. We need those who can get out and get on with the job, and we also need the older and wiser members who can give counsel and help the younger ones count the cost—and press on when the first flush of enthusiasm is past. "Never be lacking in zeal, but keep your spiritual fervor, serving the Lord" (Romans 12:11). Enthusiasm is contagious, it doesn't require much intelligence to attain it, and it is a hallmark of any flourishing church. It is one of the reasons for the enormous growth of the Pentecostal churches in Latin America.

In connection with zeal and wisdom we also need a balance *between submission and individual guidance*. This topic can arouse tremendous controversy. There is clear teaching from Paul on submission: "Respect those who work hard among you, who are over you in the Lord and who admonish you" (1 Thessalonians 5:12). Equally, leaders must not lord it over their flock, or they will begin to lose their credentials for being leaders. They will be serving themselves rather than God. In Operation Mobilization we meet the issue of submission fairly constantly, and those of us who are leaders do our best to appreciate an individual's sense of guidance and to pray with those under us to see what the Lord's will is. We are concerned not to be unreasonable, but to warn those under us if we see them going into situations that could get dangerous or embarking on unwise courses of action. From the viewpoint of those under authority, be careful not to follow blindly or to let the leader carry all the responsibility for guidance. That would be a cop-out, a denial of your own responsibility for understanding what the Lord is saying to you.

Guidance is one of the most difficult areas of the Christian faith, especially in big areas such as choosing a career or marriage partner. I am grateful to Dr. Francis Schaeffer for pointing out that prayer is not some kind of slot machine where you put in the small change of your requests, pull the handle and click! out comes your little evangelical chocolate answered prayer, which you can show round to everyone to let them know you are spiritual. God is sometimes much more concerned with our humility or with our faith than with our prayers for this or that: you may pull the lever hundreds of times before you learn what you need to know about the way God works. We can't box God in. He will break out of all our little systems with denominational or personal labels. He is not a *tame* God.

You will already be familiar with the balance needed *between warfare and the rest of faith in the Christian life*. There is plenty of language in the Bible about fighting: "I have fought the good fight," says Paul to Timothy. Frankly, I don't like all this military terminology, but God in his sovereignty has chosen, and so I must accept it and use it, as I have in this book. Certainly we are in a war situation. At the same time, our finger need not be always on the trigger. Isaiah 26:3 is a verse that has often ministered to my own heart, and I suggest that you too meditate on it frequently: "You will keep in perfect peace him whose mind is steadfast, because he trusts in you." Deep trust is necessary preparation for battle.

Then, too, we need balance between basic Christian principles and the policies of a particular church or movement. I deal with this point at greater length in my book *The Revolution of Love*. We need to be able to discern which is which! In OM we have found that it was sensible for short-term staff during the summer to use sleeping bags, because they were moving around so much of the time. Then we had one girl who felt that sleeping bags were God's way, that they were perhaps a symbol of a nomadic existence not tied down to possessions and status, and so when she went home she asked her mother to have her bed removed from her room so that she could sleep on the floor. You can just imagine what her mother must have thought.

This may seem a nit-picking point to make, but I am amazed at how Christians can get so uptight about such trivial matters. Length of hair, style of dress, using pews or chairs in church, all can cause confusion and division. Paul's approach is very clear as he talks of food laws: what matters is that you do as your conscience says, but always make allowances for consciences that are more uneasy than your own, for your love for your brother will include concern that he should not feel uncomfortable. Read 1 Corinthians 8: 9–13.

Seek, too, to find a balance *between love and judgment*. "What do you prefer?" Paul asked the Corinthians. "Shall I come to you with a whip, or in love and with a gentle spirit?" There are times when we have to offer reproof to another believer, though always in love. Judgment is a vital part of the Christian message, and from time to time particular people will feel called to speak of judgment. David Wilkerson (of *The Cross and the Switchblade* fame) is one man who feels that this should be his theme at present; some of his tapes are quite uncomfortable to listen to. Always your judgments must be motivated by love: if you cannot speak hard truth in charity, then let someone else do so. You are disqualified. This is equally true whether the other person is a Christian or a nonbeliever. D. L. Moody's preaching was revolutionized by a little-known Englishman who pointed out that he should speak more on the subject of love. There is something in most of us that inclines towards judgment. I reckon that if we make our message and concerns 80 percent love and 20 percent judgment, then we have the balance about right.

Some of us need to learn the balance *between work and worship*. Some feel that praising God is the be-all and end-all. Others are more anxious to get out on the streets to start the Christian revolution. Both are fine: but we find activist types (like me) joining Operation Mobilization and then getting upset because of the hours we spend praising and worshipping. The truth of the matter is that if we are going to do an effective job, then it will not be by our own might but by the Spirit of God. Hence there will be much waiting upon the Lord, and much time given over to glorifying him. Sometimes we cannot get right with God until we have got right with one another, and that too takes time. Do strive to avoid polarization here: after polarization comes paralyzation, and the Devil is winning at every turn.

The next area has proved one of the most difficult to get right, especially for Christian leaders. It concerns the balance *between the church and the family*. On the evidence of what I observe, it seems natural for Christian men to neglect their families. Here you are, preaching and guiding and counselling, and your wife and children get left out of the picture. Someone once said, "Any fool can learn by experience." So if you don't yet have a wife and family, try to learn from others' experience before you make the mistake for yourself, that it is very easy—and even, by a twisted way of thinking, virtuous—to neglect them. If not, you *will* learn by experience, when your wife leaves you or has a breakdown. The same man added, "It is a wise man who learns by instruction." The Devil in these days is putting all his might against the family, and he is going to win unless you give the matter careful attention right from the start. Work at communicating, at staying in touch, especially when the pressure is on. If you are not yet married, you can still learn how to communicate. Learn how to understand different kinds of people. Learn to accept and ignore others' weaknesses; your wife to be (or your future husband) may have the same faults as your roommate has right now. If you have leadership responsibilities, it is clear from Paul's letters that one of the qualifications for your position is that your family should be obedient and respectful. Your family will not show obedience and respect towards you—let alone love—if you do not take your full share in their upbringing. Love begets love.

Try also to achieve a balance *between positive and negative*. This is a tough one, because it is so indefinable. Many people have a basically negative outlook on life, with a streak of cynicism, a tendency to look on the black side of the picture. If you feel yourself to be in that category, then let me give you three warnings. By the age of forty you are going to be a thoroughly miserable person; you are going to make a lot of other people thoroughly miserable; and I think I should be praying for whomever you end up marrying! Your children will be three times as negative and will probably end up negative about you as well. A negative spirit shows an unbelieving heart, for you are not really convinced that God can work things out. It is a contradiction to the injunction in Philippians 4:8 to think about "whatever is true, whatever is noble, whatever is right, whatever is pure, whatever is lovely, whatever is admirable." I realize that cynicism is a protection against the disappointments of life, but it carries a very high price tag. If you want to survive as a Christian on planet earth, where there is so much to be negative about, then you have to be able to say, "I can do all things through Christ who strengthens me."

There is certainly a place for negative statements, and the Bible abounds with them. There is nothing wrong with seeing the negative side provided you are prepared to work your way through to the positive side. This is an area where I am still battling to know how to find the right balance, and there are no easy answers. There's no little tree outside my house which drops a baptism of positiveness on me as I walk underneath. It is an act of the will.

Life will be a lot easier if you can exercise a *balanced view of reckless faith and common sense*. Tozer comments, "A bit of healthy disbelief is as needful as faith to the welfare of our souls. We would do well to cultivate a reverent skepticism: it will keep us out of a thousand bogs and quagmires. It is not fatal to doubt some things: it may well be fatal to believe everything." Christians are called to have faith, not to be credulous. There are a lot of naive evangelical people around who simply believe everything, especially if it sounds spiritual or concerns a miracle and particularly if it is in book form. A lot of people have been misled this way, and it is important to pray for discernment. Just because a man has a nice face, a good build, a pleasant manner, and a reputation for being godly, that does not mean that every word he says is true. Search the word of God; use the Bible as a check for all teaching, including this book.

My last point concerns the need for balance *between anointing and training*. Some Christians place such a heavy emphasis on the need for the anointing of the Spirit that they insist that Bible schools, pastoral training, and careful teaching are of the Devil. What nonsense this is! Of course we desperately need trained theologians and pastors and missionaries, especially those who are humble, broken, filled with the Spirit.

I spent two years at the Moody Bible Institute, and for me, it was a most valuable time, giving me the chance to dig deep into all kinds of good spiritual books. It was at Moody that I first caught the vision of Turkey and other lands which has been such an important part of the ministry of OM. College was a time of great worth: of many temptations, but a superb growing time.

Do not think that such training will destroy your personality or force you into some kind of mold. God wants to see your personality grow into the image of his son Jesus as you expose yourself to his Spirit and his word. Indeed, as you learn more and more about his truths, and are able to take upon yourself more and more of his Spirit's blessing, you will become a *richer* personality. You will not feel the need to prove yourself so much. You will begin to become familiar with a dual vision of yourself: both as someone who falls hopelessly short of God's ideal and someone who is a great deal nicer to know than they used to be.

In every area of our lives, there is a need for some kind of balance. Do not think of balance as a dull boring concept, or in the way they consider it in some parts of the States, where all moderation and compromise are seen as of the Devil. Balance is harmony, gentleness, a stable base for building a revolution of love.

11

FAMILY *living*

DISCIPLESHIP STARTS IN THE FAMILY: not just husband and wife, but parents and grandparents and children and grandchildren. Your family probably knows you better than anyone else in the world, certainly better than you think they do. You will not be able to keep many secrets from them, and they will see right through your pretensions. As such they are a most valuable sounding-board, apart from deserving your best efforts. A Christian home can be a glorious witness to the reality of the Lord in your midst, and also a marvellous asset in keeping your feet on the right path. If it turns sour, it gives the lie to all your fine words and destroys in the bud any chance of improvement.

In this brief treatment of the subject, I want to discuss some of the areas where, again, balance is needed. It is worth keeping them at the back of your mind as a warning system when in the heat of the argument, you find yourself saying things you wish you could take back.

One common area where most of us could use some balance is the guilt-inducing debate about "forsaking all" and yet maintaining an attractive home. At both ends of this spectrum, I come across people who seem to me to have things wrong. Plenty of Christians give quite a high priority to decorating their home; not infrequently I feel like asking some pointed questions about their standard of living. A number of books, such as John White's *The Golden Cow,* have appeared over the past years. If you are worried that your standard of living is rather better than it ought to be, then I would commend this one to you as well-written and full of good sense. Another part of the Christian community, however, seems to feel that it is unspiritual to maintain an attractive home, and that it is far better to give away as much as possible for the Lord's work. Something in me has a lot of sympathy for this point of view, but it entails certain problems. A scruffy and dingy home is a poor witness to a religion that preaches joy, and it is really hard to be steadfastly cheerful, let alone happy, in ugly surroundings. Our Lord created beauty: most of what is truly ugly in the world is man-made. From this I conclude that he loves beauty, and our homes should be as beautiful as possible. How to keep this in balance when tens of millions of people across the world have no proper homes at all to speak of is an issue I am still wrestling with very deeply.

This does not mean expensively furnished. We need to see beyond the standards of our immediate neighborhood if that neighborhood assesses furniture by how much it cost. Most attractive homes are the result of the effort and imagination that has gone into their design rather than because of the money that has been spent. Husbands should take an interest in how their homes look and allow their wives the time and the cash to decorate as well as possible. They should also lend a generous hand. You are both liberated in Christ: try to break out of some of the social molds, especially the one which is labelled "little woman at home."

In this context, it is worth pointing out that it is God who is our security. Many people in the Western world considerably overspend on insurance, burglar alarms, and sophisticated locks. Some insurance may be prudent, but don't let it become a mania. God can look after you. We have some hundred and sixty families in OM living by faith; their children are well provided for and do not lack any essentials. It is so easy to fall back on secular schemes, rather than be the concerned, caring community that we should be.

A second area of family life where balance is much needed is in the relationship between being open and honest and being kind. Of course, this issue extends beyond the family context, but kindness is the absent friend all too often at many dinner tables. Honesty without love is a curse. If you feel that a member of your family needs a few home truths (telling phrase!), then be absolutely sure that they are based in and bounded by love. This equally applies to the discipline you impose on your children. Sometimes kindness overrules honesty; if you're a man, then your thoughts probably stray from time to time to other women, but it might be more loving not to confess them to your wife. (Most politic as well.) You will be aware that emotional love fluctuates wildly; it can be thoroughly immature to share every passing feeling. A strong marriage is one based on dedication and commitment to one another rather than on a series of sexual or romantic highs. Constantly affirm your allegiance to your marriage partner; don't let it grow cold.

You should also balance your conviction with love. People matter more than principles for, like the Sabbath, principles exist to serve people. Thus it is sometimes more important to love than to win an argument. Your loyalty to your wife or your parents or your children should take precedence over everything, excepting only your loyalty to your Lord, should it come to that crunch (and occasionally it does). Love is not by any means soft or indulgent, and sometimes can be very hard. But be sure that if you are insisting on your convictions, you are doing so aware of the best interests of your family. It is important for the husband to accept and to value his wife as she is: and it is also important for the wife to support her husband. With great gratitude, I can say that my wife has always been my strongest supporter, and never once have I picked up the hint that she was not backing me all the way. Even when we disagree, she can still affirm that she believes in me.

"Not enough" and "too much" are common bugbears in marriage. If you are married or are expecting to be married some day, then the following might be a useful checklist. They are all complaints shared with me by husbands and wives over the past twenty-five years.

The "Not Enoughs"

Not enough time. Usually on the wife's lips rather than the husband's: give your marriage partner precedence over your hobbies and other friendships always, and over your Christian work unless totally unavoidable. If you have to put your Christian work first, then ensure you can catch up on the talking later. Try to work as a team and to do things together.

Not enough information. Make sure you share what is on your mind. You will probably find the need to have an area of your thinking marked "Private," but see that it is as small as possible.

Not enough money. In all probability, money, and the lack of it, will cause your bitterest arguments. Even if you keep separate bank accounts see that you discuss your expenditure together. It is most important to get this area of your life organized. Learn to trust and believe the best.

Not enough sex. This tends to be the husband's complaint rather than the wife's. So many pages have been written on this subject in the last two decades that I see little point in adding to them, except to say that the wife should absolutely never use sex as "operation carrot." It is utterly essential to find harmony in your sex lives. Sex can be either a great delight or a source of dreadful pain and temptation. Never be afraid to read a good book on the subject or seek counsel from others. Beware of marital pride.

Not enough affection. As men and women, we often need love and affection much more than sex. Here is an area where we must not presume on one another, and it would be good to think of the words of Jesus, "Not to be ministered unto, but to minister." Men need to remember that with women, little things, little encouragements, and little expressions of affection are often more meaningful than perhaps some of the big things that bring greater satisfaction to men.

Not enough water. A male problem for the most part. There is no reason why your wife should tolerate your bad breath and smelly feet. A little soap and water can go a long way. Details like this in marriage are very important.

Not enough prayer. It is often hard to pray together, especially if your individual prayer lives are not so hot. But don't give up— praying together is a wonderful center to your marriage.

The "Too Muches"

Too many people. Quite often this is the wife's fault. She takes a bit too much pride in her hospitality and in consequence forgets the needs of her husband and children. Make sure that all those guests don't hinder something more important. For Christian leaders and pastors, there is the danger of bringing too many people home.

Too much looking at other women. Men, control your eyes. Your wandering appetites can really hurt your wives. Both of you, stamp down hard on any thoughts beginning, "If only I'd married. . . ." Don't be naive about Satan's subtle traps in this area.

Too much fat. Gluttony is such a common sin that you never hear anything about it any more. Both men and women can neglect themselves, but I see a lot of women, not quite in their first youth, who are definitely carrying too much weight. It is your husband's duty and basically his wish to love you; you will make it a lot easier for him if you keep the pounds off.

Too many children. Not necessarily in total quantity, but from time to time make sure you get away for a real break. Both you and they will benefit from it. Single people can also enjoy your family and play a real part in looking after them. If you are single, see if there is a family where you could help from time to time. Offers are rarely refused!

Too many demands. Husbands tend to become fraught by meetings, and wives pay a high price for the part their husbands play if there are children to care for. Ask yourself: is my presence at that committee really needed? Is it my top priority? We easily make far too many heavy demands on each other.

Your family form your closest neighbors. Love them as yourself. If your radical discipleship does not start in the home, it has not truly begun.

12

LORD *of all*

IT IS MY PRAYER THAT THIS BOOK will have challenged you to a deeper and richer Christian life, more outgoing and more effective. The aim of this final chapter is to encourage you in this fuller commitment and the accompanying fullness of the Holy Spirit. I am afraid it is likely that some of you who read this book will have reached this stage without saying with all their heart, "Jesus, you are going to be Lord of everything." I would like therefore to be specific about what "everything" is going to mean.

Of all drugs, the search for *status* is the most addictive and the least satisfying. It is also the most common. None of us is truly free of it. Yet it is directly against the whole nature of the Christian gospel, for our only claim to fame is that God has redeemed us because he loved us. "If I must boast," says Paul to the Corinthians, "I will boast of the things that show my weakness." So worry only about what Jesus is thinking about you, and ignore what others may say. If you do hear some morsel of hot juicy gossip against yourself, forget it. Just think: if they knew all the truth they'd really have something to go on! Of all the people in the world, you are the one least qualified to judge your own worth. Don't try to.

Another major area that is one of the last to be brought under the lordship of Christ is your *social life,* specifically your relationships with members of the opposite sex. (And in some cases your own sex.) Some of the most dedicated young people I have ever met have told me that their social life is badly mixed up in this respect. One minute they are leading a Christian Union meeting or talking about Jesus, and within the hour they are in bed with their girlfriend. Sometimes they are engaged in what can be clas-

sified as "evangelical sex." If that is a new term to you, it means
not going all the way but doing everything else instead. I have had
people share with me that they have gone to bed with their girlfriends or boyfriends without any clothes on, but since they didn't
go all the way they didn't regard it as fornication, so their consciences have a loophole. That is a sin against the Living God—it
is immorality—and you are deceiving yourself if you pretend that
this is not. If you find yourself involved in heavy petting, then you
are going too far; you are playing with fire. If you believe you can
make progress in your Christian life and still compromise in this
way, even with a boy or girl that you are likely to marry, then you
are in for some big surprises.

Please don't get me wrong. There is nothing against dating,
or against doing sports together, going to church, taking a walk
in the woods. No one is telling you that it is sinful to kiss your
girlfriend goodnight—but some of you are like Jaguars with
Volkswagen brakes, and you need to get them overhauled. Don't
follow David's example: follow Joseph's. There was a man who
made his God the absolute monarch of his life, so that even when
a lovely, voluptuous Egyptian woman tried to take him to bed he
could say, "How could I do such a wicked thing and sin against
God?" even though he ended up in prison.

To some extent the churches are at fault. You find churches
which say with pride, "We teach the whole counsel of God."
When did you last hear a sermon on the following passage from
Proverbs 5:18–20?

> May your fountain be blessed,
>   and may you rejoice in the wife of your youth.
> A loving doe, a graceful deer
>   may her breasts satisfy you always,
>   may you ever be captivated by her love.
> Why be captivated, my son, by an adulteress?
> Why embrace the bosom of another man's wife?

You might also think about verse 23:

> He will die for lack of discipline,
>   led astray by his own great folly.

Marriage was given to us by God as one of his most lovely gifts. Sex is beautiful. Billy Graham calls it the "creative force" within us. It is a big part of God's plan, but it has got to be according to God's pattern, within the commitment of marriage, set free because it is within limits.

Another specific area that I'd like to question is your *free time*. Is Jesus Lord of that as well? You can tell a man's maturity by what he does with his leisure, for it is then that the truth about him can be discovered. (Bookcases are very revealing. What do you read for pleasure?) There is nothing wrong with taking a couple of weeks off to go mountaineering, sailing, or lie on a beach. But you can't take a couple of weeks off from being a Christian because the Devil doesn't take holidays. If you're not careful, your leisure time can lay you open to all kinds of temptations.

One of the commonest is simply wasting time. Without discipline and crucifixion of the self-life, you are likely to waste hundreds of God's precious hours. You will know from some of the things I've said in earlier chapters that I am all for relaxing; every Christian should have a hobby and a sport. "God has given us all things richly to enjoy." But relaxing, to my mind, does not mean hanging about chatting or flipping through some silly magazines or watching an idle television show. You are merely passing time and only occupying the surface of your mind. Find things you really enjoy and put all you've got into them. I don't necessarily mean violent activity: it might mean dreaming on a tree stump somewhere in a wood. Learn how to savor your pleasures. Real pleasure, as C. S. Lewis points out in *The Screwtape Letters,* is a splendid defence against the attacks of Satan.

Television is a particular problem. I don't think I'm neurotic about television, though I have been heard to say that the best place to hang your prayer map of the world is in front of the screen. A television is a useful thing to have: there is news to pray about, there are Christian programs, there are good plays and documentaries and sports. But so easily the television can end up controlling you. Recently I visited a dear friend whom I hadn't seen in some years, and they couldn't even turn off the football game when I walked into their living room. There is nothing at all wrong with football games, but so often in the Christian life the good can become the enemy of the best. Be self-critical about your use of the box.

Make Jesus Christ Lord of your *future*. What are you going to do with your life? God does not tell everyone to leave their nets, and in fact most "full-time" Christian workers are the more effective for having spent a few years in an office or school or on a shop floor. But be quite clear that Jesus owns those nets.

I had some very nice "nets." At the age of sixteen, I owned three small businesses. I was a little visionary capitalist, and I had 200 people working for me part time. My vision involved doing the least work possible, instead letting other people do it for me. I owned a philatelic agency, a firefighting equipment business, and one other small setup. It was great to have pockets full of money, go to New York night clubs, and blow it all in one evening.

Then one day I was prayed into a Billy Graham meeting and sat there, in Madison Square Garden, a little middle-class, bourgeois, American pagan, and met the man from Galilee.

From that moment I never knew anything except total surrender to Jesus—an ongoing process! There was no other option. I cannot understand how people can make a big thing of committing their lives to Christ and just go on as they did before, with only a few minor changes. Faith in Jesus Christ is a radical thing. When you meet the Savior, he gives you a complete overhaul. You never know how much time you have left to serve him, so your talents, your strength, your energy, your mind, your hour-by-hour existence all count for eternity.

In view of this, what are you going to do? Will you find a nice job, a nice house and a nice car, with a nice mortgage? Keep up with the other families in the road and, of course, go to church because it is respectable and in America at least you can make good business contacts? (Especially if you're an undertaker.) Jesus is not respectable, but he does care if you're at odds with anyone in your fellowship when you break bread together. He is the one "from whom no secrets are hid." It is far more important to live in love and unity with one another than to maintain appearances. Do not clothe yourself in cold respectability, but rather take part in operation defrost as the warm love of our Savior melts your hearts. And as the ice melts, you may perhaps hear his voice saying, "Follow me. I want to make you a fisher of men." Keep listening! He may be calling some of you to good secular employment, not least to earn the money to give to support those in full-time work but also simply to be a Christian presence in the market places of the world. The important thing is to be ready to hear and to obey.

Give over into Jesus's care as well all your *material possessions*. I have made a few comments on this in the previous chapter, so for the moment I will only say that probably just about everyone who reads this book should be classified as a rich young ruler by comparison with the majority of people in the world. The comparison is valid: Solzhenitsyn said, "To talk about internal affairs in the present world is just ridiculous." Do not compare yourself with those in America or Germany or anywhere else that has a higher standard of living; they are the few. (Incidentally, do not judge them for their higher standards: many of them have a greater love for Jesus than you do.) Set yourself free from the shackles of material things: make Christ Lord over your check book and credit card and that inheritance you have just received. It is a beautiful experience to be set free from clinging to possessions. "My God will meet all your needs according to his glorious riches in Christ Jesus" (Philippians 4:19).

Shortly after I was converted, my parents and my sister also found the Lord. God was just starting to work through me, and my father told me that I needed a new car for my ministry. (At that point I was driving a fifteen-year-old truck. We repaired it, and it did another 50,000 miles.) "Dad," I told him, "I can't take a new car when there are so many other needs. We need Bibles! Tracts! There are Mexicans who don't have a place to live. They don't have any food on their tables." So my father, then in his fifties, (a hard-working electrician) began to get a vision for giving his money for Christian literature and other works of God overseas, a vision that so few seem to have in our day. He had only just become a true believer, but God was working in his life. He and my mother even moved into a smaller home in order to give more money to get the gospel out.

When a revival moved through Canada, farmers put large chunks of land aside and dedicated it to world evangelism. There is one farmer out in Colorado who has dedicated a cow and everything it produces to the work of spreading the gospel.

In the same way, see that your possessions are under the Lord's control. "This is how we know what love is: Jesus Christ laid down his life for us. And we ought to lay down our lives for our brothers. If anyone has material possessions and sees his brother in need but has no pity on him, how can the love of God be in him?" (1 John 3:16,17). Possessions include skills. There is tremendous need in missionary work for people who can handle computers, for bookkeepers, for mechanics, for engineers, for radio technicians. God also needs the one-talent men—and if you only have one talent, then praise him, you have less to take care of! You may find it difficult to communicate. You may even be handicapped. I think of a man in Chicago who had no arms or legs and was also blind: yet he learned to read the braille Bible with his tongue, had a radiant testimony for God, and taught the word of God wonderfully. Of Joni, an ordinary schoolgirl who would never have been known in the world apart from her own friends in Maryland, but because of a terrible accident she has already been used to touch millions for Christ.

No matter how little you have, Jesus can use it. D. L. Moody was described by a secular encyclopedia as a man who "depopulated hell by two million souls." One day the Lord touched Moody in New England, a man who couldn't even speak proper English, and asked, "What is that in your hand?" "Just shoes, Lord," said Moody. He was a shoe salesman. God asked the same question of William Carey, the pioneer Baptist missionary to India. "Just shoes, Lord," answered Carey. He was a cobbler. "Give them to me," commanded the Lord, and Carey did so. Whether you make shoes or microchips, God can use you. Thank him, if you can, for your body, for health, for energy, for every asset you can think of, and turn them over to his care.

As a true believer, you are God's child. Jesus is within you. To you, to everyone, he is saying, "I want to be your Lord, I want to be the king of your life. I want to control your time, your talents, your money, your holidays, your work, your marriage. Come to me, to the foot of the cross, and make me Lord of your life."

HUNGER *for* REALITY

How to Escape from Spiritual
Pretence and Double-living

Dedicated to
John Watts and Keith Beckwith

. . . members of Operation Mobilization who encouraged me to put this message into print and who died in an auto crash in Poland in 1965 while fulfilling the Great Commission committed to them by the Lord Jesus Christ.

CONTENTS

INTRODUCTION

Farewell to Schizophrenia

NO ONE COULD SAY IN these days that we Christians are spiritually starved. Through the care and faithfulness of God's servants, we are generously fed, taught, encouraged, pampered, stimulated, supported, nursed along. A religious world of sermons, discussions, magazine articles, hymns, messages, books, meetings, and conferences surrounds us for our participation and growth. Yet we know very well, if we are honest, that these things have all too little effect on our lives. Why is this so?

If we give the matter a little thought, we will realize that most of us are living in "two worlds." We have split our convictions, activities, and goals into two categories. In the first we place our religious experiences: what we believe; what we sing about; what we pray about; and what we defend in argument.

The second category contains our world of secular values and actions: our use of leisure time; our actions taken to impress people; our attitude towards associates who are better or worse at their job than we are; and how we get our money and use it.

We keep these two worlds strictly apart, and though we may vaguely feel that something is wrong, we don't suspect we are suffering a major disorder—a sort of spiritual schizophrenia. In church, and occasionally among Christian friends, we talk about dedication, commitment, surrender, revival, a life on fire for God, and other expressions of loyalty and love for God. But the words and their corresponding deeds get little exposure outside church walls.

This evangelical dichotomy has had more serious results than we admit. It has produced men who are hard to get along with, women who rank themselves by the furnishings of their house and the style of their clothes, and whole families that put on smiling faces with their Sunday clothes for a few hours at church.

The late A. W. Tozer commented on this situation in his book *Of God and Men*.

> "Evangelicalism as we know it today . . . does produce some real Christians . . . but the spiritual climate into which many modern Christians are born does not make for vigorous spiritual growth. Indeed, the whole evangelical world is to a large extent unfavorable to healthy Christianity. And I am not thinking of modernism either. I mean rather the Bible-believing crowd that bears the name of orthodoxy. . . ."

> "We are making converts to an effete type of Christianity that bears little resemblance to that of the New Testament. The average so-called Bible Christian in our times is but a wretched parody of true sainthood. Yet we put millions of dollars behind movements to perpetuate this degenerate form of religion, and attack the man who dares challenge the wisdom of it."[1]

Everywhere I go I find young people who are aware of this split of Christian and secular values. Many have become atheists or agnostics because of it, while others have skidded into pits of indifference. Many Christians—leaders included—have admitted to me that their beliefs do not control their everyday lives.

Yet many are hungry for reality and genuineness in the Christian life. I met a student in an evangelical seminary who was first in his class academically, president of the campus mission group, and chaplain of the student body. In talking with me, he admitted that he had very little heart-knowledge of God, but he longed for a satisfying Christian experience.

Can this dichotomy be ended, this schizophrenia cured? Can Christ really revolutionize your life so it is consistent and productive? The answer is yes. I do not offer a formula to achieve this result, but I can offer the real Christ. I have seen him revolutionize people's lives all over the world.

These Christians once lived in spiritual barrenness, then they honestly faced Christ and confessed their besetting sins that clung from the old life. Jesus transformed them, and he can transform you. It is not a life of perfection, but it is a life of reality. It does not mean a life of ease, but it is a life of joy.

If you're tired of split-level living, ask Jesus to make you a whole person.

1
WE *are* REVOLUTIONARIES!

THE LORD JESUS CHRIST was a revolutionary! Consider, if you will, some of his most basic teachings: "Love your enemies"; "Do good to them which hate you"; "Bless them which persecute you"; "Whosoever will be chief among you, let him be your servant"; "Lay not up for yourselves treasures on earth"; "Except a man forsake all that he hath, he cannot be my disciple."

Do you suppose that all these ideas fell in with the cultural pattern of Christ's day? Of course not! The people of his day were just as enslaved by the material aspect of living as the people of the twentieth century. But the Lord Jesus broke with any cultural pattern which interfered with the life of sacrificial love which he came to give.

In the history of Christianity, there have been comparatively few who have lived according to the literal teachings of Christ. The early apostles did, of course. And the results for them were suffering, persecution, imprisonment, exile, and death. Does this seem strange? No! These are the normal results of any life based upon the principles set forth by Christ.

Why is this? The answer is simple: the individual who would live this life is of necessity a revolutionary individual, a cultural nonconformist, a "fanatic," if you please. Literal adherence to the principles laid down by Jesus Christ would, without a doubt, result in worldwide revolution—a revolution motivated by love, a revolution executed by love, and a revolution culminating in love.

And we *are* revolutionaries! We are only a small group of Christian young people in Operation Mobilization, yet we have determined by God's grace to live our lives according to the revolutionary teachings of our Master. Within the sphere of absolute, literal obedience to his commands lies the power that will evangelize the world. Outside this sphere is the nauseating, insipid Christianity of our day.

We have committed ourselves in reckless abandonment to the claims of Christ on our blood-bought lives. We have no rights. Every petty, personal desire must be subordinated to the supreme task of reaching the world for Christ. We are debtors. We must not allow ourselves to be swept into the soul-binding curse of modern-day materialistic thinking and living. Christians have been "willing" long enough to forsake all—the time has come (and is passing) when we must forsake all. Christ must have absolute control of our time and money. We must yield possessions, comforts, food, and sleep; we must live on the barest essentials, that his cause might be furthered. The propagation of the faith we hold supreme. Christ is worthy of our all. We must be ready to suffer for him and count it joy, to die for him and count it gain. In the light of the present spiritual warfare, anything less than absolute dedication must be considered insubordination to our Master and mockery of his cause.

This is our commitment, and we will press forward until every person has heard the gospel. We will soon be in many different countries, engaged in combat with all the forces of darkness. We look beyond the thousands to the millions; beyond the cities to the countries. The world is our goal. And our primary targets are the seemingly impenetrable areas of the Communist and Moslem countries which can only receive freedom as they have opportunity to receive the Truth. These countries will be reached for Christ no matter what the cost. The ultimate victory is ours.

We must say to you, fellow Christian, that we are risen with Christ; we seek those things which are above, where Christ sits on the right hand of God. We have set our affections on things above, not on things on the earth, for we are dead and our life is hid with Christ in God. What blessed hope! What *compelling truth* to lead us to total abandonment of self and unto Christ! Without this, there is certain victory for the enemy and disgrace to our Lord Jesus Christ, who gave himself for us that he might be all things to us.[2]

2

HUNGRY *disciples*

ANYONE WHO CLAIMS TO BE A disciple of Jesus Christ should be experiencing the reality of 1 John 2:6: "He that saith he abideth in him [Christ] ought himself also to walk even as he walked" (KJV). Without question, it is God's will for Christian disciples to live as Christ lived. This is not dry theory or a casual observation about Christian living; it is the dynamic standard which produces a vital witness for Christ to lost men and women.

Sometimes the men of the world are wiser in human affairs than the men of God. The agnostic H. G. Wells said in his *Outline of History:* "Not long after Jesus Christ died, those who claimed to follow him gave up practicing his revolutionary principles."[3] Yes, "revolutionary" was his description, and how right he was! The church has held on to structures and many of the doctrines, but it has lost the core of truth that Jesus taught.

Today you can meet more and more "say-evangelicals" as distinct from "be-evangelicals." As I have visited Bible school after Bible school and Christian institution after Christian institution, I have found many "talkers" of Christianity—but few *walkers!*

Not only I, but many Christian young people are acutely aware of this discrepancy. Many have been disillusioned by this contradiction between faith and life.

If we are informed, we realize that many of the young people who grow up in evangelical churches deny the faith before they are twenty-five. We wonder why, and some say, "It must be the latter days"—the days of apostasy and doom. That may be true, but that would not be sufficient explanation of our tragic losses to Satan.

Some Christians say the answer is in "good, sound, Bible teaching." But that is not enough, either. Never in the history of the church have there been so many Bible conferences, radio Bible studies, and Bible study books. Did you know there are more than a thousand books available in the English language on the Pauline epistles? And today we have excellent recorded Bible studies as well. You can hear outstanding Bible teachers in your home by the turn of a radio knob.

We have every opportunity for learning of the life and teachings of Paul, but where are the Pauls of the twentieth century? Where are the men prepared like him and his companions to face cold and shipwreck and robbers for the gospel's sake, and to thank God for the stripes that tore their backs? We have many sincere servants of God and many great preachers. But where are those who can say with Paul that he ceased not to warn men and women night and day with tears? Such men are difficult to find, if not impossible. Why? The reason, I believe, is that we have separated our Bible beliefs from our daily living. Paul never did this.

We want to serve the Lord, and we say, "I am ready to serve the Lord if only I can find my place in his service!" Not finding it, we are frustrated. What is wrong?

God is far more concerned about your finding your place in Christ himself than your place in his service. The essential thing in Christian living is not where you are going or what you are doing, but in whose strength you are living. You may go behind the Iron Curtain or just across the street to serve the Lord, but *in whose strength are you going?* Let us see how the Apostle Paul went about it. In Acts 20:19–20, Paul says, "I served the Lord with great humility and with tears, although I was severely tested by the plots of the Hews. You know that I have not hesitated to preach anything that would be helpful to you but have taught you publicly and from house to you."

Notice the words: "with great humility." The apostle does not say he is serving the Lord with great preaching, literature distribution, tremendous campaigns behind the Iron Curtain, and great exploits in Turkey and India. He says that he served the Lord with many tears and trials. Discipleship is first of all a matter of the heart. Unless the heart is right, everything else is wrong. Our hearts need to experience a deep hunger and longing for God.

Hunger for God is the genuine mark of a disciple. It confirms to me that I am his child and that he is working in me. What I do for God does not prove that I am a disciple. I may try to fulfill the terms of the Sermon on the Mount or of church creeds; I may live ruggedly and sleep on the floor, but these things do not mark me as a disciple. The way I may know I am a disciple is my having an intense, insatiable hunger for the crucified Lord of Glory. If this is your experience—if you yearn for deep fellowship with your Creator, if you desire to know him intimately and to walk with him and to breathe with him—though you may look like a failure and have made innumerable blunders, then you are well on the road to discipleship.

David was an Old Testament individual who knew God and walked with him. Did God say: "David was a man who lived in purity all the days of his life"? No, God said that David was "a man after my own heart."

As we see in the Psalms, David had a hunger for God. "My heart longeth, yea, fainteth for the living God." "As the hart panteth after the water brooks, so panteth my soul after thee, O God." Despite David's failures and backsliding, he was hungry and thirsty for God. In church history right back to the beginning, we find that the mark of a true disciple, a man of God, is a hunger to know God and his righteousness.

The man after God's heart is described in Psalm 34. He can praise God for all his experiences. "I will bless the Lord at all times! His praise shall continually be in my mouth. My soul shall make its boast in the Lord: the humble will hear it and rejoice. O magnify the Lord with me, and let us exalt his name together. I sought the Lord, and he answered me, and delivered me from all my fears" (verses 1–4 NASB). And verse 10: "The young lions do lack and suffer hunger; but they that seek the Lord shall not be in want any good thing" (NASB). *They that seek the Lord:* to seek and hunger for him, to praise him continually, these are the marks of a true disciple of Jesus Christ.

Outward marks are often deceptive. The clever Christian, the one who excels in fluent praying or vigorous preaching, or the one who can answer all the theological questions, is not necessarily a disciple. Nor is it necessarily the one who has sold everything, down to the last shirt in an act of "true discipleship." These things of themselves do not draw us close to God. But God draws near, the Scripture says, "unto them that are of a broken heart, and saveth them that are of a contrite spirit." No discovery of Christian truth has brought more encouragement to me than this one.

Do you remember Jesus' parable of the two men who came to the temple to pray? The first one went to the front and, surveying his audience, exulted, "O God, how thankful I am that I am not like that other man!" He may have remembered the rich man who turned away from Jesus because he had too many possessions, and then prayed: "God, I thank you that I am not like him either. No Pharisee would do that!" Perhaps he thought of a young fellow who had never gone on a Pharisee Crusade, inspiring him to declaim: "Thank God I am not like that!" And then he unrolled a beautiful prayer that he learned in the Pharisee Bible College and arranged himself gracefully round the microphone to pray it to his public. But the second fellow, away off in the distance, bent over abjectly and beat his breast in agony, imploring: "God, have mercy on me."

To whom did God draw near? To the theological discourser, tossing out weightless words? Certainly not! As he strode off in his robes of self-righteousness, he knew nothing of God's justification or blessing.

God drew near to the one who came with a broken heart and contrite spirit. He heard the cry: "God, you know I am a failure. You know I am a phony. You know that I am worthless. I am a sinner! Have mercy on me." That man acknowledged his sins, and God justified him. This conflicts with our human understanding, yet it is one reason why I believe the Bible: no man would originate this way of salvation. This shows us the heart of God.

Except for Christianity, every religion offers a combination of service and reward: Do this and you will get that. So the average person would reason that if you are a good disciple of Jesus and live according to the Sermon on the Mount, or if you join evangelistic campaigns and hand out tracts, or perhaps if you shine the shoes of some person to prove how humble you are, then you will be rewarded with great blessing. But blessing comes only by God's way, not man's.

You, by yourself, can never shine anyone's shoes without false motives. You will not even distribute tracts without some personal ambition. Paul asked the Galatians: "Having begun in the Spirit, will you now continue in the flesh?" Many Christians are trying to do that. "I am saved by grace," they might say, "but now I must work my way through the Christian life."

This is a serious mistake. You are saved by God's grace, and by his grace you must serve. The Lord is near—not to the successful but to those who are of a broken heart. He saves—not the energetic but those who have a contrite spirit.

"Delight yourself in the Lord," says the psalmist, "and he will give you the desires of your heart" (Psalm 37:4). The reason we often fail to find the will of God is that we delight in other things. Christians engaged in evangelism are tempted to delight in the adventure of it. Or we delight in the fellowship of the gospel and the enthusiasm we share. I assure you that if you delight in any work for God or in any organization or movement, discouragement will sooner or later catch up with you. Our God is a jealous God, and he will not share his glory with an organization, a personality, or movement, however spiritual.

This is so clear in John 5:44, when Jesus says to disbelieving Jews, "How can you believe, when you receive glory from one another, and you do not seek the glory that is from the *one and* only God?" (NASB). How can you believe God for great things—for laborers, for finances, for conversions, for victories in the lives of Christians—when you seek honor from other humans?

While we seek honor for ourselves, or try to advance the program or reputation of a movement or a preacher, we are building on the fragile merit of men. As the mark of a true disciple is his hunger for God, his goal is God's approval. When the work is done, he wants to hear God say, "Well done, thou good and faithful servant." Day after day he lives for God and his glory, seeking it as the deer craves the water of the brook.

Despite the weaknesses of Christ's people, there are many today who are hungry for God. This hunger must be cultivated both by feeding and by developing its capacity. God wants all of our being, not just our labor for the Lord, our problem-solving, or our serving behind the scenes. We can get so caught up in activities, even Christian ones, that we lose conscious contact with God himself. He waits, close but silent, ready to remind us: "My child, you are too busy to receive any strength from me."

His counsel remains: "Be still, and know that I am God" (Psalm 46:10). The only way to find the necessary power and resources for each day is to quietly wait on God. Plan for time to be alone with him; learn to delight in him; cultivate a hunger for his infinite being. Without this, your work will be superficial; with it, your deepest desires will be filled, and your discipleship will glorify him.

Our situation today is described well in these words by A. W. Tozer:

> In this hour of all-but-universal darkness, one cheering gleam appears—within the fold of conservative Christianity there are to be found increasing numbers of persons whose religious lives are marked by a growing hunger after God himself. They are eager for spiritual realities, and will not be put off with words, nor will they be content with correct interpretations of the truth. They are athirst for God, and will not be satisfied until they have drunk deep at the Fountain of Living Water.[4]

Many things have blinded our eyes; a multitude of theological distinctions and religious traditions have made a dichotomy between the doctrines of God and an intimate relationship with him. But there is hope wherever Christians are hungering for God. They are joined in a crusade to know God. This is the only cause that ultimately counts, the only link that will not be bent and broken by the ignorance and selfishness of men. Our real link is not with any organization, but with the living God. As we humble ourselves at the cross, we shall learn the reality of Jesus' power that conquered sin and death. We will receive the promise: "Blessed are those who hunger and thirst for righteousness, for they will be filled" (Matthew 5:6).

3

the **PRAYER** *of* **FREEDOM**

"LITANY" IS A WORD THAT DESCRIBES a formal prayer read by church people the same way each time. A great deal of litany was abandoned by the Protestant churches after the Reformation, and almost everything of Roman Catholic origin was rejected by the new churches. This resulted in some spiritual losses that we couldn't really afford because some of the devout Roman Catholics can teach us vital truths. The power of the gospel and the presence of the Lord Jesus Christ infiltrate even somnolent churches, and some people come to know him and love him just as Martin Luther did within the Roman Church. If we Protestants possessed some of the spiritual depth evidenced by men such as Francis of Assisi, I believe we would accomplish far more for the Lord.

I do not know the name of the Roman Catholic who wrote the following litany, but it speaks of a life that all disciples of Christ need to experience.

O Jesus, meek and humble of heart, hear me.
Deliver me, Jesus,
from the desire of being loved,
from the desire of being extolled,
from the desire of being honored,
from the desire of being praised,
from the desire of being preferred to others,
from the desire of being consulted,
from the desire of being approved,
from the fear of being humiliated,
from the fear of being despised,
from the fear of suffering rebuke,

from the fear of being forgotten,
from the fear of being wronged,
from the fear of being suspected.

And, Jesus, grant me the grace to desire
that others might be loved more than I,
that others may be esteemed more than I,
that in the opinion of the world others may
increase and I may decrease,
that others may be chosen, and I set aside,
that others may be praised and I unnoticed,
that others may be preferred to me in everything,
that others may become holier than I,
provided that I become as holy as I should.

If we sincerely prayed like this every day, I am sure the Holy Spirit would marvelously change our lives. I believe the qualities spoken of in this prayer can become ours today. This should be our goal, not the accomplishment of any particular task for God.

There are many cheap substitutes and secondary roads for genuine holiness. We can tramp down one false route after another clutching the counterfeit of New Testament discipleship instead of possessing the real thing.

When I was a student, I was hungry to know what Christian holiness was, and I searched the Scriptures to find out the heart of the New Testament message. I came to the profound conviction that the Holy Spirit wants to produce Christlike individuals—not religious robots, not doctrinal champions, not evangelistic whirlwinds, but men who are like Jesus Christ. That is basically what this prayer is about.

These attributes are characteristics of Jesus. He was the one who was not esteemed, who was unloved, who was unextolled. He would not accept honor nor any of the things that ambitious men crave. He was the one who finally was completely despised and consequently executed. This prayer was written by a person who knew God intimately.

The work that God wants to do supremely in our hearts is to

produce Christlikeness. It is a work that will take all our lives—
there are no shortcuts to this kind of spiritual growth. There is no
organization, no activity that can substitute for it. We need a constant hunger and thirst for the nature of Christ to be reproduced in
us. We need, too, an awareness of the unending spiritual warfare
surrounding us.

Men at war have to be ready to die any day. They may not
know Christ, but they are ready to lose their lives as they go out
to fight, or they are poor soldiers. We need something of the same
spirit in spiritual warfare. We who have Christ's eternal life need
to throw away our own lives. This readiness can come as we pray
and live in the direction of this prayer.

It begins, "Deliver me, Jesus, from the desire of being esteemed." We all have an innate desire to be esteemed. However
undistinguished we are, we like to be recognized. When we meet
a new group of Christians and someone says, "Good to have you
with us, brother! Would you like to share what God is doing in
your life?" we feel gratified. But if we are ignored or slighted, we
feel hurt. Whether we are extroverted or introverted, we selfishly
desire attention, and so we all need to pray: "Lord, deliver me
from the desire of being esteemed." In Philippians, Paul warns
against the product of inordinate self-esteem: "Do nothing out of
selfish ambition or vain conceit, but in humility consider others
better than yourselves" (2:3). This requires the love-power of
Jesus Christ.

The second petition of the prayer asks: "Deliver me, Jesus,
from the desire of being loved." To be loved is our basic psycho-
logical need. Children cannot develop normally without love, and
adults cannot function happily without the security of love. God
met these needs supremely by giving his Son in love for us. "This
is how we know what love is: Jesus Christ laid down his life for
us" (1 John 3:16). The greatest way God could demonstrate his
love was to give his beloved, perfect Son to redeem us from sin.
And his desire for us is that we should minister that same love to
one another, for the same Scripture continues: "And we ought to
lay down our lives for our brothers."

I believe that some Christians strive anxiously for manifestations of God's love because we do not experience the love of fellow Christians which Christ commanded to be given. When there is little love flowing between us, we may feel impelled to seek special favors and blessings from God as confirmation that we are loved.

God's plan, according to the Scriptures, is for Christians to love one another, even as Christ loved the Church and gave himself for it. The revolution of love is caught and passed on horizontally as well as vertically.

Most men who are on fire for God caught the spark from another man on fire. Great men of God grew to be like Christ because they had been with a man of God as well as with God himself in communion. God meets us in prayer and in his Word, but he also meets us through the person and example of another brother.

I owe more than I can tell to the love and encouragement of other Christians. One of them is Billy Graham, though I do not know him personally. I have read his life story and followed his progress. Once I shook his hand in a crowd, and I felt his love even there.

I had gone to his office in London on business, and many people were there ahead of me. The whole office force was caught up in the pace of an evangelistic crusade, and nobody had spoken to my friend and me except the receptionist. Then Graham came in and immediately started shaking hands with everybody. He came straight to us, greeted us, and said something very kind. Here is a famous man who is fifty times busier than most people, but he had time to shake hands with the nobodies in his outer office. This was especially heartening to me because I had found Christ as my Savior through Graham's preaching.

People will come to know Jesus if we go where they are and love them in this way, but the revolution of love cannot spread if we are intent on gaining love from others. We all need love, but the Christian disciple concentrates on giving love because he has received abundant love from God. A severe test comes when we feel unloved and rejected, as Jesus was. But at that crisis we may prove how wonderful the Lord's love is by giving ourselves for others.

The next snare we must be delivered from is "the desire of being extolled." I define "extol" as flattering or praising. How much we enjoy this! It is almost like feasting at a banquet. Jesus, we are told in Philippians, was just the opposite. He was "everything" in heaven, and he became as a criminal on earth. The Bible says: "Except a grain of wheat fall into the ground and die, it abideth alone." In order to be fruitful, the disciple must die to himself. Do not seek to be lifted up; be submerged.

This may be practiced every time we are overlooked or not given credit for our deeds. It is hard on the ego—which is just what the ego needs. This prayer helps to cut us off from the cancerous craving to be somebody, to gain a status superior to others. It checks the treacherous invasion of Satan among Christian workers.

Very close to this is the next plea: "Deliver me from the desire of being honored." God said: "How can you believe if you accept praise from one another, yet make no effort to obtain the praise that comes from the only God?" (John 5:44) Jesus' testimony was: "I receive not honor from men." Often when a Christian has accomplished something for God, he is tempted to exploit it for heightened personal honor. This temptation is from Satan. Some honors and recognitions are very subtly harmful. They come from well-intentioned people or Christian organizations, and the commendations become food for self-exaltation. Sometimes we can receive more honor from fellow Christians than from the world system, and the "sanctified" source makes the praise all the more insidious.

There is even a danger of our seeking spiritual experiences for self-aggrandizement. We are tempted to testify of deliverance from sin, answered prayer, or some other experience of God's grace in a way that brings vast satisfaction to ourselves rather than honor to God. His grace is to be prized, but it is not to be flaunted as a sign of our merit.

I sometimes get letters from young people seeking training,

who write recommending themselves. They tell me how great they are, and how many qualifications they have. Can you imagine getting a letter like that from the Apostle John? There was, of course, a time when, like the others, John sought credit and even precedence for having followed Jesus, but that was before the cross brought about a revolution in all their lives. It is not wrong to be encouraged. What is wrong is the seeking of praise and commendation from others. Do we praise God as much when we are alone as when we're with others? Do we continue our work alone with as much enthusiasm as we did when we were being observed? I dislike working alone and believe in working two by two. But sometimes we are alone, and then we are tested as to whether we are concerned for our honor or for God's.

The next prayer is very close in meaning: "Deliver me from the desire of being praised." This is related to everyday associations and deeds. If we are hungry for praise, we eagerly accept crumbs of approval from anyone, whether they are sincere and honest or not. Such praise turns rotten on the tongue of fickle and unprincipled men.

We also pray: "Deliver me from the desire of being preferred to others." How do we feel when we are qualified and someone else is chosen? Do we rejoice when a fellow Christian receives honor? This blessing to another may cut us deeply. A. W. Tozer said, "The cross will cut into our lives where it hurts the worst, sparing neither us nor our carefully cultivated reputations." Worldly men put great stock in their ranking, but John the Baptist easily declared: "He that cometh after me is preferred before me."

"Deliver me, too, from the desire of being consulted." Our experience and knowledge are hindrances when we expect others to defer to us and acknowledge our wisdom. Being overlooked is especially trying when our advice seems to be so obviously right. But this is another form of self-serving, as we can trust God to employ our advice if it is needed for his glory.

Most of us need deliverance also from "the desire of being approved"—of being assured by others that we were right, after all. Disciples must continue to be learners in God's school of life.

When people ask me what degree I am studying for, I reply "The A.U.G.—Approved Unto God." It will not be awarded in this life, but it is the only one that matters eternally.

A common burden we carry is "the fear of being humiliated." We want to look good to others, even desiring to make favorable impressions "for God." But God does not have this problem; in his perfection and power, he is never humbled. And his Son did not shrink from the humiliations of men when he was on earth.

God often takes us the same way his Son went. The humiliations dramatize the contrast between God's ways and man's, and point the way to safety. Records show that swimmers who have practiced life-saving are vulnerable to drowning because they are overconfident in the water. God would save us from overconfidence in self, and so he humbles us. He undermines and weakens our naturally strong points for our good and our growth in him. Let us not fear the humiliation that can bring this valuable benefit.

Deliver us, too, Lord, from "the fear of being despised." Oh, how we need this fearlessness for witnessing. So many people scorn the Christian who witnesses for Christ. The distributor of tracts may be despised, but we who know their value should give them out as though they were bank notes. Some people resent the "invasion of their privacy" concerning spiritual matters, but the Christian witness is investing in eternity. May God's love fully cast out this fear.

The "fear of suffering rebuke" clutches at most Christians, yet we need correction to avoid lagging in our discipleship. Christians must learn to speak to one another both in love and rebuke. Though we learn primarily from the Spirit of God, he may use a brother or sister to teach us. Earnest disciples can expect God to speak through his Word, through prayer, and through the exhortations of a brother.

God has given me, I believe, increasing grace to take rebukes, but it has taken years. I reacted like a rattlesnake to the first rebukes I got as a Christian. There's a great difference between a rattlesnake and a worm. The Bible compares Jesus to a worm in the treatment he received (Psalm 22:6). If you strike a worm, it wriggles or dies, but if you strike a rattlesnake, you are struck in return. How significant it is that Satan is described as a serpent!

Our twenty-five reasons why the other fellow is wrong and we are right are always near the tip of our tongue. But our readiness or reluctance to defend ourselves is a measure of our spirituality. Let us implore God to make us unafraid to receive rebukes.

Then there is the almost universal "fear of being forgotten." In India, where living conditions are so poor, some people hoard money to make sure a beautiful memorial over their grave will remind the living of their name. Some Christian churches also are filled with memorials that perpetuate the names and prestige of the dead.

Most of us fear being forgotten by friends. If we don't struggle to prove our worthiness or helpfulness, our past contributions may be forgotten—and us, too.

But life is not lived in the past. Service, satisfaction, and sharing are experienced in the present. Forgetting the things that are past—though we can never forget the people—we press on for today's goal. Let us fear being remembered only for the past. God remembers every good thing we do, and that's sufficient.

"Deliver me, Jesus, from the fear of being ridiculed." Wise is the person who can laugh at himself. Sometimes there is such good cause. Sometimes the ridicule is malicious and is intended to hurt. It may be difficult to realize at such times that the ridicule is a boomerang, injuring the source. The Bible says: "The Lord looks on the heart," and if my heart is right, I may be filled with peace. As we bare our hearts to him, he is quick to reassure when man is quick to ridicule.

"The fear of being wronged" may keep us from trusting people. This fear can be crippling, preventing us from taking a step of faith immediately before us.

The closely related "fear of being suspected" immobilizes some Christians. But we are always going to be misunderstood by someone, no matter what we do. Praying often in meetings will cause some to think you are trying to display your spirituality. We cannot afford to be bound by fear of what others may think. "Rejoice," said Jesus, "when men shall say all manner of evil against you falsely for my sake." We can come to that place of liberty where, because we love the Lord Jesus and act in faith, we are not anxious about what other people think or suspect.

The second section of the prayer deals with worthy desires. "Jesus, grant me the grace to desire that others be loved more than I." This reminds us of the need people have for love which we can help to supply. Wherever I go I meet people who need love and attention—to be visited, listened to, written to, prayed with. How can this enormous need be met? Only by God's grace working in me that others may be esteemed more than I.

"Grant me the desire that in the opinion of the world others may increase, and I may decrease." The testimony of John the Baptist is unequivocal: "I must decrease." The following phrases of the prayer: "That others may be chosen, and I set aside; that others may be preferred to me in everything; that others may be praised and I unnoticed" are summed up in this principle that Jesus Christ must increase, but I must decrease. I must hide behind the cross, that my Lord may be seen and worshiped. I must recognize myself as nobody, so Jesus will be my all.

The final clause is revolutionary: "That others may become holier than I, provided that I become as holy as I should." There is always a danger that Christians may have such a hunger for spiritual reality that we tread on other people in our search for it. The Christian life is not a competition with others; we have a common goal and we grow together in the strength and grace of the body of believers. We must drink together at the Fountain of Living Water.

Can we honestly pray this amazing prayer? I am reminded of some words of A. W. Tozer that I have written in the front of my Bible:

> The Church at this moment needs men who feel themselves expendable in the warfare of the soul. Such men will be free from the compulsions that control weaker men, the lust of the eyes, the lust of the flesh, and the pride of life. They will not be forced to do things by the squeeze of circumstances. Their only compulsion will come from within and from above. This kind of freedom is necessary if we are going to have prophets in our pulpits again instead of mascots. These

free men will serve God and men from motives too high to be understood by the rank and file who today shuffle in and out of the sanctuary. They will make no decision out of fear, they will take no course out of a desire to please, accept no service for financial consideration. They will perform no religious act out of mere custom. Nor will they allow themselves to be influenced by the love of publicity, or by the desire for reputation."[4]

The link between this passage and the prayer is clearly etched. It is as though these two spokesmen, the earlier Catholic and the modern evangelical, learned in the same school. And they have, for they both studied at the feet of Jesus.

4

the **LAND** *of* **REST**

IF THE PROMISED LAND WAS A country to conquer under the leadership of Joshua, it was also a place of rest and victory for the Israelites. A "Promised Land" also awaits the Christian who is willing to move from the wilderness wanderings of self-effort and frustration.

> Let us therefore fear, lest, a promise being left us of entering into his rest, any of you should seem to come short of it. For unto us was the gospel preached, as well as unto them: but the word preached did not profit them, not being mixed with faith in them that heard it. For we which have believed do enter into rest, as he said, As I have sworn in my wrath, if they shall enter into my rest: although the works were finished from the foundation of the world. For he spake in a certain place of the seventh day on this wise, And God did rest the seventh day from all his works.
>
> And in this place again, if they shall enter into my rest. Seeing therefore it remaineth that some must enter therein, and they to whom it was first preached entered not in because of unbelief: Again, he limiteth a certain day, saying in David, Today, after so long a time; as it is said, Today if ye will hear his voice, harden not your hearts. For if Jesus had given them rest, then would he not afterward have spoken of another day. There remaineth therefore a rest to the people of God. For he that is entered into his rest, he also hath ceased from his own works, as God did from his. Let us labor therefore to enter into that rest, lest any man fall after the same example of unbelief. (Hebrews 4:1–11 KJV)

So many Christians are carrying burdens. Though we try to drop them or run away from them, they cling like mud on our feet and fear on our mind. These burdens are carryovers from our pre-Christian days, and God intends Christians to be rid of them.

The account of Israel's coming out of Egypt and entering the Promised Land, Canaan, is a graphic picture of the full redemption we have in Jesus Christ. It vividly describes God's intervention into human affairs as well as the variety and complexity of problems encountered by God's people. Paul reminds us that "these things were written for our example."

Moses, the man who received from God the Ten Commandments inscribed on stone, did not understand God's ways in his earlier years. He did forsake prestige and privilege in the Egyptian hierarchy to identify himself with God's people, but he recklessly asserted himself on behalf of the Israelites instead of acting by God's direction. The result was a forty-year exile in the Sinai wilderness. There, from a burning bush, God called and commissioned Moses to return to Egypt and deliver Israel.

Moses was afraid, so keenly was he aware of his past failure. When God told him to go, he said, "They won't listen to me." He pleaded, "I can't speak. . . ." Moses was like so many ambassadors of God who have begun with: "I'll never be a witness for Christ; I can hardly speak. I'll never be a missionary; I don't like spiders and snakes; I can't sleep on the floor. I'll never do this because I am afraid of that." Yet God did such stupendous things through Moses.

Israel's exit from slavery in Egypt is a picture of the Christian's deliverance from sin's bondage. God's judgment fell on the unrepentant Egyptians but not upon the people who were marked by the blood of the Passover lamb. After the angel of death struck Egyptian homes, Pharaoh capitulated and ordered: "Let them go," and the nation of slaves started for the Promised Land.

They had not gone far before Pharaoh changed his mind and started after them. If Moses thought his troubles were over after getting out of Egypt, his education was just beginning.

Leading one of the largest mobilization operations in history, Moses was doing quite well shepherding a million people and innumerable animals toward the open spaces and safety. Then billowing dust from the fast-moving war chariots of Egypt signalled the pursuit of a vengeful army, and fear swept through the refugees. "Moses," they cried, "you've brought us out here to be killed. Why didn't you let us stay back there? Things in Egypt weren't that bad!"

Hedged in by grumbling people, advancing Egyptian soldiers bent on slaughtering or recapturing them, and rolling waves that blocked their flight, Moses appeared in a desperate strait. But the appearance was deceiving.

Moses cried to God for help, and then obeyed God's command to wait for deliverance. Another miracle took place as the waters of the Red Sea parted, and the wind made a dry path for the Israelites to walk over. They hurried across, hardly able to believe their eyes, and the chariots of Pharaoh raced to overtake them. All at once the waters swept back, and chariots, Egyptians, and Pharaoh were gone!

Satan is not finished when Christ first delivers us from his clutches. The night I was converted, I stepped out of Madison Square Garden in New York where I had accepted Christ and bumped into solid opposition. It was in the form of a belligerent youth anxious to demonstrate his masculinity. I objected to a crude remark made about girls, and this street pugilist deposited me on the concrete with one blow. That was my introduction to the Christian life—I learned early that it's a warfare!

The problems Moses faced in the wilderness were problems every Christian leader has. The people complained about the arrangements, questioned Moses' motives, and wistfully recalled the few pleasures they'd left behind. Somewhat like the twentieth-century Church, they whined, "Of course, we want to be free, but can't we take a little of Egypt with us? We don't want to live back there, but some Egyptian styles can't hurt!"

But God had promised them a place of rest, a land overflowing with milk and honey. He never intends his people to subsist indefinitely on manna rations. The wilderness crossing to Canaan was short, and they could have entered directly. But the advance scouts saw only hazards and enemies in the Promised Land. There are giants over there," they stammered. "We are like insects in their eyes. We can never possess such a land." And they were immobilized by distrust of God.

Today we hear and see the same disbelief. "It cannot be done!" There are giants in the land—Buddhism, Islam, Communism." "We must forget the countries closed to the gospel." Like Israel, the Church often does not see that the place of challenge is also the place of rest.

There were two "fools for Christ" in Israel: Caleb and Joshua. They were prepared to believe God and act, and they later entered the Promised Land. The great majority were doomed to wander, struggle, and die in the wilderness. How many men of faith and vision in our generation have pointed to the place of spiritual rest and gone unheeded? Still the Promised Land waits.

We cannot live a life of victory in the "wilderness" of unbelief and disobedience. If we go to serve the Lord in Asia or Europe or America—or wherever—and we go in doubt, burdened with problems and wrestling opposition in our own strength, we shall experience steady failure and discouragement.

Hebrews 4:10 declares that "he that is entered into his rest, he has ceased from his own works as God did from his." Any work for God that depends on our own efforts, our own zeal, our own ability, and resources will fail. The place of victory and rest is the place of *God's* works, not ours. We are active and completely involved, but the victory does not depend on us, and the cause for anxiety is gone.

We can enter into God's rest now because Christ has entered it for us. When we contemplate what Christ did for us on the cross, we realize that God has genuinely identified us with Christ. Through our faith in the One who died for us, we have been "crucified with Christ"—identified with him in his death. If you are a Christian, you have been crucified with Christ! It is not something that can occur in the future if we trust enough, pray effectively, or memorize another seventy-eight Scripture verses. No, we are to see ourselves dying to sin with Christ on his cross, and, as the truth dawns, we can find ourselves entering into his spiritual rest just as the people of Israel found the Jordan parted and their inheritance open to them as they crossed over. This entrance takes place when we recognize that Christ is our *All*—our strength, our guidance, our hope, our victory—and although the battle is not over, the anxiety and fear are.

Some people know the exact day on which they were born again. For me it happened on March 5, 1955. Others have just as real an experience, but cannot tell the date of it. They do know it happened. It is the same when we enter this experience of victory—we may not be able to explain it or tell when it happened, but we know that we are in a new relationship to God.

No man can offer truly effective service to the Lord unless he has entered this life of restful trust in God, this victory of the risen Christ. Because then, just as we are truly identified with Christ in his vanquishing of sin and death, so we are identified with him in his risen life. We cease our struggle in self-centered accomplishments and live by the power of Jesus' resurrection. That is real victory.

This is the only way to success in Christian living. It is the way of faith, the same kind of faith that brought us salvation. "The just shall live *by faith*" (Romans 1:17). "As you have therefore received Christ Jesus the Lord, so walk ye in him" (Colossians 2: 6). Then we shall say with Paul, "I live, yet not I, but Christ liveth in me" (Galatians 2:20). When we have entered God's place of rest, we cease from our selfish strivings and the worries that accompany them.

There are times when I have a hundred letters on my desk, many of them about problems. Where should evangelism teams go? Where is the money to support them? How shall we find the vehicles to move teams and literature to their destination? I have learned from 1 Peter 5:7 what to do with them: "Casting all your care upon him; for he careth for you." Sometimes I can say, "Lord, those letters, those telegrams, are all yours. I'm going to bed."

Sleep is a wonderful blessing, and we must not let worry rob us of it. I do not believe in worry because I believe in God's place of rest. I believe that Jesus Christ was crucified for all the worries of the world; if the Lord Jesus did that, then why should I be anxious about them? This applies to every area of life, every frustration, every inferiority feeling, everything that bothers me. All these things cannot defeat me unless I leave the place of rest—my security in Christ.

As Christians, we know that we walk daily in a wilderness world, but the attractions of the wilderness need not walk in us. Whenever they intrude through our eyes or ears or mind, the citizen in the Promised Land must pray: "Lord, I used to enjoy that diversion in slavery, but I have died to that in Christ; hold me in your rest and resurrection life." It is ours for the asking and the trusting.

The Promised Land of rest on this earth is not for sleeping; it is for fighting—but it is the place where you hear God say: "I shall fight for you." Opposition, danger, temptations, and hardships surround you, but your spirit rests in the fortress of God's love and power. Will you choose this sanctuary instead of trying to straddle the Jordan and keep one foot in the world? It's the most important thing you can do in response to this book.

5

front-line **PERILS**

HAVE YOU DECIDED TO WALK THE road of discipleship? Are you determined to follow Christ wherever he leads? Then be prepared for obstruction washouts and falling rocks! For it is absolutely certain that you have a rough road ahead of you.

One of the ways God helps the disciple is to give a glimpse in Scripture of the perils encountered on the way to a victorious Christian life.

> Moreover, brethren, I would not that ye should be ignorant, how that all our fathers were under the cloud, and all passed through the sea; and were all baptized unto Moses in the cloud and in the sea; and did all eat the same spiritual meat; and did all drink the same spiritual drink: for they drank of that spiritual Rock that followed them: and that Rock was Christ.

> But with many of them God was not well pleased: for they were overthrown in the wilderness. Now these things were our examples, to the intent we should not lust after evil things, as they also lusted. Neither be ye idolaters, as were some of them; as it is written, The people sat down to eat and drink, and rose up to play. Neither let us commit fornication, as some of them committed, and fell in one day three and twenty thousand. Neither let us tempt Christ, as some of them also tempted, and were destroyed of serpents. Neither murmur ye, as some of them also murmured, and were destroyed of the destroyer.

> Now all these things happened unto them for ensamples: and they are written for our admonition, upon whom the ends of the world are come. Wherefore let him that thinketh he standeth take heed lest he fall. There hath no temptation taken you but such as is

common to man: but God is faithful, who will not suffer you to be
tempted above that ye are able; but will with the temptation also
make a way to escape, that ye may be able to bear it. (1 Corinthians
10:1–13)

Notice particularly that Paul says these experiences are examples "for our admonition." He is warning about the many hazards
that beset Christians. Although these Israelites shared in God's
revelation of power to Moses in the pillar-cloud and the retreating
sea, and though they received the same spiritual sustenance, they
failed to pass the stern tests that Moses overcame. In a similar
way, the Christian leaves Egypt—the world—and crosses the Red
Sea—which speaks, I believe, of salvation. He begins to sing of
his liberation, just as the Israelites did when they saw the Red Sea
rolled back and the enemy wiped out behind them. But he fails to
realize that mighty enemies are still ahead.

Ancient Simeon Stylites lived on top of a flag pole for thirty
years, yet he did not escape trials. You may isolate yourself anywhere and still face conflicts. Why? Because the enemy roves
within you. The people of Israel fled from the giants of Canaan
but suffered defeat after defeat in the deserted wilderness. Only
Joshua and Caleb survived of the pioneer travelers because they
trusted in God.

These two men illustrate the reality of heart commitment to
God. They could easily have differed with each other, but their
hearts were right with God. Caleb, for example, said, "Let us go
up at once, and occupy it; for we are well able to overcome it."
Some observers might have accused him of self-confidence, but
God knew his faithful intention. Joshua focused his words on
God: "If the Lord delights in us, he will bring us into this land and
give it to us."

What thrills me is that both men walked with God, both entered
the Promised Land, and both were richly blessed. They did not
judge the other's motives by a variation in terminology. And neither should we. A young Christian with wrong vocabulary and ill-
expressed doctrine may actually be trusting in the work of Christ
more than Mr. Deeper-Life who has it all turned out to the last

syllable. Caleb's and Joshua's key to entry into Canaan was the same: their sincere, persevering response to God's promise.

I believe the land of Canaan speaks of the Christian's victorious life. The salvation of God has taken us across "Jordan," but most Christians languish on the border of the Promised Land. We stubbornly disbelieve the mountain ascent will bring us to our inheritance, and we hide among the rocks in the valley.

We must go on, though we are not entering a picnic ground or holiday camp when we cross Jordan. Battles, struggles, trials, and defeats are ahead in the Promised Land, but so are victory and joy and power. After truly entering this land, you will know more of God's fullness and power, thrilling answers to prayer, and intimacy of true discipleship. Yet you will be amazed that the battle can be so fierce. At times there may be no more than bare necessities supplied. Here we realize we are in a fight to the finish with sin, self, and Satan.

The realization that we are involved in a constant spiritual warfare can be a great source of strength and comfort. When some difficult situation arises or fiery darts from Satan pierce us, we realize that this is part of God's wonderful plan for us. My wife and I can testify that it is doing wonders for us in our married life. Friends often give advice: "You should do this . . ."; "All parents do that . . ."; but we are able to go on our knees and say, "That's right, Lord, in times of peace, but this is war!"

We are helped when we reflect on this century's two world wars. Think of the demands made upon young men; think of the anxieties suffered by wives and children. And we have been given the privilege of fighting in the battlefield alongside the Lord of glory, the Captain of our salvation. What sacrifice can be too great for him? Compared with what Christ did on the cross for us, our service for God is nothing.

Someone has said, "The devil doesn't waste his fiery darts on nominal Christians." The history of war confirms that armies make opposing leaders their targets. Satan uses the same tactics. He does not waste time on those who are not counting for God; he aims for the active disciple. When the devil sees someone steadfastly following Christ, he goes into a strategy meeting with the demons of hell and together they plan a fullscale attack. If we understand something of the enemy's movements and are armed against them, we shall not be caught unawares.

Two tactics we are told to use against the devil are to resist and to run. I have always been a better "runner" than "resister," but I want to learn more about resisting in God's strength. The Word of God tells us to "flee" Satan's temptations (2 Timothy 2:22). It says to resist him, not in our own power, but in the power of the cross of Christ (James 4:7). The atoning blood of Jesus Christ removes the guilt of our sin, and the cross severs Satan's control over us. The crucified life of a disciple is maintained only as other camouflaged perils are recognized and avoided.

The first is pride. The Word of God says, "Pride goeth before destruction" (Proverbs 16:18). We need to ask God to search our hearts and root out this subtle peril that has time and again ruined Christian men. I have seen young men, dedicated, zealous, filled with the Spirit, and seemingly being used by God, become totally ineffective because of pride. They have seen answers to prayer and are sure they are getting through to God. Or they have been greatly used by God in the salvation of souls. Or they have been told that they are exceptionally gifted in some way. Then spiritual conceit invades and takes over.

One mark of spiritual and emotional stability is to remain unaffected by commendation. Such a person can take the praise and honor of men realistically. He knows where the true honor is due.

The unstable person receives praise and clutches it protectively. If he is told he is weak in a particular area, he will nurse the memory of someone telling him this was his strong point! A balanced Christian knows how to accept the praise of men with diffidence and to welcome their criticism with concern. When you begin to accomplish something for God, watch for pride to follow and repent of it before the cross.

There is a kind of pride that elevates us while debasing others. We must be careful of criticizing Christians for not having attained something spiritual which we believe we have gained. But we have not gained it if we indeed do possess it; we have received it from God.

It helps me sometimes to think what I will be like forty years from now: will I preach with as much zeal, as much urgency, as much exercise of spirit as now? I can't know, and I must be careful what I say about others.

Someone has pointed out to me that the defects which we sometimes see and judge in others may be battle-scars suffered in faithful service to Christ. Perhaps the Christian has seen more and harder battles than we. He may have won many battles, but not without scars and wounds in the process.

We might consider older men of God old-fashioned and short on zeal. Younger Christians must show mercy to the older generation, and I ask them in return to have mercy in their dealings with us. God wants both the older and younger generations to realize neither would be anything without Christ and his grace.

The kindred peril to pride is a critical spirit. It seems easy to see distinctly everything that is wrong with other people. But psychologists tell us that the things we most readily criticize in others are sometimes things which are wrong in our own lives. This is called projection, and some Christians unwittingly specialize in it.

When I tested myself on this, the results scared me. If, day in and day out, I was seeing something wrong in other people, was it really a reflection of some weakness in my own personality or habits? I saw others' inconsistencies so readily. One man tended to be superficial; another seemed to say things that he did not mean; a third was weak on economizing time. But could it be true that these weaknesses supposedly contrasted with my strengths, but the comparison was neither fair nor kind?

Paul instructed Christians in Philippians 4 to think positively:

> Finally, brethren, whatsoever things are true, whatsoever things are honest, whatsoever things are just, whatsoever things are pure, whatsoever things are lovely, whatsoever things are of good report; if there be any virtue, and if there be any praise, think on these things.

I believe this represents part of the revolution in men's lives that Christ came to bring. It is a revolution that replaces complaint with wholesome and affirmative thinking, a revolution that passes over people's mistakes and follies to bring God's light and love on the scene.

One time I was running to catch a train in Stockholm, and hot criticism welled up within me against the brother who had mixed up the schedule and got me to the station ten minutes after the train was due to leave. "Why cannot people who have lived in Stockholm all their lives read their timetables?" I thought to myself. I wanted to get to Gothenberg the next morning in order to investigate a ship that might serve our goal of world evangelism.

I left the station, battling with myself, until the Lord brought Romans 8:28 to my mind. Some might say that this verse is a "crutch" for the crippled, but I was feeling crippled as I sought victory over the feelings in my heart. I leaned on the promise: "All things work together for good to them that love God, to them who are the called according to his purpose." And in faith I was able to praise God that I did not catch the train.

That night the train I had missed crashed. I offer no explanation for the crash, but I learned to be more careful about concluding that disappointing events are mistakes. We make mistakes, but our God does not. And with infinite patience and foresight, he specializes in overruling ours.

The Bible tells us God has entrusted the treasures of the Holy Spirit to the clay pots of our bodies as containers. In our work for the Lord, we often mess up his purpose. There are times when I could weep for marring the wonder of his truth with my corroded personality, my beat-up pot. But God's sovereign power overrules and makes the crudest, weakest, lowliest, most out-of-place testimony for him count for eternity.

If we have a greater vision of our sovereign God, our negativeness and criticism would diminish or vanish. When we fully realize that our human leaders are learners like the rest of us, we can concentrate on God and be delivered from a critical spirit.

Another peril to the victorious Christian is becoming accustomed to spiritual things. As we see the power of God at work, answering prayer and accomplishing the impossible in people's lives, we may find ourselves being callous about the miraculous.

A team working in Operation Mobilization met for prayer in Zaventem, Belgium, and quite a few stayed to pray until 3 a.m. The financial needs of the work were acute, and God stirred us to a great exercise of faith. When we went to bed, we had a thrilling consciousness that God was going to work. The next morning, I had to phone our central office in England for some other business. On the phone someone asked me if I had heard about the large gift which had come from another country. The telegram announcing the gift had come into our office that very day. The amount was some $6,000. The money did not come from someone who was stirred up in the prayer meeting, but from someone thousands of miles away, who had sent it sometime earlier. We have seen things like this happen for over a decade, and we simply praise God for his answers to prayer. But there is a grave danger of becoming familiar with the miraculous, casual about God moving in wonderful ways.

The Bible says that there is rejoicing in the presence of the angels over one soul that repents, but sometimes we do not rejoice unless it is a dozen. I remember at Bible College when I went out and was able to help someone find Christ. I really got excited and would barge into a fellow student's room bubbling with joy. "Come on, drop your work. Let's have a prayer meeting, brother. Let's give up some time to praise the Lord." A week later, another brother would come to see me. He was not as loudmouthed as I: "Praise the Lord, George; a fellow down the street accepted Christ tonight." What was my reaction? "Oh, praise God; that's good. Amen." And back I went to my studies. May God forgive us for letting ourselves become over-familiar with holy things, or rejoice over our victory and not over that of the other fellow.

Such familiarity can be heartbreaking in gatherings of God's people. Sometimes we meet around the Lord's Table to remember his death, and there is less praise among us than if we shared a meal of ham and eggs after a long night. The Israelites in the wil-

derness took God's miracles for granted: they became accustomed
to manna and craved meat. God gave them the meat they desired,
and leanness filled their souls. It can happen to us, too.

Another peril of the Christian life is asceticism. If we seek
hardship because it builds our reputation, we are not suffering for
Christ's sake. An example of this was a young man on a witnessing tour who was invited to stay overnight at a Christian home
where the hostess went to a lot of trouble to prepare a comfortable
bed. The young man stiffened proudly and announced that he no
longer slept in beds. He had forgotten—or had never learned—
that Paul knew how both to be abased and to abound. This balance
is difficult, but it is possible as we make love our way and Christ
our goal.

Asceticism is not nearly such a problem as its opposite—laziness and the love of ease. This is one of the most deadly perils
for a Christian in the position of independent responsibility.
Discipline is good for us, and laziness is a great sin. One reason
the Church lacks foot soldiers is that it lacks people who want to
work hard. Nehemiah's men finished their task because they had
a "mind to work." When the pressures of duties relax, laziness
becomes a tremendous danger to many Christians.

Then there is the serious peril of disqualification. When God
begins to use you significantly, the devil closes in to discover
some flaw that he can exploit and scandalize. Evangelist Alan
Redpath has pointed out that King David's sin with Bathsheba
was preceded by his sinful withdrawal from battle. While his
troops were fighting the enemy, he was at leisure, and his relaxation physically and spiritually opened him to the whirlwind of
temptation that swept him into sinful lust and God's judgment.

This illustrates the peril of being away from the place God has
called us to, of breaking communion with the Lord Jesus Christ,
of self-indulgence, and of arrogant criticism. These give Satan his
chance to invade our spirit and inflame sin that will dishonor God
and ruin our testimony. Though the sin can be forgiven, the consequences may hinder the gospel for years.

Perils still beset the Christian living in the Promised Land,

and we must be aware of them. We must remember the warning in 1 Corinthians 10:12: "Let him that thinketh he standeth take heed lest he fall." God's provision for us amid the dangers is constant: There hath no temptation taken you but such as is common to man: but God is faithful . . . he will make a way of escape" (10:13). Choose it, and God's grace will bring victory.

6

LOVE *that* CONQUERS

IN JOHN 13:34–35 WE READ THESE words of Jesus: "A new commandment I give unto you, That you love one another; as I have loved you, that you also love one another. By this shall all men know that you are my disciples, if you have love one to another." This is the touchstone of Christianity and the dynamic of the revolution that was begun by Jesus Christ himself.

Some Christians seem to have misread this verse. They apparently see: "By this shall all men know that you are my disciples, that you have no possessions," or ". . . that you read and carry your Bibles," or perhaps ". . . that you have sound doctrine," or maybe that ". . . you traverse land and sea to win converts to Christ."

But Jesus said none of those things. He said that there is one major thing that will convince the world we are his disciples, and that is the love we have for one another. We are not the disciples of a theory or doctrine or institution, but disciples of the loving Jesus! His love led Jesus to give his life for us, and that kind of love is commanded between Jesus' followers.

People sometimes ask me, "How do you conceive of the love of God?" My answer is found in 1 John 3:16: "In this we perceive the love of God, in that he laid down his life for us." As a consequence, says John, "So we ought to lay down our lives for the brethren." This is the supreme love, Jesus told us, for "greater love has no man than this, that a man lay down his life for his friends" (John 15:13).

Love is the essence of discipleship: it is the wall that surrounds a disciple, the roof that protects him, and the ground which supports him. The Bible says emphatically that though I speak with tongues of men and of angels, have all wisdom, make tremendous sacrifices, give my body to be burned, and relinquish all I own, I am worth nothing if I have not done them in love.

Most of us have to admit that we know very little about actually loving people. We know that we have often loved because of the benefits that come to us. Divine love is impartial; it loves the repulsive and the attractive, the beggar and the merchant prince.

Is this love really possible? And does it work? When I give myself for the sake of another, when I "fall into the ground and die" in order to bear fruit, when I deny myself and take up the cross and follow Jesus—does it make a revolutionary difference? Or would it turn me into a blind fanatic rushing from one good deed to another and getting trampled by the strong?

This love is possible, and it is very practical. It does not come naturally, nor does it come instantly in a rededication service or some particular experience. Real love comes from God, who is love, and it is developed in the hard school of life over many years. There may be a crisis of appropriating God's love, but a process of expressing love follows or it all becomes an abscess.

The Bible speaks clearly on how to acquire and develop God's love. The first thing it tells me is that love is a fruit of the Spirit (Galatians 5:22). As every Christian has the Spirit, every Christian may have this love. Ephesians 5:18 gives one of the few commands about the Holy Spirit in the New Testament: "Be not drunk with wine, wherein is excess; but be filled with the Spirit." The filling produces an overflow that touches other people.

What are evidences of the filling of the Spirit? "Speaking to [among] yourselves in psalms and hymns and spiritual songs." This is joy and encouragement shared with other Christians. And it also communicates with God: "singing and making melody in your hearts to the Lord; giving thanks always for all things." These signs accompany the love given by the Holy Spirit.

The Scriptures also teach that prayer will develop this love. Paul is our example: "I bow my knees unto the Father of our Lord Jesus Christ . . . that he would grant you . . . to be strengthened by his Spirit . . . and to know the love of Christ, which passeth knowledge" (Ephesians 3:14, 16, 19).

As the Lord blesses the person prayed for, he will also work in your heart. We are sometimes partly responsible for others' weaknesses, and weaknesses in a brother's life may reflect weaknesses in our own. If I have been spiritually discerning of something wrong, through prayer I can help to change it. Let us pray earnestly for the people we do not like or do not understand, and God will make changes in the situation. We have many examples of this in Scripture, and we are exhorted to pray for all men, even our enemies, said the Lord Jesus.

Another helpful step is to pray with the person concerned. If you are having trouble with someone in your church or group, try to pray with him about various needs and joys. This effort to share and understand will be rewarded by fellowship and a growing love.

The love of God believes the best about people, and discounts adverse reports and rumors. Love sympathizes and assists. Perhaps there are intense problems handicapping the person. Poor health may be dragging him down. Background environment or heredity may still control the individual. Prayer together can open the channel of love and wisdom from God to both.

Belief in the sovereignty of God enables us to rest in the confidence that he is in charge of all that is going on in the earth. Sometimes the devil seems menacingly near, but he is weak in comparison with the God who is in charge of our lives. Though Satan makes headway, he cannot overcome the Christian who is trusting God. He can say, "The Lord is in this," and look for the Lord's way out. Philippians 1:6 assures us that God has begun his work in us, and he will complete it.

Another step that develops love is personal interest in the welfare of others. This is shown by both words and deeds. Sincere attention builds a bond that involves us in others' lives. If someone's personality rubs against yours, ask questions about your common concerns and look for things to compliment. You'll find love sprouting from the interest, and you may receive love in return.

Some of us find it easy to make fun of people: the shape of their ears, the style of clothes, or the odd mannerisms. Jokes about others are good fun unless they wound the victim. Amy Carmichael said:

> If I enjoy a joke at the expense of another, if I can in any way slight another in conversation or even in thought, then I know nothing of Calvary love. If I belittle those whom I am called to serve, talk of their weak points in contrast to what I think are my strong points; if I adopt a superior attitude, forgetting, "Who made thee to differ? What hast thou that thou didst not receive?" then I know nothing of Calvary love.[6]

Another stimulus to love is to give something to another. There is a story of a husband and wife whose marriage was on the rocks. The husband never remembered anniversaries or birthdays, and he was always complaining. She became more and more discouraged. One day he inexplicably decided to bring her some flowers. It was so unusual that when he came to the door and held out the flowers she wept hysterically. "What a miserable day!" she moaned. "I've been having trouble with the children all day, the clothes washer broke, I burned the supper, and now you've come home drunk!" Don't wait so long to rebuild a relationship that your gift can't be believed! Give something of practical help or a memento that shows you care.

How blind we sometimes are to the plain words of Scripture! Jesus commanded the help of his people to one another by saying: "Inasmuch as ye have done it unto one of the least of these my brethren, ye have done it unto me" (Matthew 25:40). This is a revolutionary passage of Scripture, and if we let it penetrate our minds daily, it would change our lives. Our attitude toward the weak and the needy, God says, reveals our attitude to his Son. This should lead us to repentance. "He who loves not his brother whom he has seen, how can he love God whom he has not seen?" (1 John 4:20)

And have we forgotten what is called the Golden Rule? "Therefore all things whatsoever ye would that men should do to you, do ye even so unto them: for this is the law and the prophets" (Matthew 7:12). This verse offers us a simple check on our speaking or acting: Would I enjoy this if it were directed at me? This would eliminate cruel gossip and destructive criticism and would spare us from future judgment

The Bible tells us we are to correct someone in the spirit of love when it is necessary. "Brethren, if a man be overtaken in a fault, ye which are spiritual"—which excludes quite a few Christians—"restore such an one in the spirit of meekness; considering thyself, lest thou also be tempted" (Galatlans 6:1). Amy Carmichael wrote: "If we can go to someone to correct them without a pang in our hearts, then we know nothing of Calvary love." The love depicted in 1 Corinthians 13 allows no rejoicing hearts over the failure of another person. Love never speaks with the attitude: "I told you so; you should have listened to me!" It sorrows with those who mourn, and lifts up those who fall.

In his love, God can transform sorrows and failure, so we can help and comfort others. God, says Paul, "comforteth us in all our tribulation, that we may be able to comfort them which are in any trouble, by the comfort wherewith we ourselves are comforted of God" (2 Corinthians 1:4). How can a woman who has had four children, with no complications at birth and no problems as they have grown up, help a woman who has had three still births and now has a handicapped child? She has not been prepared for this opportunity. But a woman who has lost a child herself or has suffered deeply in some other way can communicate the love of God that she has experienced. She may speak directly, but with compassion, to the sufferer.

To rebuke and exhort another Christian is one of the hardest things to do properly. It is easier to overlook the fault, but love must correct at times. Amy Carmichael comments: "If I'm afraid to speak the truth lest I lose affection or lest the one concerned should say, 'You do not understand,' or because I fear to lose my reputation for kindness; if I put my own name before the other's highest good, then I know nothing of Calvary love."

Love acts. When I see a little child running toward a busy

street, I do not just stand there and suggest: "Wouldn't it be better to stay on the pavement?" I move into action. I grab the child back from the street in order that its life may be saved. The Bible says that we are to snatch men from the fire of hell. To think such action too drastic is a misconception of love.

The love of Jesus was not of the Hollywood variety. His love led him to serve. I believe it was also love that sent Jesus into the Temple to clean up the mercenary mess there and to chase out the greedy merchants with violence. It was love for righteousness; it was love for those who were being cheated. His love led to action all through his life.

Love grows—when it is exercised. Supplying all-conquering love is God's part; expressing love is our part. As we walk with God, he will make us confident "of this very thing, that he which hath begun a good work in you will perform it until the day of Jesus Christ" (Philippians 1:6). And God will work in the lives of others by love, for his perfect love never fails.

7

WHEN *I am weak . . .*

MANY YOUNG PEOPLE BEGIN CHRISTIAN service believing that they are dedicated and keen Christians. They have been encouraged to think so by their complimentary friends or church officers. And perhaps they did rise above the average Christian in their surroundings. But service on the firing line makes them more and more conscious of Jesus' words: "Without me you can do nothing" (John 15:5).

All Christian workers come eventually—if they are honest—to the place where they can no longer casually affirm their dedication to the Lord. They realize only too well that they are not Hudson Taylor or George Müller or C. T. Studd. The result may be extreme depression: since great exploits constantly elude them, they may conclude that there is no hope for them.

There is an antidote for this. Robert Murray M'Cheyne once said that for every look he took at himself, he took ten looks at the Lord Jesus. He had abandoned hope in himself, but his hope in Christ was boundless. For M'Cheyne and for us, total failure may be necessary to bring us to the realization our only hope is in Jesus. And it is not Jesus plus money, or Jesus plus an efficient organization, or the proper equipment, but only Jesus.

Thanks to the Apostle Paul, we have an example who has proved this way to victory: "And he said unto me, My grace is sufficient for thee: for my strength is made perfect in weakness. Most gladly therefore will I rather glory in my infirmities, that the power of Christ may rest upon me" (2 Corinthians 12:9).

When you are in a tight situation, when the demons of discord, criticism, misunderstanding, and confusion maul you in a pressure cooker, remember those words: "My grace is sufficient for thee." Without this knowledge and confidence, you cannot survive the warfare that awaits the disciple of Christ.

Can the cost of Christian warfare be less than that of nations in conflict? If it is, it is not warfare. Alexander Duff, the Scottish saint of God, knew the cost. Weeping as he faced a crowd, he asked if Scotland had any more sons to give. "When Queen Victoria calls for volunteers for India, hundreds respond," he reminded them. "But when King Jesus calls, no one goes." The silence was deafening. "If there is no one who will go," he continued, "then I will return. I will return and lay my bones by the Ganges, that India may know that Scotland has at least one who cares."

Whether we remain at home or go abroad, Christ's claim upon our lives is a call to battle. The enemy is powerful; he is dragging and tricking souls into hell; he is devastating the hopes and plans of men on earth. Yet Jesus can defeat him through any Christian who puts on the spiritual armor (Ephesians 6:11–18). Our hope, then, is in the all-sufficient Lord Jesus, not in ourselves. Whatever the circumstances, "My grace is sufficient for thee," promised God.

Someone has said that "grace is God's riches at Christ's expense." This definition underlines the great gift imparted to us by Christ. It is the riches of the infinite God, inherited through the death and resurrection of his Son. It is all too easy to become indifferent to what Jesus did on the cross. It is all too possible to gather thoughtlessly around the Lord's Table. When this happens, we void the riches of the grace of God.

There is another way of voiding God's grace: by underrating it. If we get to the point of desperation and say, "O God, what's the use? I can't go any further—and you can't help me, either," we deny the grace of God. And just at that moment, we could discover his grace, his sufficiency, his life, and his power are available to take us through. This is tragic and sinful.

The demands and standards of Christ are admittedly extreme— in fact, impossible. But Jesus does not ask us to live the Christian life; he asks us to let him live it in us. There was no grace for the self-righteous man who prayed, "Thank you, Lord, that I'm not like the rest." But there was grace for the man who wept, "I'm a sinner; Lord, have mercy on me!" The complete sufficiency of the Lord Jesus Christ makes up for our deficiency. We cannot earn his grace; we can get it only by coming empty to the cross.

Paul speaks an amazing truth in Colossians 2:9–10: "For in him (Christ) dwelleth all the fullness of the Godhead bodily. And you are complete in him." Complete! Do we realize this when we strive to build a reputation? Do we realize it when someone deprives us of recognition? Do we realize it when we feel uncomfortable in a group? Perhaps we feel worse when we suffer persecution or ill health for serving God. Or we may languish in jail for righteousness' sake. Our plans fail; our witness is rejected. How do we feel then?

You are complete in Christ! Our completeness is not in Christ plus friends, Christ plus service, Christ plus position, Christ plus converts. We are complete only in Jesus! In him is all the fullness, so Jesus is all that we need. Everything else may fail us; Jesus will never leave nor forsake us.

Whatever arises that might discourage us, we can echo with the conviction of Paul: Jesus is sufficient for that, too. The question is not in his sufficiency, but only in our trusting him. We cannot go on, we just will not make it. We may want to quit: the Lord is asking too much of us. Each time, *he is sufficient.* He says to us, "You are complete in me." We have been made acceptable to God in Christ the Beloved One.

We all seek acceptance; all of us want to be needed, liked, cared for. If we expect we are going to meet the ideal husband or wife to meet those needs, we are going to be disappointed. Not even a husband or wife can fulfill our heart's deepest longings, because we were made for God. Only he can reach down and fill that deep void; only he can satisfy.

In Jesus Christ, we have been accepted by God *now.* We have been accepted, not by some social group, but by the infinite *God.* We have been accepted, not in our spotted virtue, but in the perfect Lord Jesus Christ. With this confidence motivating us, nothing in the heights or depths, in life or death, nor in the whole universe can stop us, for nothing can withstand him. His grace, abundant and overflowing, is ours—if we will receive it.

8

STEPS *to* REVOLUTION

HAVING READ THESE PAGES, you might be asking yourself: "What do I do next?" To read about the all-sufficiency of Jesus Christ is one thing; to obtain and experience it in your own life is another.

More than anything, this book is a plea and a guide for reality in the Christian life. The standard of vital Christianity described in these pages will not be reached easily. It will not occur through a short prayer of commitment or by any kind of crisis experience. God may use a crisis to jolt a Christian into action, but *a crisis plus a process* is necessary to keep him moving as a revolutionary disciple of Jesus Christ.

If this book is to be significant to you, you must declare a *personal revolution*. This will take all your dedication and the application of every means of grace offered in the Word of God. There cannot be a revolution for those who merely "play the game" or go through the motions. Nor is revolution possible for the Christian who is not willing to deny self, take up his cross daily, and follow Jesus.

We are not ready for revolution if we have not yet seen the spiritual schizophrenia within and around us. God must convince us that "the heart is deceitful above all things, and desperately wicked." Spiritual fog seeps into our hearts from the world, and only God can dispel it in response to earnest prayer.

To be ready for revolution, we must accept the blame for not living a dynamic Christian life. Christ lives within the Christian, and *he* is the revolutionary. We must be willing to die to self-interests and self-determination and let Christ live his life through us.

Many Christians are entering the ministry and the mission fields and other places of Christian service without being spiritually prepared. We must realize that we are in dangerous territory if our service for God is taking us beyond our experience of God. Satan waits there to attack us—and we are very vulnerable. The revolutionary spiritual life issues from a deep relationship and experience with God, who makes the disciple a faithful soldier of Christ.

I am absolutely convinced that Christians who take the following steps to revolution will find that they "work." They work because Christianity works. These steps are basic biblical principles which Jesus Christ and the apostles repeatedly emphasized to those who wanted to be disciples of Jesus.

1. *A Revolution in Our Prayer Life.* One of the most depressing signs in the Church today is the lack of prayer, both in private and in groups. It is almost incredible to see how little the average evangelical church relies on prayer for doing God's work.

When there is a prayer meeting, a small minority of the people are involved. Nights of prayer, home prayer meetings, days of prayer and fasting—so much a part of the early Church—seem nothing more than Christian relics today. Because people are busy, they think they are too busy to pray. The Church has sought innumerable substitutes for prayer to accomplish work that can be done *only* through prayer.

If we are serious about being spiritual revolutionaries, we must determine to learn how to pray. There are many excellent books on the subject, but there is no substitute for getting on our knees and starting to pray. Samuel Chadwick said, "The one concern of the devil is to keep the saints from prayer. He fears nothing from prayerless studies, prayerless work, prayerless religion. He laughs at our toil, mocks at our wisdom, but trembles when we pray."

The mountain peak of our prayer life will be worship. Specific times should be given each day to climbing the summit of spiritual reality through worship, praise, and thanksgiving. King David declared, "I will praise the name of God with a song, and will magnify him with thanksgiving. This also shall please the LORD better than an ox or bullock that hath horns and hoofs" (Psalm 69:30–31).

Reality in worship will create a spiritual revolution in the inner man, the likes of which few people seem to have experienced in the twentieth century. It will not be attained in a year or two, nor perhaps in ten or twenty years. However, since this is the highest calling of the Christian, it is worth any number of years to learn reality in daily worship. There is no more important aspect of spiritual revolution than this.

There is a sense in which we can "pray without ceasing" and offer prayer and praise to God at any time of the day. Yet there is also a need for separating ourselves from other humans and being alone with God. The entire Church and the cause of Christ around the world is suffering for lack of this kind of prayer. If the only response made to this book were a determination to take a definite time each day for prayer, praise, and feasting on God's Word, the book would be eminently successful. For through prayer, we can come to see the other principles of spiritual revolution which will lead us from victory to victory as God's Word is mixed with our faith.

2. A Revolution in Our Bible Study. At any cost, spiritual revolutionaries must become "men of the Book." D. L. Moody declared, "Either sin will keep you from this Book, or this Book will keep you from sin." Most Christians place a low value on memorizing and meditating on the Word of God. In contrast, Muslims by the thousands leave their universities with the whole Koran memorized. Actors and actresses memorize thousands of lines to earn fame and wealth. Despite the spiritual rewards promised for students of God's Word, few Christians seek them. The result is churches peopled by spiritual dwarfs, some having been "growing" ten or twenty years in the faith.

In some cases spiritual dwarfs become leaders of the congregation, and the contrast with New Testament churches is shocking. If anyone points this out, he is regarded as a fanatic, an extremist, or a meddler.

On the other hand, I have found increasing numbers of believers around the world who are tired of eating spiritual breadcrumbs and want to get into God's Word in a new and revolutionary way. The important thing, however, is not so much our "getting into the Word of God" as "the Word of God getting into us." This means we must engage in more than Bible reading; we must meditate intensively on the Word of God, as the Psalmist instructs in 119:9, 11.

Our Bible study must be as honest and unprejudiced as possible. We cannot come to the Word of God with our favorite viewpoint and expect the Bible to shed new light. We must come to the Scriptures in humility and openness, and attempt to obey in our daily living each truth we find there.

An evangelist has warned: "We have taken the Word of God, the Sword of the Spirit, and used it to carve one another up instead of going forth in a great offensive in the name of Christ." How much easier it is to go to war over pet doctrines and favorite verses rather than continuing to receive the whole counsel of God, and advancing against the enemy.

We must not only determine to obey those verses we enjoy, or that strike us as being important, but we must be ready to obey verses that sometimes strike us in the opposite way.

We are sometimes eager to accept those verses that speak about blessing and to neglect verses that speak about suffering. We welcome the first part of 1 John 3:16, "Hereby perceive we the love of God, because he laid down his life for us"—and the rest trails through and out of our consciousness: ". . .and we ought to lay down our lives for the brethren." The next admonition also gets scant attention: "But whoso hath this world's good, and seeth his brother have need, and shutteth up his bowels of compassion from him, how dwelleth the love of God in him?"

This is also God's Word! What excuse do we have for our failure to love not merely in word but in deed and in truth? Obedience here is revolution.

3. *A Revolution of Discipline.* For many, discipline is an unpleasant word. Yet church history shows no undisciplined man or woman who amounted to much for Christ. The basic support of discipline is motivation, and the best motivation is the constrain-

ing love of Christ.

Christ said, "If ye love me, keep my commandments." He also said, "If ye continue in my words, then are ye my disciples indeed." This is critical, as we can realize from Paul's concern in 1 Corinthians 9:26–27: "I therefore so run, not as uncertainly; so fight I, not as one that beateth the air: but I keep under my body, and bring it into subjection: lest that by any means, when I have preached to others, I myself should be a castaway." Paul was disciplined, but he recognized the danger of slipping and falling into sin.

True discipline is possible only because of the promises of God. We find ourselves unable to keep a particular commandment or engage in a form of self-discipline, but we can be sustained by such a promise as: "I can do all things through Christ which strengtheneth me" (Philippians 4:13). For every battle and difficulty in life, there is an assurance of God's grace and sufficiency we can claim.

We are hearing more and more in Christian circles about a victorious life being attained through a particular sanctification theory or crisis experience which launches an effortless joyride with God. But for every Bible verse that speaks of rest, abiding, trusting, and allowing God to work through you there is another word nearby that speaks of battle, testing, obedience, and the need to present our bodies as a living sacrifice to do God's will. These are complementary and essential for the balanced life.

We do not pit Joshua against Caleb because they used different terminology and concepts to challenge the people to enter the Promised Land. The spiritual revolutionary learns the balance between God's action and his own. He depends on God's strength and wisdom to work out the salvation life within him.

For example, if you lie in bed tomorrow morning and pray that the Lord will lift you out of bed, you are likely to have a very late breakfast. The recital of "Not I, but Christ" will bring about few changes unless you *move*. But when you move, the recognition of "Not I, but Christ" will produce eternal results by God's Spirit.

One of the important disciplines is repentance. When we sin

or fail, we can recover and go on if we immediately find forgiveness at the cross. Many a Christian has languished in depression and defeat because he hadn't learned the discipline of repentance. Not even Jesus Christ "felt" like going to the cross, but he went because he loved us and was obedient to the will of God. We may not "feel" like going to the cross, but we will because of our love for Christ. There we receive total forgiveness and joyous renewal that will enable us to live in discipline.

4. *A Revolution of Love*. Jesus Christ said that people would know Christians were his disciples because of their *love* for one another. The greatest indictment of evangelical Christianity is that Christians have failed to have this kind of love. Yet when I have seen this love in a few Christians, it has impressed me as the expression of genuine Christianity.

It is amazing to see how the Lord Jesus Christ can change an unloving, lost soul. In country after country, I have seen the power of this revolution of love. If more of us would enter in and fan the flames of this love, I believe we would see spiritual revolution around the world in our generation. This does not necessarily mean the conversion of masses of people, but rather individuals everywhere transformed by the revolutionary principles of the New Testament and living them before others.

Unless we "declare a revolution" in the areas of life already mentioned, however, we will not see a revolution of love. For it is only as we get to know God at a deep level and trust Christ to work through us that we can receive and demonstrate revolutionary love. Until we do experience this love, the spiritual revolution will not reach very far.

Nothing obstructs revolutionary Christianity like the opposite of love: resentment, envy, anger, fear, jealousy, and hatred. The mutual toleration evidenced in handshakes after the typical Sunday morning church service also falls far short of the revolutionary love that unites brethren in dynamic fellowship. Yet a greater display of interest in one another is not the real answer; revolutionary love is the outcome of obedience to and communion with Christ.

The greatest possible impact on the world would be made if Christians of many races, backgrounds, churches, and temperaments were working together in love and harmony with Jesus as King and Lord. The Bible says, "Love casteth out fear," and we could move forward on that promise, finding that divine love would cast fear out of our hearts—the fear of people we do not understand, who are from a different race, or who worship differently. We must break out of our cliques and work with all of God's people. We must unite under the banner of Christ's love and the cardinal doctrines and principles of New Testament Christianity. The pride that scorns Christians outside "our group" will have to die at the cross before we can join in revolution. If any of us has received more light, exercised more gifts, or been granted more recognition, it should be demonstrated by more humility and more love.

This is the essential principle of Christian living and spiritual revolution; without it, there is no power.

5. *A Revolution of Honesty.* Spiritual honesty is one of our greatest needs. We evangelicals have grown accustomed to our religious masks, pretending to be one thing while living quite another. It has continued so long that we hardly know now where reality is. Can you imagine what a revolution of honesty would do in our churches? If we were honest, many of us would have to change the words of "Onward Christian Soldiers" in somewhat the following manner:

> Backward Christian soldiers, fleeing from the fight,
> With the cross of Jesus nearly out of sight:
> Christ our rightful Master stands against the foe,
> But forward into battle we are loathe to go.

> Like a mighty tortoise moves the Church of God;
> Brothers, we are treading where we've often trod,
> We are much divided, many bodies we,
> Having different doctrines, not much charity.

Crowns and thrones may perish, kingdoms rise and wane,
But the Church of Jesus hidden does remain;
Gates of hell should never against that Church prevail,
We have Christ's own promise, but think that it will fail.

Sit here, then, ye people, join our useless throngs;
Blend with ours your voices in a feeble song.
Blessings, ease and comfort, ask from Christ the King,
With our modern thinking, we won't do a thing.

These words might seem harsh, but you will find stronger words
in the New Testament. "I know thy works, that thou art neither
cold nor hot: I would thou wert cold or hot. So then because thou
art lukewarm, and neither cold nor hot, I will spew thee out of my
mouth. Because thou sayest, I am rich, and increased with goods,
and have need of nothing; and knowest not that thou art wretched,
and miserable, and poor, and blind, and naked" (Revelation
3:15–17).

We must declare war on that kind of self-deception described
in these verses. To do this, we must determine to become spiritually honest. We must face ourselves as we are, and we must allow God to begin to bring revolutionary changes. Many of us are
trying to live at a particular spiritual level when we know we are
nowhere near it! This leads to all kinds of unreality, confusion,
and sometimes even to nervous breakdown.

Sometimes the Christian most anxious to improve his spiritual
life ends up with the greatest problems—because he tries to make
the changes himself. The need is not for spiritual extremists,
but for spiritual revolutionaries who know the reality of spiritual balance. The spiritual revolutionary knows that according to
Ephesians 1:6 he is fully accepted in the Beloved, and therefore
he ceases striving to gain merit through his spiritual activity. He
recognizes that he is a sinner, but in Christ he is a victor.

Christian leaders may fall into this trap quicker than the average Christian. When Christians make heroes of leaders, they may
feel forced to act out their roles while despising their hypocrisy. It
is a very unhealthy and precarious route to follow.

One of the reasons many Christian young people forsake the church and their parents is widespread spiritual pretense. A normal young person understands failures are inevitable, but continual inconsistency and spiritual dishonesty deeply confuse him. Some are so repelled by the double life that they "drop out." They would rather befriend an "honest" agnostic than live in the shadow of spiritual schizophrenia. A spiritual revolution may be necessary to recall these rebels to fellowship in the Church. I challenge the rebels to follow Christ and help spring this revolution.

6. *A revolution of witness.* When the revolution takes place in the areas described, it will spontaneously bring a revolution of witness. Half the world still remains in spiritual darkness as far as a knowledge of Jesus Christ is concerned.

When we have gone forth, we have often taken the nonrevolutionary form of Christianity. A. W. Tozer wrote: "The popular notion that the first obligation of the Church is to spread the gospel to the uttermost parts of the earth is false. Her first obligation is to be spiritually worthy to spread it. . . . To spread an effete, degenerate brand of Christianity to pagan lands is not to fulfill the commandments of the Lord."

Tozer was a twentieth-century prophet who spoke for God from the pulpit and through his books. If we put into practice the principles he set forth (allowing for human error), we would see a spiritual revolution. This in turn would lead to witnessing in every form which would gather many people into the Church of the Lord Jesus Christ. Down through history, men who had different theological perspectives have lived out the same kind of dynamic, revolutionary Christianity, and we should be able to lay down our doctrinal pop-guns and work together in world evangelism and spiritual revolution.

The Jehovah's Witnesses, with all their false doctrines, boast of being ninety percent mobile. That is, ninety percent of their membership is involved in definite outreach and witness. What can we say of our evangelical churches' mobility? In some churches it seems that only the pastor and perhaps a few others know how to win others to Christ. But the New Testament clearly teaches that each believer in Christ is a witness. The fact that people have come to Christ just through reading a piece of Christian literature should show us that no Christian need arrive in heaven without helping someone else get there.

There are many ways to witness, and, though some ways may be better than others, the teaching of Scripture is that we primarily witness through life and through word. Far more than a crusade, a special project, or outreach program, true witnessing is a spontaneous outflowing of the indwelling Christ.

Let's stop clutching our weaknesses, shyness, lack of training, fear, or any other excuse and start believing the God of the impossible who specializes in using weak vessels. There is not a single Christian who cannot become an effective, revolutionary witness for Jesus Christ if he really wants to.

In conclusion, I have two requests. The first is by far the more important. I request you to unite with me in repentance at the foot of the cross and *believe God* to bring into our lives and the lives of other Christians a spiritual revolution. Let us bow in daily repentance, recognizing our failures, and believing God for great and dynamic changes in the days to come.

Second, I ask you to take a few minutes and write to me, care of the publisher, expressing what you feel after reading these pages. Perhaps this could be your first act of discipline after reading this book. I have a tremendous desire to pray for anyone who truly wants a spiritual revolution in his own heart and life. Those of us who want spiritual revolution in the twentieth century must unite and work together toward this goal. God is on our side—and if he is for us, who can be against us!

END NOTES

Revelation of Love

1. P. Billheimer, *Love Covers*.

2. Francis Schaeffer (1912-1984) wrote and lectured extensively on theology, culture, and apologetics. His many books include *A Christian Manifesto*, *True Spirituality, The God Who is There*, and *How Should We Then Live?* based on the influential film series.

3. A.W. Tozer, *The Set of the Sail*.

4. Roy Hession, *The Cavalry Road/Be Filled Now*.

5. Tozer, *The Set of the Sail*.

6. R. Steer, *A Living Reality: The Life of George Müller*.

7. Patrick Johnstone, *Operation World*. See *Operation World, 21st Century Edition* (Waynesboro, GA: Authentic, 2001 for the most up-to-date figures.

8. Johnstone, *Operation World*.

9. Johnstone, *Operation World*.

No Turning Back

1. M.V. *Logos* was the first of two ships (the other being m.v. *Doulos*) commissioned by Operation Mobilization to provide Christian literature and educational facilities in ports all over the world.

2. Tozer, *The Pursuit of God*.

3. Quoted in Eddie Gibbs, *I Believe in Church Growth*.

4. H.A. Hodges, *The Unseen Warfare*.

5. Tozer, *Avoiding Spiritual Deformity*.

6. Tozer, *The Root of the Righteous*.

7. Josh MacDowell, *Evidence that Demands a Verdict* and *More Evidence that Demands a Verdict*.

8. Samuel Logan Brengle, source unknown.

9. M.V. *Logos*.

10. Tozer, *Born After Midnight*

11. John Stott, *Balanced Christianity*.

12. Tozer, *Gems from Tozer*.

Hunger for Reality

1. Tozer, *Of God and Men*.

2. This manifesto for world evangelism, with minor changes here, was drawn up by twenty-five students in 1961, the beginning of Operation Mobilization, which the author now coordinates.

3. H.G. Wells, *Outline of History*.

4. Tozer, *Of God and Men*.

5. Amy Carmichael, *Calvary Love*.